NATIVE POLICIES
IN AFRICA

NATIVE POLICIES
IN AFRICA

BY

L. P. MAIR
M.A., Ph.D.,
Lecturer in Colonial Administration,
London School of Economics

NEGRO UNIVERSITIES PRESS
NEW YORK

Originally published in 1936
by George Routledge & Sons Ltd.

Reprinted 1969 by
Negro Universities Press
A Division of Greenwood Publishing Corp.
New York

SBN 8371-2180-9

PRINTED IN UNITED STATES OF AMERICA

To
B. MALINOWSKI

CONTENTS

vii

CONTENTS

CONTENTS

LIST OF MAPS

AUTHOR'S NOTE

THIS book is intended to be rather a study of main lines of policy than a work of reference. Accordingly I have not attempted to give data on exactly the same points for each colonial area, but have concentrated on the fuller treatment of those which seemed most significant and on which the information available was sufficiently full to make an estimate of their significance possible. Certain essential facts and statistics have been collected in appendices for purposes of comparison. For other such data the reader is referred to Mr. R. L. Buell's *The Native Problem in Africa,* and (on labour questions) Major G. St. J. Orde-Browne's *The African Labourer,* both works to which I am much indebted. The very important Report of the 1935 Commission on Emigrant Labour from Nyasaland was published too late for its contents to be included in the section on that territory.

I have to acknowledge the help given to me in the collection of data by Miss Pauline Blackmore, and the kindness of the Rockefeller Research Committee of the London School of Economics through whom her services were made available to me.

I should like also to express my gratitude to the staff of the Colonial Office Library for their ever-ready help in the pursuit of official documents.

LUCY MAIR.

LONDON
June 1936

ERRATA.

Page 45, line 18, for "independent" read "interdependent.

Page 79, line 29, „ "1912" read "1902."

Page 88, line 1, „ "931" read "939."

Page 88, line 6, „ "130-160" read "130-150"

Page 103, line 22-3, „ "just under two" read "twenty-four."

Page 108, line 28, „ "1921" read "21."

Page 223, line 19, „ "75,000" read "750,000."

Native Policies in Africa

CHAPTER I

EUROPE'S TASK IN AFRICA

"Empire-consciousness" in the Post-War Era.—The post-war period has seen among all the nations which have possessions in tropical Africa a great increase of public interest in the affairs of those territories. The conception of her colonies as an assured source of cheap raw materials, and market for the manufactures of the metropolis, only took firm root in France as her politicians began to look round for means of restoring the economic losses of the War. In Belgium the change from the Free State regime in the Congo had hardly time to make itself felt before 1919, and the intensive exploitation of her colonial empire began only about 1920. For Portugal modernization of the colonial system, in the sense of the active development of communications and encouragement of the cultivation of crops for export, has had to wait even longer. The necessary concomitant of such economic development, the creation of "Empire-consciousness" by popular propaganda, has had its counterpart in Great Britain in the Wembley Exhibition and the activities of the Empire Marketing Board.

The Critical Attitude towards Colonial Policies.—In Britain, where the admonition to think imperially was uttered a generation earlier, public interest is beginning to take a more critical line. In 1919 the conviction that this country was uniquely fitted by Providence to bear the White Man's Burden no doubt accounted satisfactorily to the man in the street for the cession of the German colonies; though even at that time Mr. Leonard Woolf had pointed out that the need for a new system of control over colonial administration arose not from the alleged atrocities of Germany but from defects common to all existing systems.[1] Certainly that cession could only be justified if it resulted in a demonstrable improvement in the administration of the areas concerned; and while the actual distribution of the Mandates obviously represents not a disinterested desire to see them in the best hands but the satisfaction of annexationist claims, the terms on which they are held, and, still more, the interpretation placed by the Permanent Mandates Commission on those terms, represent a definite reorientation in the theory of colonial government. The practice of the Commission demands more than lip-service for the principle of trusteeship, and the standard which is set by its discussion and criticism of administration in the areas under its supervision must be taken into account by a colonial power which has declared that it regards that principle as equally valid in other areas under its control.

In this country, as a matter of mere historical development and longer experience, and not of any inherent ethical superiority, public opinion has passed beyond the stage where it accepted as automatic and inevitable the connection between intensive economic exploitation of tropical territories and the advancement of their inhabitants. Dr. Norman Leys' criticism of policy in Kenya first aroused a widespread public interest, which has been kept alive by the long series of debates on the desirability of a closer administrative union between Kenya and the neighbouring territories, and whose extent can be measured by the general indignation that was expressed in 1932 at the decision to amend the Kenya Native Lands Trust Ordinance in order to allow gold-mining to be undertaken in the Kavirondo Reserve. The result is a growing conviction— not of course confined to this country, though elsewhere it has not penetrated in the same way to circles which have no direct interest in colonial questions—that the responsibility of a colonial power for its subject peoples involves something more than simply facilitating their introduction to European enterprise, and that this process, so far from being purely beneficial, creates its own peculiar problems, for which satisfactory solutions have yet to be devised.

[1] *Empire and Commerce in Africa*, p. 258.

The Real Problem of Culture Contact.—Yet the nature of the problem has not so far been clearly grasped by many of those who are most anxious to see it solved in accordance with the best interests of the African peoples. Some, turning in distress from the locations of Johannesburg or the native quarter of Nairobi, or from some account of the disintegration of African family life, say: " Let us give Africa only that in our civilization which is good," or even, " Let the Africans be free to reject what seems to them to be unworthy of imitation in our ways." Others hold that we have deliberately withheld from the African, in order to perpetuate our domination over him, those gifts of our own culture which could have enabled him to rise to our level—an education equal to that which we give our own children, and the opportunity to control his own political life through those democratic institutions which some of us still claim as civilization's greatest achievement. Almost all accept it as the starting-point of argument that there are certain respects in which European civilization is undoubtedly superior to any other, and that it is a positive duty to spread its superior elements through all those regions where European domination extends.

In all these views there is an element of truth, but all fail to grasp the essentials of a problem which is not one of point of view, of more or less liberal conceptions of fair play, but of the objective analysis of facts. In the debates which rage over policy in Africa, the partisans of economic interest and of disinterested humanitarianism alike focus their attention upon what ought to be to the exclusion of what is. Both sides are convinced that the policy which they advocate must produce the best results, but neither, so far, has paid much attention to the effects which policies now in operation do produce. Nor could they do so; for the necessary knowledge is in most cases not available.

The Contribution of Social Anthropology.—The study of social anthropology has of recent years devoted especial attention to the problems which arise when a human society is invaded by an alien culture at a far more advanced stage of development. Analysis of these situations, in which the contact of cultures

3

presents itself in a particularly dramatic form, must be of extreme theoretical importance in the light which it can throw on the processes of cultural change and assimilation in general. It is also, surely, indispensable to persons who make the direction of such change their aim.

The study of human culture along the lines first traced by Professor B. Malinowski in the functional theory of anthropology throws an entirely new light on the problems of colonial policy. The interpretation of culture as a mechanism of co-operation for the satisfaction of social needs, in which every element is linked with and conditioned by the rest, implies the necessity of giving more serious consideration to the indigenous institutions of uncivilized peoples than has usually been accorded in the past.

So long as it was assumed that all native tribes lived in a condition of chaotic savagery which they themselves found very disagreeable, it was easy to regard the ultimate triumph of civilization with its obvious advantages as assured, and to look on any resistance as a mere temporary difficulty which would vanish when the natives learned to take the reasonable view. I should not maintain that this comfortable belief was by any means obsolete now. It has guided throughout, for example, the attitude of the Kenya Government to the visible dislocation of native life in the Kavirondo Reserve by the establishment of a mining township at Kakamega, in its very heart. *The Times* Nairobi correspondent, in an article which forecast a further extension of prospecting, wrote:

"The problem of settling families among their neighbours may possibly involve some readjustment of ideas among the natives concerned. . . . There is no reason to suppose, however, that the natives will fail to realize that the situation which has arisen is something quite outside the scope of native law and one which must be dealt with on an entirely different basis."

Of course the natives will realize, as they have had to realize over and over again within the last two generations, that they are confronted with a situation entirely alien to their experience. But it is expecting a good deal of human nature to assume that

4

this realization will cause them to make the modifications in their economic organization, in their methods of owning land, in the system of mutual ties which regulate individual relationships, that would be necessary for an arbitrary redistribution of the inhabitants of a densely populated area to be carried through without throwing the whole social organization badly out of joint. I say nothing of the manifold transformations that would be required in order with any degree of success to harmonize the life of a people practising agriculture at a primitive level with the labour demands of a European industrial enterprise. It shows a complete failure to understand the nature of human society to suppose that it can assimilate foreign elements which are unexpectedly thrust upon it by some such happy process as is open to the oyster.

The juxtaposition of two civilizations creates its own problems which require a special technique for their solution. Of course the conatct of cultures has happened before. We are constantly reminded of the part that it has played in the development of European civilization, and the backward condition of the peoples of Africa is ascribed, in contrast, to the absence of external stimulus. It is obvious too that no social change can come about without some dislocation of an existing system, and no one would be so foolish as to argue that for that reason all changes must be deplored. But the peculiar position of African society today arises from the rapidity and extent of the changes that are being forced upon it by powers which it is unable to resist. Changes initiated from within rarely, in the nature of things, produce a complete break with the past. The most radical of reformers is himself a product of his own society, and takes for granted those aspects of his environment which he is not actually engaged in modifying. Moreover, he is expressing a desire for change which has been felt by some at least of his fellows. Such reforms, whether they achieve their object or not, are part of the process of continual adaptation in which social evolution consists.

The methods of colonial powers have in the main been characterized by a complete unawareness of the existence of such processes of adaptation, or of any relation between social institutions and the circumstances for which a given social system has to provide. They have been actuated by an unquestioning belief in the inherent superiority of British justice, *la civilisation française*, Christianity, the dignity of labour, individual enterprise, the ability to utilize natural resources to the full, over any other form of government, education, religion or economic organization, and they have set themselves to impose the institutions of which they approve on all the peoples over whom they exercise authority. They have been indifferent to the nature of the societies which they thus determined to transform, except in so far as they indulged in practices like sorcery or head-hunting which had to be suppressed, have not paused to consider whether the institutions which they found were actually inadequate to the needs of the people who evolved them, and in the one direction where it was of vital importance that a satisfactory adjustment should be made—in the response of African society to the new economic forces which colonization has brought with it—they have concentrated entirely on assisting the process of penetration and left the result to take care of itself. Bringing with them a culture separated by centuries from that to which it is introduced, they have sought to substitute for the evolution by which they themselves reached it a series of strokes of the pen. They have attempted to mould a material of which they were ignorant into a form determined without reference to the ends which it would have to serve.

Rational Control in Human Development.—The deliberate manipulation of human society is a task which it has been left to this generation to undertake. It is the essence of that " sacred trust " which colonial administration has been recognized to be. Of course it cannot be performed under laboratory conditions. The largely irrevocable mistakes of the past, the constant pressure of influences which no government can control, the demands, often misguided, of the people themselves, must be accepted as data in the problem as it confronts the administrations of today. What they have to do is to envisage native development, not as a process which must eventually culminate in the adoption of European institutions, but as a series of adjustments to the new circumstances which native societies are being called upon to face. The criterion of policy therefore should be not any vague general principle, but an estimate of its results in terms of such a development, based on a knowledge of the structure of the society concerned, of the inter-relation of its various elements—government, family life, economic organization, religion and magic—which can indicate the directions in which an innovation will cause dislocation and create a need for readjustment.

It would be futile to envisage as an ideal the regulation of human affairs by the dispassionate application of scientific principles. The material is too intractable, and, in the conditions in which modern government is carried on, decisions of policy are less often the result of a considered plan than of a more or less fortuitous combination of circumstances which makes action of some kind imperative, and are seldom uninfluenced by pressure from conflicting interests. Yet even in these conditions, the existence of an objective criterion of policy can be of some value in determining the nature of the compromise that will eventually have to be made. For colonial governments the data on which to base such criterion will be supplied, as I have suggested, by an analysis of the process of culture contact. To be equipped to meet the situations which this process creates is as necessary for such governments as it is to command the services of engineers, agriculturalists or public health experts. For most of them, however, the realization of that necessity is still in the future, and the indiscriminating dissemination of " civilized institutions ", assumed *a priori* to have an intrinsic value, is being pursued nearly all over the world.

This study, therefore, will only to a very slight extent describe measures deliberately designed to counter the disruptive effect which European contact has had upon African society. Its aim is to describe the theory and practice of the various Powers which govern territories in tropical Africa as they are at the present time, and it must deal with policies dictated by other conceptions of trusteeship than that which I have tried to outline. In many cases it will not be possible to discuss in detail the results of different policies, for their results have not yet been sufficiently investigated, and at best one can conjecture what they are likely to have been from such general knowledge of comparable situations as is available. Within these limits, however, the treatment of the subject will be governed by the principles that I have set out; it will attempt to discover what the various governments in Africa are making of the African.

The Major Problems of Policy.—Before embarking on a description of the methods followed in different territories it will be as well to understand what are the major points of policy which any African administration has to decide. First and most fundamental of all is its attitude towards European settlement and European enterprise, for on that every other aspect of policy depends. If government is to take upon itself to encourage colonization it must undertake to provide the facilities which make colonization worth while—land for economic development and labour to work it. In practice these considerations will come to dominate the outlook of the administration, and its aim will be envisaged as the creation of a community in which Africans are willing to work for Europeans. So great are the difficulties of accomplishing this aim that little attention can be spared for the development of African life in any other direction. In Kenya, indeed, such an attempt has been suggested, and there the "dual policy" of encouraging independent native production side by side with European enterprise has not come much nearer practical expression than its enunciation in a White Paper. This is an issue on which no compromise is possible. An African tribe can be made into a reserve of labour or a community of independent producers, but not both.

The attitude towards actual colonization is to a certain extent dictated by climate, for it is generally assumed that Europeans cannot live permanently in tropical Africa at a height of less than 4000 feet. Only in the east of Africa, and in the Portuguese territory of Angola, is there sufficient area of land above this height to make possible any question of establishing a colony of settlement comparable to the British

Dominions. Kenya, Tanganyika, the Rhodesias and Nyasa-land are the areas for which such a possibility is discussed. Both in the mountains of West Africa and the small portion of the Belgian Congo which runs up to the Nile-Congo water-shed white settlement would be possible, and has to some extent been encouraged, but geographical conditions alone would prevent these areas from even being more than islands in a predominantly African sea.

Territories of Colonization.—A policy of intensive European settlement creates its own special problems, for whenever there is a numerous white community it eventually demands the right to control its own affairs—a right which must carry with it control over the destinies of the native population. Here the interpretation of the principle of trusteeship becomes a matter of bitter controversy. Can the immigrant community be associated in the trust, as the British Government has declared is possible in Kenya, and a just balance still be held between native and non-native interests? Does the paramount duty of trusteeship make it impossible to grant self-government to the European population until the distant date when the native communities are capable of sharing in it? Or can some middle course be found?

But even where permanent white settlement is out of the question, a demand has always to be met for the allocation to Europeans of large areas of land for economic exploitation, whether by the cultivation of crops for export, the collection of forest produce such as rubber, ivory and, more recently, palm nuts, or for extracting the minerals of whose existence in the African soil no one was aware till the scramble for possession was over. This demand at once raises the question how the land is to be partitioned between the native inhabitants and the newcomers. Are native rights to be respected, or must they give way before the right of conquest, the coming of a more advanced system of ideas with regard to land tenure, or the moral right to undeveloped territory of those who can make the best use of it? Is the distribution to be made according to needs, and in that case, shall the first provision be that native requirements are met or that no hindrance is put in the way of European expansion? Is the area estimated as necessary for native requirements to be demarcated and the rest thrown open for settlement, or, on the other hand, is the area available for settlement to be restricted to regions where there is no possibility of over-population? The history of many an African territory could be epitomized in the answers which have been given to these questions.

After the demand for land comes that for labour. In no part of Africa has the native, in the initial stages of contact, gone willingly to work for wages. He has his own occupations, which provide him with the satisfaction of the needs and desires of which he is aware, and in which he is keenly interested, and the suggestion that he should abandon these to undertake a kind of work which he does not understand, at a distance from his home, for a payment in money for which he has no use, does not commend itself to him. He has therefore in some way to be persuaded to give that co-operation without which the material development of the colony, and the consequent increase in prosperity for everyone in it, are impossible. Here it is for government to decide to what extent, and by what means, it is justifiable to put pressure on native populations for this purpose. There is no government which has not regarded taxation as having the incidental advantage that it obliges the natives to engage in some kind of work by which they can raise money. Some go no further than this, and leave the native entirely free to choose his own method of meeting the tax. At the other extreme is the policy which openly applies compulsion, either by recruiting labour for plantations or by the system of forced deliveries of wild produce that was practised in the old Congo Free State. Intermediate between these two methods are others which shade off from persuasion to compulsion, and those means of indirect compulsion which consist in penalizing natives who have not worked for European employers or making it impossible for them to meet their obligations in any other way. Such methods are, for example, exhortations, often accompanied by threats, to go out to work pronounced by government officials, pass and vagrancy laws which make it difficult for a man to leave his reserve except in search of work, and render him liable to arrest if he is found outside it and is not engaged in European employment, the obligation to perform labour on public works from which he can obtain exemption if he has been in employment for a stated period, increases in taxation frankly imposed for this purpose, or prohibitions against growing certain crops.

On the attitude towards the encouragement of European enterprise depends very largely the policy pursued with regard to the recourse to compulsory labour which is generally admitted to be sometimes necessary. There are cases where government could not be carried on at all if an official was not empowered to requisition porters to carry his goods over roadless country. Again, sometimes a piece of engineering construction—a road or a bridge—must be completed at high speed if the rains are not to destroy the whole of the dry season's work, or immediate action is called for against plague or locusts. In such circumstances it is generally recognized that the authorities are justified in requiring compulsory labour as a last resort. The conditions on which recourse to compulsion is justifiable were defined in a Convention adopted by the International Labour Conference in 1930 as follows: the work must be urgent, it must be of important direct interest to the community called upon to undertake it, it must not impose too heavy a burden on them, and the supply of voluntary labour available must have been found to be insufficient.

But these limitations are not accepted by all governments. Even where they are recognized in theory, the conception of what is directly beneficial to the community can be stretched to cover works whose anticipated result will be simply an increase of revenue to the territory, from which, it is argued, the native community is bound to profit. Hardly any African railway has been built without compulsory labour, and of very few of the existing lines could it be said that they primarily serve the needs of the native producer. The French Government expressly rejected the Forced Labour Convention on the ground that it prohibited what they regard as an indispensable means of carrying through the public works necessary to the economic development of their colonies. And while there is no inherent logical reason why a government which approves the conscription of labour for public works of all kinds should also allow it for the benefit of private enterprise, it is in fact the case that in colonies where such conscription is freely used commercial enterprises expect to be able to call on government for assistance at times when there is an exceptional demand for labour.

Development under Indirect Rule.—The alternative to the furtherance of European enterprise is the economic development of the colony through the agency of the native "working", as Lord Lugard has put it, "in his own time, in his own way, for his own profit and with the assistance of his family." [1] This system is generally known as Indirect Rule, though the name, literally interpreted, only describes a single element, and that perhaps not the most significant, in the policy which was initiated by Lord Lugard in West Africa and developed with such striking results by Sir Donald Cameron in Tanganyika. Its makers themselves now describe it by other phrases, and such terms as "association", "parallel development" and "co-operative devolution" do suggest better the principles on which the system is based, but none of these has succeeded in displacing "Indirect Rule" in current parlance, and if the essential characteristics of this policy are clearly understood, there is no harm in calling it by the most familiar name.

The basic aim of the Indirect Rule policy is the development of an African society able to participate in the life of the modern world as a community in its own right. In territories where it is followed government does not accept the encouragement of European enterprise as a duty, but judges its value in the light of the contribution which it can make to African development. The other aspect of Indirect Rule—the preservation of African institutions where the needs of the Africans themselves do not call for their modification—is almost a natural corollary of this attitude towards European penetration, for it is only where government is committed to its furtherance that the far-reaching measures of interference with native life become necessary which have just been described.

[1] "Education and Race Relations," *Journal of the African Society*, January 1933.

Under Indirect Rule the land of the territory is recognized as the property of the native tribes, and, though alienation is still permitted, the ruling principle is always that such alienation must produce beneficial results to the native community and must be accompanied by adequate compensation. Neither the wholesale transference of native populations nor the curtailment of their reserves to dimensions which make them unable to gain subsistence by their accustomed economic methods are permitted under such a system. Village life on the lands protected by the ancestral spirits, work organized through traditional systems of co-operation and fitting into the accustomed rhythm of alternating effort and recreation, by methods improved, perhaps, not under the strain of necessity but through the incentive of increased returns, become the bases of an economic development, which, if properly guided, can be integrated into the structure of an African society instead of remaining an external disintegrating force.

In most of the territories governed by Indirect Rule there is, in fact, little European enterprise and consequently little demand for wage-labour—a fact which may be explained by density of population, but which does suggest that where native interests are effectively safeguarded there is not found to be much land available for alienation. The failure of Lever Bros. to obtain from the Gold Coast Government facilities which seemed to them adequate, and their transference of their palm-oil industry to the Belgian Congo, is perhaps significant. In Tanganyika, however, considerable alienations of land had been made by the previous administration, and, while some areas are now closed to further settlement, there are others where it is held that European colonization can still be increased without prejudice to native interests. Here, therefore, the demand for labour does arise. But governmental action with regard to it has aimed not at making alternatives to wage-labour difficult or impossible, but at increasing its attractions by establishing a high standard of conditions on plantations, by providing transport facilities, building rest-houses on main routes for labourers travelling on foot, and so forth. In this territory careful and detailed studies have been made of the effects of wage-labour on the various tribes; studies which, it is true, do not dispel all doubts as to the possibility of reconciling the periodic exodus of a large proportion of the adult men of an African tribe with its development as a community to a higher cultural level, but whose merit lies in the spirit of objective inquiry in which they were carried out. The abolition of the Labour Department, which put an end to this work, has been one of the worst pieces of mistaken economy indulged in by any colonial government of recent years.

The element in the Indirect Rule policy from which it takes its name is the maintenance in their position of the authorities recognized by the native population, as the basis of development of a native administration fitted to perform the functions of a modern government. This too is evidently an essential feature of a system which makes the evolution of African society its aim. Here too one might say that only the exigencies of European enterprise have made necessary the supersession of the traditional authorities by government agents appointed from outside. Only where government policy is constantly at variance with the interests and desires of the native population does it become necessary to enforce it through the orders of aliens. Elsewhere, despite one or two notorious cases—notorious just because of their infrequency—where chiefs have proved unequal to their new responsibilities, the gain in continuity of development, in willingness of the native population to accept new measures, in their respect for authority and confidence in justice, has more than outweighed the disadvantages of a certain inefficiency in the initial period. The mere requirement of an organization of competent native officials has never necessitated the destruction of recognized authorities.

This is the aspect of Indirect Rule which has met with most criticism, most imitation and most misunderstanding. It is assumed that the whole system consists in this and this only, and an advance in policy is thought to be achieved when an official who is a mere mouthpiece of the alien authority is selected from the ruling house rather than from the ranks of government clerks, or when native councils which have no particular standing in the eyes of the population are set up to give formal endorsement on behalf of their tribes to policies decided upon by government. Elsewhere the colonial power is thought to have done its whole duty when it has confirmed the position of existing authority, even if it has disregarded altogether the changed circumstances which call for modification in its privileges and functions. In the very region where Indirect Rule was invented, it now meets with the criticism that it merely perpetuates the domination over its subject peoples of what was already an alien oppressive authority. Elsewhere the system is represented as perpetuating antiquated institutions and retarding the progress of peoples already fit to adopt a more advanced civilization.

Both imitators and critics have taken for the essence of the system a single feature of it which, reproduced in isolation, can have practically no effect on a policy directed in all other matters to the destruction or wholesale transformation of native society or to the furtherance at all costs of non-native interests, while, on the other hand, a change in this one respect could not set right what is wrong where the system has been misapplied. The real meaning of Indirect Rule cannot be summed up in the phrase, "Find the chief". It consists in an understanding of the structure of native society and the interrelation of its parts, which precludes the possibility of assuming that it can be suddenly modernized from the outside, and at the same time reveals the points at which changed circumstances call for readjustment, and the bases on which necessary innovations can be firmly established.

The Aims of Native Education.—The last important point on which policy has to decide is what are to be the aims of education and the treatment accorded to its product. Here again the answer depends very largely on the presence or absence in the colony of European economic interests. Where the main preoccupation of policy is with the demand for labour, the type of education favoured by Government tends to concentrate on developing the kind of skill that will be useful to the employer, while neglecting such crafts as could have a value in improving the material basis of village life and deliberately avoiding teaching of a type which might make the pupil aspire to a higher place in the social scale. It is "vocational", not in the sense that it looks to native life and the part which superior knowledge and skill could play in its advancement, but in that of an endeavour to train natives for just those few vocations in which there is a place for them in the European community. Thus natives may do well as engine-drivers in the Belgian Congo or as compositors in Nairobi; but as soon as the European population is large enough they begin to come into competition with its least efficient elements. The "Poor White" problem arises, and the European standard of living has to be protected by the exclusion of the native from the exercise in European surroundings of crafts for which there is no place at all in his own reserve. That all education in such territories is not confined to producing an efficient proletariat is due partly to the share taken in it by missionary societies, partly to the enunciation—as regards British policy—by the home government of principles which are considered by them to be of universal application.

Elsewhere education does make its avowed aim the development of all the native's powers to their fullest capacity, but the form which that development should take is still a matter of much controversy. Indeed, there is no direction in which less application has been made of even the available knowledge of native society. Education has up till now been taken to consist in the imparting of a certain quantity of knowledge considered to be intrinsically valuable. In French territory the French language and literature, French history and the characteristics of French institutions, are regarded as the most important subjects of education. In English colonies there has been less insistence on a spread of English culture which would be inconsistent both with Indirect Rule and with the policy of European settlement as it has been outlined. Here, however, owing to the practice which has been widely followed of leaving education to missionary activities, religious teaching takes up a proportion of the curriculum greater than would be allotted to it at home. In East Africa, through the influence of Professor

Julian Huxley, elementary biology has now become popular as a means of encouraging both greater attention to hygiene and a rational attitude towards phenomena which are at present ascribed to supernatural causes. In all colonies the standard of achievement in higher education is set by the examinations recognized in the home country.

Only in one or two African territories has there been any attempt to envisage education in its bearing on the needs of native life, though this conception of its aims is beginning to spread. At present the educational system of the majority of colonies aims at rendering the educated individual superior to his community, not at making him a more valuable member of that community. It assumes that the knowledge which he acquires at school will enrich his life by broadening his mental outlook. In a very limited sense this is true. The intelligent native is intensely interested in what is going on in the world outside his village or tribe; he is eager to learn as many facts of present-day importance as he can. Whether the past history of other peoples than his own appeals much to him is doubtful; but it is almost certain that imaginative literature, so far from developing his æsthetic feelings, leaves him entirely cold. It does enrich the African's life to enable him to read the newspaper; but the English language conceived as a key to the treasures of Shakespeare and Milton is wasted on him.

The "humanistic" contempt for "vocational" education is reasonable enough so long as what it condemns is a training whose sole end is conceived as that of increasing the market value of the product. Yet this is in fact the effect of a literary education on the average African. He prizes it not for its own sake but as a means of obtaining a highly-paid job in some town; and if he fails to do this he is no better equipped for life in the village than if he had never been to school at all. A remodelling of the whole of African education to bring it into close relation with African life is one of the most urgent and difficult tasks of current policy.

While a system of education devised in this spirit would no longer serve as exclusively as the present one the needs of the minority who are destined to follow a profession in European or Europeanized surroundings, provision has to be made also for them. Towards them, again, different attitudes can be observed in different colonies, though one could hardly go so far as to speak of policies deliberately adopted. The extreme case is that of South Africa, where it is simply impossible for the educated African to practise any of the professions for which he might be qualified. Elsewhere French and British colonies present a striking contrast. The French carry to its logical conclusion the principle that French citizenship is the right of all who merit it by adopting French civilization. If their policy has given too little thought to the interests of the majority who do not reach this standard, at least it provides a place in the social scheme for the small number who do. They do not abandon their own mode of life and cut themselves off from their own community, only to find that European society excludes them from any participation in its life beyond what goes with the exercise of their profession. In the British colonies, on the other hand, though the existence of native barristers, clergymen, doctors, politicians and newspaper editors may be accepted and no obstacles put in the way of their pursuing their avocation, there is a rigid social cleavage between them and European society. British preoccupation with the preservation of tribal institutions, coupled with a tradition of racial superiority bred of two centuries in India, tends to make of the educated native a thorn in the flesh, a complicating factor in a situation which should have developed otherwise. Hence the intense suspicion of the British Government among the Europeanized natives of West Africa and their inability to see in the Indirect Rule system—which is no longer applicable to themselves—anything but an instrument of British domination. Here is another problem which has never yet been squarely faced.

These considerations may be said to constitute the salient data of the present-day problem of the development of African life. The object of this book is to describe the theory and practice of the various administrations concerned with regard to them.

CHAPTER II

THE WHITE MAN'S COUNTRIES

IT has been pointed out that, apart from Abyssinia and Portuguese Angola, all those parts of Africa which contain large areas thought to be climatically suitable for permanent settlement by Europeans are under British control. Of these territories the Union of South Africa lies altogether outside the tropical zone, and while it contains hot and unhealthy regions, the greater part of it indubitably satisfies the necessary climatic conditions. Within the tropics it is generally held that Europeans can reside permanently, and bring up children, at any height above 4000 feet. It is not yet by any means certain that the combination of altitude and tropical sun has no injurious effects, but that there are none is an article of faith with most Europeans already established there. Of the four territories which contain considerable areas of highland, Kenya, Tanganyika and the Rhodesias, all but Tanganyika follow a policy directed primarily towards the encouragement of European settlement with a view to the ultimate attainment of responsible government—this has already been achieved in Southern Rhodesia—on terms which will maintain the European population in a dominant position, while the natives continue to supply the manual labour necessary to its existence. Although the Imperial Government has more than once declared, with reference to those African territories which are still Crown Colonies, that in case of conflict the interests of the native population must be paramount,[1] difference in practice between independent South Africa and Southern Rhodesia and colonial Northern Rhodesia and Kenya is one of degree rather than of kind.

[1] Cmd. 1922 of 1923, Cmd. 3573 of 1930.

NATIVE POLICIES IN AFRICA

I. SOUTH AFRICA

Only in South Africa, however, can a historian write several hundred pages before coming to the section on "the natives." Only in South Africa could a farmer refer to the natives as "the curse of the country". Only there could anyone dare to write without a blush, "The conception that native policy should be determined in South Africa *by the people of South Africa as a whole* may be said to have prevailed," [1] or the Minister for Native Affairs remind a Native Conference that "this being a constitutional country after all the final say rests with [the Europeans]".[2]

Having it Both Ways.—In South Africa policy represents the determination to have it both ways pushed further than anywhere else on the African continent. The native is to be "segregated" from the European sufficiently to prevent his stealing stock, but not enough to prevent his "coming out to work". The native is to be forced to abandon such barbarous practices as the giving of a bride-price for his wife—till someone points out that the need to acquire cattle for *lobola* is a valuable stimulus to "work". The native is to "progress" far enough to want to buy European goods, but not far enough to have ideas about parliamentary representation. He is to be educated enough to be "industrious", but not enough to be "cheeky". He is to become an efficient manual labourer, but he is not to undersell the unskilled European. He is to have enough land to save him from destitution, lest he should be driven to crime as a means of livelihood, but not so much that he has no need to "work". The principle of the freedom of contract is invoked against proposals to raise his wages by legislative action, but not against measures making it impossible for him to live without working for wages.[3] He is to be protected from the dangers of inter-racial animosity by a policy which shall scrupulously avoid any measure that might be unpopular with the Europeans.

[1] Hofmeyr, *South Africa*, p. 157. (Italics mine.)
[2] Report of Native Affairs Commission, 1927–31.
[3] See the Report of the Native Affairs Commission, 1903–5, par. 370.

The nemesis of all these mutually contradictory desires is the condition of the "Land of Good Hope" today.

Historical Influences.—The development of South African native policy has been complicated not only by the conflict found everywhere between native inclinations and European needs, but by the conflicting interests of different groups of Europeans, by the fact that in different circumstances the same interests demanded diametrically opposite measures, by wide variations in the attitudes of successive Imperial Governments and the personality of their representatives, by the fundamental divergence of views between Downing Street and the Dutch population as to the relationship between black and white, and by the historical accident that the trek-Boers when they left the Cape Colony founded not one but three Republics, one of which—Natal—was early annexed by Great Britain. The federation of the four colonies led to a certain assimilation of their legislation affecting natives, though there remains the complicating factor of the three Native Territories of Swaziland, Basutoland and Bechuanaland, for which the Imperial Government is still responsible. Basutoland and Swaziland form enclaves within the Union. *Despite the principles which theoretically govern the administration of mandated areas, the legislation of the Union is applied without modification to South-West Africa.

In the early days of the colonization of South Africa the direct contact of the colonists was with the Bushmen and Hottentots. The early farmers looked for labour to imported slaves, while the Bantu were regarded primarily as cattle-thieves against whose depredations the colonists must be protected. In the Cape Colony various measures were adopted to this end at different times. Their common feature was the progressive extension of boundaries behind which the Bantu were pushed back. At one time an attempt was made to leave a belt of territory as a "neutral area" between the boundaries of black and white; at others the frontiers were planted with farmers who accepted land there in return for the duty of turning out on "commando" against stock-thieves. Demands for compensation, often exaggerated, more than once provoked wars.

Cape and Transvaal Policies.—The perpetual northward migration of Boer farmers, which from 1836 onwards had in it an element of political defiance of the British Government,[1] led to the foundation of two independent Republics, the Transvaal and Orange Free State, based on conceptions of the relation between black and white fundamentally different from those of Downing Street. The Cape policy, later to be expressed in Rhodes' famous phrase "Equal rights for all civilized men south of the Zambesi", may be said to have developed from the famous 50th Ordinance of 1828, which cancelled all legislation differentiating against Hottentots and laid down their right to own land.

Article 9 of the Transvaal Grondwet—"There shall be no equality between black and white either in Church or State"—adequately sums up the attitude that governed policy in the Republics. It will be noticed that Rhodes' dictum refers only to the Europeanized native. The ideas governing the Cape policy of the nineteenth century were essentially similar to the French theories to be discussed later. The difference in their practical expression is due in the main to the fact that in the Cape there is, as there is not in West Africa, a permanent European population. Only in Natal, the fourth of the political units which now form the Union, were native customs and native institutions regarded as in themselves worthy of respect —and here the degree of respect shown, and the sphere in which in its inception it was manifested, have been based on such arbitrary and unintelligent conceptions of their meaning that the result is in many ways no more satisfactory here than in the other Provinces.

In practice the Cape policy has worked out in a manner not widely different from that of the Boer Republics. The practical disadvantages under which the native population is placed are similar throughout the Union, though the legislative enactments affecting their position are less severe in the Cape than elsewhere. The assimilation of native policy which has taken place since the Imperial Government ceased to take an active interest in it seems to indicate that the earlier divergence

[1] See Macmillan, *The Cape Colour Question* ; and Walker, *The Great Trek.*

was due not to the inherent liberalism of the British race but to the influence of disinterested opinion at home. The one question which continued to be dealt with by the Cape on lines different from those followed in the rest of the Union was that of the native franchise, and one of General Hertzog's first acts as Prime Minister was to introduce a Bill to remove this difference. The franchise question, however, affects only a limited number of natives, and will be better dealt with after those matters of economic policy which affect the entire native population have been discussed.

Land Distribution.—Inevitably, in a colony whose history has been largely dictated by the need to extend effective control over a European population constantly pushing forward into native territory, deliberate administrative action with regard to the distribution of land has consisted in little more than the recognition of *faits accomplis*. The demand for a final delimitation was not put forward till 1901, and received satisfaction only in 1913.

A complication peculiar to South Africa lies in the fact that in many areas migrant Boers came into contact not with settled but with migrant Bantu. All through the earlier half of the nineteenth century the native populations of south - eastern Africa were in a constant state of upheaval and flight before the conquests of the great military despots. This circumstance would have presented a real difficulty had there been any question of recognizing existing native rights, and did provide a convenient legal argument for the assumption of all rights by the Crown; but only a fool could suppose that it removed the necessity, for a pastoral and agricultural population, of land to occupy.

The land now in native hands in the Union has been so preserved in a number of different ways. Cape policy was avowedly to respect existing native holdings,[1] but that did not prevent the alienations necessary for the establishment of frontier farms, nor the displacement and division of rebellious tribes.

The existing native locations of the Ciskei represent the

[1] Native Affairs Commission, 1903–5. Report, par. 81.

result of such displacements, along with nine districts where natives who had taken the British side in the numerous Kaffir Wars received grants surveyed and allocated in individual tenure against quit-rent. A final delimitation was made in 1878. In Griqualand West some fifty farms were demarcated as native locations in 1877. The largest native area in the Cape, and indeed in the whole Union, is the Transkeian Territories, which include the Transkei proper (or Fingoland), East Griqualand and the native areas of Tembuland and Pondoland, which for a long time had remained technically independent of British rule.

The Glen Grey System.—Here has been to a large extent applied the system of individual tenure originally devised by Cecil Rhodes for the District of Glen Grey in the Ciskei. The Glen Grey Act of 1894 established not only individual tenure but a system of local self-government which will have to be discussed in its place. That part of it which deals directly with land tenure provides for the allotment of land in surveyed holdings of 4 to 5 morgen (about eight acres), any surplus land being common grazing. The native holder pays the cost of survey and title, plus a quit-rent of 15s. per 5 morgen allotment and 3s. for each further morgen. Only seven districts have been surveyed. . Elsewhere, though the eight-acre holding is the theoretical standard, adjustments are still made in accordance with native custom, in a way which is held by competent observers to meet the difficulties of land shortage more adequately. The survey will probably not be completed.[1] The principle of "one man, one lot" rigidly applied would mean that a polygamous group of whatever size could obtain no more land than an monogamous household, but regulations promulgated in 1928 sanctioned what had already become administrative practice, the grant to a polygamous household of one lot for each wife.[2] These regulations also apply the principle "one man, one lot" so interpreted to all native locations in the Cape Province. Under the Glen Grey Act

[1] See Fazan, *Survey of Land Tenure in the Transkeian Territories*, in Kenya Land Commission (1933) Evidence, vol. I, p. 1096; and Rogers, *Native Administration in the Union*, p. 138.
[2] Rogers, *Native Administration in the Union of South Africa*, p. 122.

land can be forfeited as a punishment for rebellion, stock theft, non-beneficial occupation, or failure to pay rent or survey expenses. This land cannot be devised by will but must pass to the eldest son. The others have to apply for new allotments. In accordance with the principle "one man, one lot" the heir, if he has already a holding of his own, must abandon one or other. An amendment of 1905 allows a widow to remain on her husband's land till her death; under the original system she was unprovided for. Registration of holdings, re-allotment, collection of rent and administration generally were placed in the hands of native Location Boards of three members for each district—a system which had already been legally established in 1879 for districts where individual tenure prevailed.

In 1903 it was reported that these Boards consisted of illiterate natives who did not understand their duties, received no explanation of regulations published only in English, did not always represent native authority, and were interested in contravening the regulations in such respects as letting out the common ground for revenue which they appropriated themselves.[1] In 1933 it appears that the members are still illiterate and that the holding of regular meetings and keeping of minutes is not really expected of them. Mr. Howard Rogers, of the Native Affairs Department, nevertheless writes of them: "They act as commonage rangers and water bailiffs; they serve as the mouthpiece of the people and frequently advise the Magistrate in land administration."[2]

Native Areas Outside the Cape.—The other relatively large native areas in the Union are in Natal. In Natal proper (excluding Zululand) those lands found to be in occupation of native tribes when the territory was annexed as a Crown Colony in 1864 were reserved for their benefit and vested in a Native Trust administered by the Governor in Council. Native occupation at that time was concentrated on the hill-tops, and the fertile lowlands were held to be available for alienation. A certain amount of land was granted to missions

[1] Evidence before Native Affairs Commission, questions 11863, 12207 ff., 12537, 14388.
[2] Rogers, *Native Administration*, p. 39.

and peopled by them with Christian natives who supplied them with labour and were encouraged to live a life approximating to that of the European farmer. In 1903 these mission reserves passed under the authority of the Natal Native Trust. The Province of Zululand was divided in 1879 among thirteen chiefs by Sir Garnet Wolseley, who promised them the undisturbed possession of their lands. When it was annexed to Natal in 1897 a commission was appointed to delimit "sufficient Reserves for Native Locations", and instructed "to provide liberally for the Natives and in doing so . . . to consider their present and future requirements for some years to come".[1] Their interim reports were rejected by the Natal Government. They nevertheless adopted a report stating that "if the Natives in this Province are to be fairly dealt with . . . they cannot be deprived of any more land than that we recommend be thrown open for European occupation, and what we have delimitated as Reserves is none too much for their requirements." The principle which they followed was "to group adjoining tribes into more limited areas wherever it was possible to do so", and as a result they were able to recommend the alienation of a large area, from which a considerable number of natives were required to move to the Reserves. Some 4000 square miles were eventually alienated, the remaining 6000 being left in possession of the natives. This has been administered since 1909 by a Zululand Native Trust.

In the Transvaal about 2000 square miles have been set apart as native reserves. In this Province natives have been allowed to acquire land, though up till 1901-5 the purchase had to be made through a Native Location Commission—later the Secretary for Native Affairs—who held such land in trust. Mostly by means of tribal subscriptions, natives have acquired in this way 853 square miles of land scattered throughout the Province. The Orange Free State absolutely forbids the purchase of land by natives, and within its territory only the two tiny areas of Thaba Nchu and Witzies Hoek, together comprising 244 square miles, are set apart as native locations.

Land Shortage.—Already in 1903 the Commission on Native

[1] Report, Zululand Lands Delimitation Commission, 1904, p. 43.

Affairs was hearing from all over the country reports that the native locations were insufficient to support the population. In Butterworth District in the Transkei the land was "practically all absorbed", and even at the time of the original survey there had been insufficient in some wards to satisfy all claimants; [1] in Lady Frere the only remaining lots were "practically useless".[2] In Keiskama Hoek "scarcity of land" was advanced as a reason for failure to pay taxes.[3] In Natal 400,000 natives were estimated to be living outside the locations, as against 265,000 inside them.[4] Umballa, the Ndhlambi chief of King Williamstown, stated that his people had applied for more land "over and over again".[5]

Only of Zululand was there said to be a surplus of land, and the Delimitation Commission's Report demonstrated shortly afterwards that estimates of the amount of cultivable land available there had been very much exaggerated.

The Native Affairs Commission made a point of asking witnesses what future they anticipated for that surplus population which it would soon be patently impossible to accommodate in existing locations. Some Cape witnesses light-heartedly proposed "moving them northwards".[6] Their views make an ironical contrast with those of the Transvaal farmer who equally confidently referred to the "millions and tens of millions of natives beyond the Limpopo" who ought to be attracted southwards to supply the needs of the mines.[7] The Commission itself reminded the advocates of deportation that there would be a certain demand for labour in urban areas. The aim which commended itself to most European opinion was put thus by Mr. Hamilton, one of the Transvaal members of the Commission: [8]

> "If we provide them with areas to live on, but not with a sufficient quantity of land to maintain their stock and grow crops upon; ground enough for them and for their families to live on, but not enough for them either to produce

[1] Questions 13007–8.   [2] Question 11696.   [3] Question 7901A.
[4] Report, par. 106.   [5] Question 6610.
[6] See questions 7962, 8869.   [7] Question 40444.
[8] Question 24729.

sufficient food for themselves or to run cattle; simply places from which they might go out to work and to which they might return. . . ."

Unfortunately for the European employer of labour, "segregation" has not worked out in such a simple way. The native has not learnt to live entirely by wage-labour, nor do the wages paid him make this possible; and he has not been willing to give up his stock.

This Commission was not perturbed by reports of the shortage of land; some of its members welcomed the news as indicating that a greater supply of labour could be anticipated in the near future. The Minority Report indeed recommended the extension of individual tenure for the very reason that it would "reduce the number of natives tied to the Locations and Reserves"—in other words, crowd them out—and "release a large number for work more valuable to themselves and to the country".[1] It recommended the final delimitation by legislative enactment of land reserved or to be reserved for native occupation "and that thereafter no more land should be reserved for native occupation".[2]

Territorial Segregation.—No action on these lines was taken by the Union until the passing of the Land Act of 1913. The aim of this Act was to lay down definite lines of "territorial segregation"; that is, to divide the whole of the Union into native and European areas, and restrict further purchases by either class to their respective areas.

Existing reserves and land privately owned by natives were scheduled as native areas, while a commission—the Beaumont Commission—was appointed to report on the extent of further provision of land for native occupation which might be necessary. The prohibition on transfers between natives and non-natives came into force at once, but a decision of the Courts in 1917 ruled that it does not apply in the Cape.

In the other three Provinces the Beaumont Commission recommended the release for native occupation of between 10 and 11 million morgen of land.[3] The proposals were

[1] Report, par. 414. [2] Report, par. 207.
[3] Rogers, *Native Administration*, p. 171.

regarded as far too generous, and local committees were appointed to revise them. As a result the proposed new scheduled areas were scaled down to a total of about 7,000,000 morgen, those in the Orange Free State being reduced to nearly half the area recommended by the Beaumont Commission and those in Natal to less than a quarter. In the Orange Free State the area now proposed was already occupied by natives; that proposed in the Transvaal—an area of 4,000,000 morgen—consisted of unoccupied farms owned by Europeans on which some 68,000 natives were already established.[1] Even these proposals failed to be accepted; consequently the further provision contemplated in the Act of 1913 has never been made. There remains the right of the Government to sanction the acquisition or leasing of land by natives in special cases. As a matter of administrative practice this right has been exercised in the case of applications referring to land proposed for schedule by the Local Committees.[2] General Hertzog in 1926 introduced a Bill proposing to release an additional area of just over 6,000,000 morgen where natives might compete with Europeans for the purchase of land. But since he made this Bill dependent on another which aimed at removing the Cape franchise, and the latter failed to obtain the necessary majority, it did not become law. In 1935 he re-introduced the same measures in a modified form, reducing still further the area of land to be thrown open, but for the first time providing that European owners might be compensated in order to provide it, and establishing a Native Trust to facilitate its acquisition and supervise its development. The trust will also be entitled to sell native land.

The area to be acquired by the Trust is fixed at a *maximum* of 7,250,000 morgen. The revenues of the Trust are also specified. They are to be derived in part from a share of mining and prospecting fees and licences for operations carried out on native land, rents paid by non-natives on scheduled

---

[1] Native Affairs Report, 1921, p. 5.
[2] Rogers, *Native Administration in the Union of South Africa*, p. 167. According to Professor Edgar Brookes, some time between 1930 and 1932 this policy was reversed by " a quiet administrative ruling which only leaked out some time later ". *The Colour Problems of South Africa*, p. 60.

areas, and fines under the 1913 Land Act and the new Bill, and in part from moneys to be voted by Parliament. Thus the revenue which the Trust is actually assured of receiving is very small.[1]

In the meantime a native population of nearly 6,000,000 is legally entitled to occupy an area of some 34,000 square miles,[2] while the remaining 440,000 is either owned by Europeans or reserved for their ownership. The European population numbered 1,800,000 at the census of 1931.

This state of affairs has not, however, led to the happy consummation anticipated by Mr. Hamilton in 1903, with the reserves as purely residential areas whence the native would go to his work as the city clerk does from his suburban bungalow. To the majority of the native population agriculture is still the basic means of subsistence and wage-labour is a supplementary activity, undertaken, not necessarily unwillingly, but with a view to meeting some specific need; while the possession of cattle continues to be regarded as desirable in itself and to be necessary for purposes of religious ceremonial and for the payment of bride-price. A Native Economic Commission reported in 1932 that in all the reserves overstocking was so serious as to threaten famine in the near future. Those natives who are sufficiently Europeanized to want to live in European style, and sufficiently well educated to earn a wage which would enable them to do so, are to a large extent prevented by restrictions on their employment in skilled occupations. For it is as a source of cheap unskilled labour that the native is in demand, not as a competitor in those economic spheres which the European has arrogated to himself. And even in the field of unskilled labour he is now beginning to be feared as a competitor by Europeans who are qualified for nothing better.

If it has been found impossible to modify native life in the reserves in the direction desired—if experience has once again demonstrated that necessity is not infallibly the mother of the most efficient invention—no effort has been spared to secure

[1] See analysis in " The Native Bills ": Race Relations, August 1935.
[2] Figures given in morgen in Rogers, *Native Administration in the Union*, p. 119, and converted into acres in Evans, *Native Policies in Southern Africa*, p. 21.

that outside them the native shall not be able to exist except
as a worker for wages.

The Labour Problem.—Here the Union has its peculiar complication in the competition between the urban and mining
areas, paying relatively high wages, and the agricultural
districts. It has been mentioned already that the 1903–5
Native Affairs Commission, faced with endless complaints
from farmers of shortage of labour, rejected the idea of
regulating agricultural wages as a solution, on the ground that
the freedom of contract should not be infringed. The crux
of the whole problem of agriculture in South Africa, as in
the other "White Man's Countries", is that the native population is unwilling to work for the wages which the European
is willing to pay. Somebody must therefore be constrained,
and the principle of freedom of contract precludes putting the
screw on the employer. Although mining interests have complained of shortage of labour and have joined in the demand
to increase taxation, direct and indirect, and limit reserves so
as to "bring the native out", the most severely restrictive
legislation that has been imposed has been designed to assist
the farmer.

To the farmer the root of all evil from times past has been
the practice of "squatting". All over the Union Europeans
finding themselves in possession of more land than they could
work have turned the surplus to advantage by allowing natives
to reside and cultivate there and graze their stock. Sometimes
the return made was a share of the crop, sometimes an agreement to give labour when required, sometimes a cash payment.
In Natal a syndicate, the Natal Land and Colonization Company,
bought up large areas of land of which they made no other use
than to rent it to natives.[1] Here a strong motive to leave their
locations was the obligation imposed on natives living within
their boundaries to give six months' labour in the year for
public works at half the ruling rate of pay, which was believed
to represent an adaptation of tribal custom to modern conditions.
In every province except the Orange Free State there has also
been a certain amount of squatting on Crown lands; here

---

[1] Native Affairs Report, 1903–5, questions 19936 ff.

the term denotes simply the occupation by natives of land not recognized as theirs.

Whereas in Europe absentee landlordism is usually condemned as detrimental to the interests of the tenant, in South Africa it has been neighbouring landlords who have protested against this system. The first objection to it was that it removed natives from the reach of administrative control; that large concentrations of natives in these "private locations" were hotbeds of crime, above all of stock-theft. As the control exercised by farmers over their squatters became severer the complaint was that labour was wastefully "tied up" by landlords who did not themselves require it, while squatting on Crown land was held to enable the native to live too easily "without working".

The Status of the Squatter.—In the Cape Province squatters on Crown land have been placed under no disabilities, merely being taxed on the same basis as natives in locations. In Natal and the Transvaal legislation intended to prevent squatting on Crown land has been largely inoperative,[1] and the course followed has been to charge an annual rent. In Natal the original rent was £1 per hut, increased to £2 in 1903. In the Transvaal the rent was £1 for each adult male till 1903, when it was raised to 30s. per adult male, plus 10s. for every five head of cattle above ten, and 2s. 6d. for every ten head of small stock above twenty.

It is of course in connection with squatting on farms that the labour problem is directly relevant. Here the general aim pursued has been to let every farmer have enough squatter labour for his legitimate requirements. Everywhere except in the Cape the number of native families which might live on any one farm was limited—in Natal to three, in the Transvaal and the Free State to five—unless special permission was granted for a larger number. This regulation as an ideal was warmly praised by all farmer witnesses before the 1903–5 Commission, but it was admitted that it was never enforced.

[1] See Rogers, *Native Administration*, pp. 149–50. Compare, however, this description by a witness (not necessarily reliable) before the Native Affairs Commission of 1903–5. "Commissioners would take Kafirs living in Government grounds and give them to people who had no Kafirs, at a certain wage per year." Questions 26953–8.

The line adopted first in the Cape, and subsequently followed in the other Provinces, was not merely to limit numbers but to differentiate between those in the employment of the farmer and "squatters pure and simple". Provided the squatter is working for his landlord, it is held, his labour is not running to waste and no injury is done to neighbouring farmers. It is still argued that the squatter system enables farmers who have vacant land to offer to tie to their farms natives whose labour they require at most intermittently; to which the answer is made that they must be able to count on the necessary labour at busy seasons.

The Cape Native Locations Act of 1899 set no limit to the number of families that might reside on a farm, provided that the head of each was in continuous employment by the owner. "Labour tenants" who occupied land in return for an agreement to work for wages for a limited period were permitted up to the number sanctioned by a Government Inspector, while for "squatters pure and simple" a licence fee of £1 per annum was charged for each adult male and the landlord was made responsible for their hut tax. Under the law at present in force, the Private Locations Act of 1909, a licence is charged of 10s. per annum for each labour tenant, and £2 per annum for each squatter, now dignified by the description of "ordinary tenant". The authorities may refuse to issue such licences. The effect of this legislation has been to reduce the total population of private locations in the Cape from 35,418 in 1907 to 6630 in 1931.[1] In the Transvaal a Law of 1908 doubled the tax payable by a squatter who did not enter into a contract to give at least ninety days' service a year to the farmer on whose land he resided.

Outside the Cape the Land Act of 1913 has at one blow made illegal not only the leasing of land to natives outside scheduled areas, but the system of "ploughing on the halves" whereby a native was allowed to graze stock and cultivate land in return for a share of his crop. Labour tenancy, on the other hand, was expressly sanctioned by an article excluding from the operation of the law in the Transvaal a native resident on a farm who renders the owner at least ninety days' service per

[1] Rogers, *Native Administration*, p. 154.

annum; while in the Free State a measure was adopted which had been recommended by a Native Affairs Commission of 1909, providing that residence on a farm should "presuppose a contract" subject to the penal provisions of the Masters and Servants Act. An amendment to this Act in 1926 made its penal clauses applicable to squatters' contracts also in the Transvaal and Natal. Owing to the practical difficulties of registration, these contracts are seldom written, so that if either party claims a breach of contract the courts can only choose between the farmer's word and the natives. It is not difficult to see how this system must work out in practice.

The attraction of squatting to the native is said to have been in the past the comparative freedom from control, and in Natal the exemption from corvée (isibalo).[1] At present the principal advantage which it offers is grazing for stock, which in the reserves becomes constantly scarcer. While certain natives are becoming urbanized in numbers which the municipalities responsible for their housing and policing find seriously embarrassing, the majority continue to prefer an agricultural existence even at the price of the increasing disabilities put upon them. In 1929 fourteen-fifteenths of the native population of the Orange Free State, nearly half of that of Natal proper (without Zululand), and more than two-thirds of that of the Transvaal were resident on farms.[2]

Outside the Cape such persons can only obtain land for their subsistence on conditions which become increasingly onerous. In the Transvaal ninety days' labour is the legal minimum that can be required of them. Sometimes the agreement is that the squatter will work when called on throughout the year or give two days' work in each week, a system which effectually precludes his supplementing his meagre wages by work elsewhere. There are some areas in the Transvaal where whole families are contracted to serve in this way for no return other than the right to occupy land. Their services were calculated, in terms of the ruling rate of wages paid to hired labourers, as equivalent in value to an annual rent of £9, 15s. In the same district land companies charge such a tenant £3, 10s. In other

---

[1] See p. 42.   [2] Macmillan, Complex South Africa, p. 233.

parts of the Transvaal the service contract is for twelve calendar months. In Natal the usual contract is for six months' service, where formerly a rent was charged of at most £3.[1]

Since 1901 Transvaal natives domiciled on farms have been obliged to get a pass from the owner in order to travel to any other districts. The Masters and Servants Act prohibits the employment of any native whose identification pass shows him to be domiciled on European land unless he produces a written statement by the landlord to the effect that the latter has no claim on his services. In areas which may be defined by proclamation landowners may be fined £5 for every able-bodied male domiciled on their land (except school teachers) who does not work for six months in the year under a service contract. No such area has yet been proclaimed,[2] but the Land Bill introduced in 1935 proposes to require the payment of a licence for all squatters other than labour tenants, which in the tenth and subsequent years from its enactment will amount to £5.[3] The Department of Native Affairs is to see that accommodation is provided in native areas for any natives who may be turned off European land.

In the areas where land is being farmed more intensively by Europeans the labour tenancy system is losing vogue and wage labour is taking its place.[4] But this has as its necessary corollary a still greater shortage of land for native occupation, and if it means a more efficient use of labour it does nothing to solve the problem of subsistence for an increasing population confined by law to a limited area of land of rapidly decreasing productivity, but unable to earn a wage that would render them independent of the garden at home.

Natives in Industrial Areas.—So the "desired result of forcing these men into large labour centres", as Mr. "Matabele" Thompson put it in 1903,[5] has been achieved—yet nobody is

---

[1] Addendum by Mr. F. A. Lucas to the Report of the Native Economic Commission, 1930–32, pp. 202–3, and Report, pp. 52–3.
[2] Rogers, *Native Administration*, p. 161. The Act in its final form is very much less severe than the measure originally proposed. For a summary of the latter see Macmillan, *Complex South Africa*, p. 251.
[3] *Race Relations, loc. cit.*
[4] Report of Native Economic Commission, 1930–32, p. 56.
[5] Native Affairs Commission, question 29287.

satisfied. The urban European population wants to have within reach just that number of natives whom it can employ and not one more. So the policy of "bringing the native out to work" by making it impossible for him to live on his own land is accompanied by legislation designed to make it impossible for him to live in the urban centres. The town locations are intended to be mere temporary abiding places for natives in employment, who are now—with the exception of domestic servants—not allowed to sleep in the European cities. Restrictions on the residence of natives there were intended at first to discourage vagrancy and prevent the growth of a criminal population. Since Union legislation has imposed upon municipalities the duty of providing a decent minimum standard of accommodation in native locations, there is a new motive—the desire to avoid unnecessary expense. Today the pressing problem is said to be to check the drift to the towns by improving conditions in the reserves.[1] The wheel has come full circle.

Control over the town population is exercised by means of the registration system which since 1923 has superseded the earlier Transvaal and Orange Free State Pass Laws. On first arriving in a location a native must obtain a permit to seek work, which is valid for four days in the first instance but can be renewed by the authorities. Natives complained before the Commission of 1903–5[2] that this system had the effect of forcing them to accept work at a low rate of wages on penalty of being imprisoned on the expiry of the pass. The Commission of 1930–2 reports that it is possible for an unemployed man by obtaining successive renewals to "wander about for a considerable time at the expense of the community".[3] The evidence given before this Commission has not been made public. Once he has found work the written contract, which it is obligatory for him to make with his employer, establishes his right to reside in the location. Failure to produce such a document on request is a criminal offence. In the Transvaal it has to be renewed monthly at a cost of 2s. which, though

[1] Native Economic Commission, 1932, p. 80.
[2] Question 42059.   [3] Report, p. 78.

payable by the employer, is deducted from wages. In mining, which is the principal urban occupation, the average period of contract is from nine to twelve months.

The Urban Areas Acts of 1923 and 1930 have obliged municipalities to provide native locations giving a reasonable standard of housing, water-supply and sanitation, and transfer to them the population of the slum areas which had grown up in all the large towns. The new locations must be at least three miles from the European area, which means the addition of a considerable cost of transport to the native's living expenses. When sufficient such accommodation has been provided in any urban area, the area in question is "proclaimed" by the Governor-General. It then becomes illegal for natives to reside anywhere outside the location. Exemptions from these provisions are granted to natives owning immovable property valued at £75, and in the Cape to registered voters. Natives resident in the locations are obliged to carry a permit to seek work or a labour service contract always with them in order to establish their right to be in such an area; and the local authority may refuse to permit any further natives to enter the area except upon specified conditions. These passes are not required in the Cape. Curfew regulations, however, forbidding natives to be out at night without a special pass, apply in all the Provinces. Since 1925 it has also been a criminal offence to fail to produce a tax-receipt.

It is quite true that some system of registration may have advantages in the case, for example, of natives dying away from home, where compensation or arrears of wages may be due to them. But it is absurd to pretend that such advantages can only be secured by a system which restricts the freedom of all natives not in European employment and assumes that they are criminals until they furnish documentary evidence to the contrary.

Efforts to discourage urbanization at the same time as encouraging wage-labour have not succeeded in preventing the growth of a permanent urban population of natives who have severed all connection with the reserves. They are perhaps the worst sufferers by the existing system, since the prevailing rate of wages is that accepted by the reserve natives, who look to wage-labour, not for their entire subsistence but to supplement agriculture in a life whose material standard is in most ways lower than that of the town native. The Native Economic Commission, however, rejected as a remedy for this state of affairs the extension to natives of the machinery for wage regulation which applies to Europeans in the Union; [1] and the penal clauses of the Masters and Servants Acts make striking a criminal offence and thus draw the teeth of any organization for collective bargaining. In January 1930 the Johannesburg Chamber of Commerce refused to discuss a proposal from the native Industrial and Commercial Workers' Union for the institution of a minimum wage, on the ground that higher wage-rates would reduce the supply of natives from the reserves by making it possible for them to earn the amount they required in a shorter time.[2]

In order to protect Europeans from the competition of natives willing and able to do the same work for a lower wage, the "Colour Bar Act" of 1926—formally an amendment of the Mines and Works Act—empowers the Minister to make regulations excluding natives from occupations requiring special skill and responsibility, and thus gives legal sanction to the established practice of reserving surface work for Europeans. Other trades were barred to natives by the Apprenticeship Act of 1922, which requires that an apprentice should have had education up to Standard VI—a blessing enjoyed only by very few natives. Since 1922 the ratio of European to native employees in the mines has been fixed, by an agreement between the Chamber of Mines and the European Trade Union, at 1 to 10·5. But the natives cannot be prevented from competing with those Europeans who are not themselves capable of any work more skilled than that in which the employment of natives is normal.

The Poor Whites have been protected to some extent by the activities of a wage Board which has attempted, by fixing at a "civilized" level wages in occupations where black and

[1] Report, p. 147.
[2] Ballinger, *Race and Economics in South Africa*, p. 37.

white compete, to restrict employment there to Europeans.[1] Some employers, however, continued to employ natives at the higher wage. On the other hand, the effect of wage regulation by the Industrial Conciliation Board, which applies only to Europeans, has been the displacement of Europeans in favour of natives whose wages were not covered by its awards.

In the construction of public works a policy has been followed of employing European in preference to native labour; the tax-payer meets the cost. Its most paradoxical result is the situation in the urban locations, where houses constructed by European labour cannot be leased at an economic rent to tenants earning native wages.

The Native Economic Commission recommended measures tending to stabilize the urban and rural populations and, by cutting off the supply of casual labour, to enable the urban native to earn a rate of wages that should gradually approximate to that of the unskilled European. The measures which they advocate are the provision of more land for native occupation and agricultural development in the reserves; but not wage regulation.[2]

Meantime at any given time up to 70 per cent of the adult male natives are absent from their reserves, and the average length of employment, excluding travelling, is between ten and eleven months.[3] This in itself reduces the efficiency of cultivation there: and it was stated in evidence that natives hesitated to make improvements lest Europeans should cast greedy eyes on their lands.[4] And there is a general demand that the three Protectorates be handed over to the Union with a view to the assimilation of native policy through South Africa.

European Law and Native Custom.—In the sphere of what is narrowly known as native administration—the degree of respect shown for the political institutions and laws of the various native tribes—there has been a wide divergence of policy

---

[1] Ballinger, *op. cit.*, pp. 49–50.
[2] Report of Native Economic Commission, pp. 80–81, 147–8.
[3] *Ibid.*, pp. 173, 212–13.
[4] *Ibid.*, p. 184. On the other hand, in Natal many farmers are beginning to show considerable benevolent interest in such developments as Native Agricultural Shows.

between the "liberal" tradition of the Cape, which held that
the law of the Colony should be applied without distinction to
all its inhabitants, and the Natal system, in which native law
was codified (with such modifications as the dictates of "natural
justice" seemed to require), the relation of the European to
the native regime was expressed in terms supposed to be
suitable to native comprehension, the Governor being designated
Supreme Chief, and exemption from the scope of native law
was granted by special authorization to natives held to be
sufficiently advanced to qualify for it. The Transvaal and
Orange Free State provided for the recognition of native law
without going so far as to have it studied and codified.

The two native institutions which have been especially
influenced by the line of policy followed have been the chieftainship and the polygamous family, with all the regulations relating
to the marriage contract, the guardianship of women, and
inheritance that are bound up with it. In the Cape every effort
was made to reduce the authority of native chiefs. Their
judicial powers of course vanished in a system where the
European magistrate's was the only competent court. Their
authority over land was destroyed where land was given out in
individual tenure. Where new institutions of local government
were devised, traditional authorities were originally given no
place in them, though later modifications have recognized
their position, at least in the more "tribal" areas: the original
District Councils established by the Glen Grey Act consisted
in the Ciskei of members nominated by the Location Boards,
and in the Transkei of district headmen appointed by a "rough
ballot" and defined as "acting partly as constables and partly as
collectors of revenue".[1] Since 1932 they have been elected by
local taxpayers.

The impossibility of settling native civil cases on the assumption that only European law could be applied to them was bound
to strike any intelligent magistrate. Eventually a special Native
Court was set up at King Williamstown, where, "by agreement between the parties", cases might be heard and determined
on the basis of native law. Here native cases of divorce and

---

[1] Native Affairs Commission, question 6056.

40

succession and claims for the return of *lobola* (bride-price) cattle were decided to the satisfaction of natives, while in the next district claims for *lobola* were dismissed on the ground that an "immoral contract" could not be upheld by the courts. The general practice in the Cape was to refuse to register marriages concluded in accordance with native custom, with the result that under the only law recognized as applicable to the Colony the couples were not legally married. A Christian marriage, on the other hand, involved the application to the parties of the Roman-Dutch law of succession by which property must be divided among all the children, and ruled out the native system according to which one son succeeded to the administration of all his father's property and the guardianship of the other children. In the Transkeian Territories native law is recognized, though its administration is in the hands of European magistrates.

In Natal the policy of respecting native law, as put into practice, has been in many respects hardly better. The idea that to call the Governor-General the "Supreme Chief" could create a relationship between him and the natives comparable to that between them and their own chiefs, and provide a ground for claiming acquiescence in all new orders imposed by the European authority, seems too childish to be credible. That spirited lady, Miss Harriet Colenso, told the Native Affairs Commission thirty years ago that it was "the foundation of our many mistakes".[1] Yet this absurd fiction, which had also been adopted in the Transvaal and was extended to the Orange Free State in 1907, was confirmed in the Native Administration Act of 1927; and while in the Transvaal and Free State it had been admitted that a doubt might arise whether every action of the administration could be justified by appeal to a paramount authority supposed to be derived from native custom, such doubts have been swept away by an amending Act of 1929, defining the powers of the Supreme Chief in all the Provinces as being such powers as may be vested in him in the Province of Natal. The definition in the amended Natal Native Code merely continues to beg the question, since under

[1] Question 23967.

41

it the Supreme Chief's powers include "all powers, authorities, functions, rights, immunities and privileges which, according to the laws, customs and usages of Natives are exercised or enjoyed by any Supreme or Paramount Native Chief". It is universally assumed by Europeans that such powers include the right to issue orders of any kind and claim unquestioning obedience to them—a misconception which, as I have tried to show elsewhere,[1] has vitiated many attempts to impose European ways by using African chiefs as their mouthpiece. Moreover, the Supreme Chief does not exercise his powers as a newly constituted overlord at the head of a pre-existing native hierarchy. For the Natal system, no less than that of the Cape, has aimed at reducing the powers of native chiefs. They have been largely deprived of judicial functions, in which they have been replaced by magistrates purporting to be "representatives of the Supreme Chief", and as Mr. Justice Beaumont acutely pointed out in 1904, "Every Act dealing with natives that is passed more or less undermines the authority of these chiefs."[2]

At the same time they have been entrusted with the duties of collecting taxes, and rent on Crown lands, of encouraging their subjects to seek paid employment, and—so long as it remained in force—of organizing the *isibalo* labour system, whereby every adult male, supposedly in accordance with tribal custom, was liable for six months' labour on public works, from which those who had been in employment in the previous year were exempt. A chief was entitled to impose a fine of £2 on any subject who disobeyed his orders. Soon natives were accusing the chiefs of demanding a bribe of £2 to exempt them from *isibalo*; and contractors pointed out that "it pays them better to pay the chief £2 and evade the work at £1 a month"—the Government rate—in order to find better employment elsewhere.[3]

The Natal Code recognized marriage by native custom but, as amended in 1932, it lays down that the full *lobola* must be

---

[1] See my article, "Chieftainship in Modern Africa," to be published shortly in *Africa*,
[2] Native Affairs Commission, question 18090.
[3] Native Affairs Commission, 1903–5, questions 26133, 26524.

paid on the day of marriage. The basis of this prohibition appears to be the belief that to hand it over on a series of occasions, as native custom prescribes, allows the father-in-law to impose on the husband, and leads to unnecessary litigation; it leaves out of consideration entirely any correlation that this series of gifts might have with events of social importance in the lives of the couple and their relatives.

While the Transvaal in theory recognized native law, and based European authority on the fiction of the Supreme Chief, the magistrates who applied the law held that polygamous marriages were contrary to civilization and therefore could not be recognized. The Orange Free State only explicitly recognized native law in the matter of guardianship of minors and succession.[1] Not until 1927 was legislation introduced which made some provision throughout the Union for the administration of native law by native authorities. The Native Administration Acts of 1927 and 1929 make possible the establishment of chiefs' and headmen's courts with civil, and a limited criminal, jurisdiction, at the discretion of the authorities. In civil cases the appeal lies from these courts not to magistrates but to Native Commissioners. Such courts with civil jurisdiction are established only in areas where there is "a considerable non-detribalized population", and criminal jurisdiction under these Acts is conferred only in Zululand and British Bechuanaland.[2] An important feature of the Native Administration Act (1927) is that it prohibits the Courts from declaring that *lobola* is repugnant to natural justice.

The Goal of Native Development.—But "native development" in South Africa has always meant, not the adaptation of native institutions to modern conditions, but their progressive abandonment in favour of those of European society. The instruments of native development in the Union have been the franchise, provision for exemption from the scope of native law or from differential European legislation, and the system of District Councils.

The Native Franchise.—Only in the Cape has the franchise been granted on terms which have enabled any considerable

---

[1] Rogers, *Native Administration*, p. 221.   [2] *Ibid.*, pp. 225, 227.

number of natives to obtain it. Here the qualification is
literacy, together with the ownership of property to the rateable
value of £75, or an income of £50 per annum. About 16,000
natives are registered voters. It is doubtful how far, even now
the vote is valued for the sake of its political influence; but
because, under the provisions of the Hofmeyr Act of 1887, it
carries with it exemption from the restrictive legislation to
which the majority of natives are subject, the Cape natives cling
most tenaciously to their privileged position. The Hofmeyr
Act is usually associated with freedom from restrictions on the
sale of liquor, for the sake of which a considerable number of
natives registered as voters immediately after it was passed.
But this exemption applies also to restrictions on the acquisition
of land, to pass regulations and to the provisions of the Urban
Areas Act obliging natives in such areas to reside in locations.
It is a significant fact, worthy more attention from those who
assert that what the native demands is European civilization as
such, that it is to freedom from differential European legislation
and not from their own laws that they attach this importance.

The three other Provinces have had legislation, providing
in Natal for exemption from native law,[1] carrying with it
exemption from pass laws, the liquor laws and the restrictive
provisions of the Land Act, in the Transvaal and Orange Free
State for exemption from pass regulations. All these laws
have been repealed by the Native Administration Act of 1927
which, as amended in 1929, provides that regulations may be
made providing for the grant of exemption from differential
legislation *except* as regards the land and liquor laws. Thus
the Cape franchise remains as the sole ground on which any
native can claim immunity from differential legislation.

The fear that so large a number of natives would become
voters as to swamp the European vote began at an early date to
exercise public opinion in the Cape. Its reflexion is seen for
the first time in the Glen Grey Act, which expressly provides
that the value of land held under it cannot be counted for the
purpose of qualifying for the franchise. The type of obstacle

[1] In Natal an exempted native can obtain the franchise by a very cumbrous process. Only four have ever done so.

put in the way of registration by magistrates dominated by determination to "make the native work" is illustrated by the practice reported to the Native Affairs Commission, whereby an income of £50 was not accepted as a qualification *unless the applicant had worked for the whole previous year at the rate of £50 a year.*[1] As for opinion in the other Provinces, the opposition between them and the Cape, whose policy was favoured by the Imperial Government, nearly shipwrecked the National Convention which drafted the Act of Union. Finally the attempt to reach a uniform policy in the matter was abandoned, and instead a provision was inserted in the Act that legislation altering the Cape franchise could only be passed by a two-thirds majority of both Houses sitting together. Up till 1936 it was not possible to obtain the requisite majority.

It has been pointed out that to many natives the franchise is of value chiefly in virtue of the exemption from differential legislation which it carries with it. Presumably on the ground that exemption and the franchise are independent, a native, Ndobe, contested the validity of the Native Administration Act on the ground that it had not been passed by this special procedure, but the Courts upheld it. The extension in 1930 of the vote to European and not to native women and its extension in 1931 to all adult European males—measures which do not refer to natives but merely omit them—were passed by the ordinary procedure. Thus a differential franchise has for some time existed even in the Cape.

Native Councils.—The policy adumbrated in the Glen Grey Act, and now the avowed aim of General Hertzog, is to offer local self-government as an alternative for the renunciation of claims to participation in the European political system. Against local self-government in itself there is nothing to be said; though it should be remembered that the form in which it has been established in no sense represents the development

[1] Question 1622. This interpretation of the income qualification has now become law in the form that the £50 must have been earned in the preceding twelve months with not more than one month's intermission. Between 1930 and 1933 some 600 natives were removed from the register by the strict application of this provision. *Race Relations*, August 1935, p. 22.

of natives along their own lines. What has been done, first in the "model administration" of the Transkei, and later in all native locations, has been to set up local councils of European type to be managed by natives under the supervision of Europeans.

The Glen Grey District Council consisted of twelve members, six appointed by the Government and the remaining six by the Location Boards. When the system was extended to the Transkei, a series of Councils of six members was set up, two being Government nominees and the rest selected from among themselves at a meeting of district headmen, the latter having been appointed to their posts by the Government. In 1906 the method of appointment of these four members was altered to election by a meeting of ratepayers. These Councils were represented by two members each on the Bunga, or General Council for the whole of the Transkei. Owing to native opposition the Council system was not introduced into Pondoland until 1911, when tribal tradition was so far recognized that in Western Pondoland the Paramount Chief was given the right of nominating the four members of each Council not directly appointed by the Government. Later the system was assimilated to that of Eastern Pondoland, where the Paramount Chief appoints two members to each Council, and two are nominated by "the representatives of the people". The Paramount Chiefs are additional members of the Pondoland General Council or of the District Councils of the districts in which they reside. The Chief of Tembuland is similarly a member of the Umbala District Council. In each case the Magistrate of the district is chairman of the Council. In 1931 all the District Councils of the Transkei and Pondoland were amalgamated into a single General Council, with the Chief Magistrate of the Territories as chairman. The District Magistrates are entitled to be present and take part in all meetings of the General Council.[1]

The small Orange Free State Reserves are administered by Boards of five to seven native members with a European chairman and vice-chairman, all nominated by the Government.[2]

[1] Rogers, *Native Administration*, pp. 49 ff.   [2] *Ibid.*, p. 79.

The Native Affairs Act of 1920 and subsequent amendments
provided for the establishment by proclamation in any native
area of local Councils with or without the maximum powers
which the Act allows to such Councils. Ten such Councils
have up till now been established with limited powers, and
ten with full powers. They consist of not more than nine
natives, with a European official to preside and "generally act
in an advisory capacity".

These Councils obtain their revenue from the right to levy
from every adult male under their jurisdiction an annual rate
of 10s. in Glen Grey, the Transkei and Pondoland, £1 elsewhere,
and from the payment to them of a "local tax" of 10s. per hut
from natives who do not hold land on individual tenure, together
with the quit-rent due from those that do. The payment of
quit-rent to the local Councils may be said to correspond to
a rebate on general taxation, since this was previously collected
by the State. Their other sources of revenue represent obligations imposed on the native population over and above the
contribution which they make to the general exchequer.

The competence of these Councils includes the construction
of roads, establishment of schools and hospitals, water-supply,
sanitation, dipping of stock, agricultural development, afforestation and the prevention of erosion, while in the Transkei, where
they are associated with a system of individual land tenure,
they are responsible for the allocation of land and the regulation
of grazing commonage. In the Transkeian Territories the
District Councils are merely subordinate organs of the General
Council or Bunga, which allocates duties among them and has
sole financial responsibility. Its revised constitution in 1932
established an Executive Committee, meeting at least once every
two months, consisting of four magistrates and four native
members nominated by the Bunga. This Committee is
responsible for the administration of agricultural development and public works, the grant of scholarships, appointment
and dismissal of pensionable officers, and the institution of
legal proceedings. Five members form a quorum, and decisions
are taken by a majority, the chairman having the casting vote.
This of course means that, in case of a division of opinion

between the native and official points of view, in a full meeting the official view must prevail.

The other important amendment in the constitution of the Council was the express recognition that it is entitled to initiate and consider "any matter relating to the economic, industrial or social condition of the native population of the Union or any part thereof", and to consider "any proposed legislation or existing law which specially affects the native population . . . in so far as it affects natives within the area of jurisdiction of the Council". Resolutions of the Council on these matters have no executive force. They are discussed at a meeting of the official members, which forwards them with comments to the Secretary for Native Affairs.[1]

The Representation of Native Interests.—Within its limited sphere the Bunga has been a valuable organ for the expression of native opinion. Its complement for the whole Union was provided by the Native Affairs Act of 1920, in a general Native Council to meet annually and discuss any matters affecting natives. This Council has not been summoned since 1930. The Representation of Natives Act passed in March 1936 re-establishes a Native Representative Council which must be summoned annually and must be consulted on all legislation affecting native interests before this is submitted to Parliament or to a Provincial Council. It may also initiate discussion and recommend legislation. The new Council is to consist of twelve elected and four nominated native members, with five Chief Native Commissioners, who may speak but not vote, and the Secretary for Native Affairs as Chairman with a casting vote only. The native members may be disqualified for misconduct or "other cause". The expression of native opinion by less constitutional means is barred by the Riotous Assemblies Act, which makes "incitement to ill-feeling between black and white" an offence punishable with banishment, and outside the Cape by the right conferred on the Supreme Chief by the revised Code of Natal to imprison for three months without a hearing any native deemed to be "dangerous to the public peace".

[1] Rogers, *Native Administration*, p. 57.

Further provision for the representation of native interests was made in 1920 by the establishment of the Native Affairs Commission, consisting of the Minister of Native Affairs as Chairman and three members nominated for their expert knowledge of native affairs. This Commission has the right to be consulted on all measures affecting native interests, and, if not so consulted, may intervene *suo motu*.[1]

General Hertzog's Natives Parliamentary Representation Bill, which was first introduced in 1927, and in 1929 passed the second but failed to pass the third reading, proposed to abolish the Cape franchise in return for a communal system whereby natives throughout the Union should be entitled to elect a certain number of Europeans to represent their interests. In 1935 the Bill was introduced in a new form; it is now proposed that the native population should be represented, not in the Lower House, but through four members of the Senate. This measure has been hailed with indignation as the final betrayal of the native cause. It is certainly intended to eliminate, once and for all, the possibility that the native vote might come to outweigh the European, and if it is passed it will at once remove from Union politics an important influence making for liberalism in native policy. In thirteen out of the sixty-one constituencies in the Cape the native votes represent a proportion of the total electorate sufficiently high for a "pro-native" candidate to be almost sure of election. Since such a candidate cannot hope for a successful political career, in the commonly accepted sense of the word, most of the representatives of these constituencies have been men of strong character, actuated by a genuine interest in native welfare. While it is not likely that in any matter of native policy the House would be so evenly divided that these thirteen members would hold the balance in voting strength, their presence has always guaranteed that the native point of view on any given measure would be both courageously and persuasively represented—probably more effectively, in such an environment, than it could have been advocated by Africans themselves. Whether the "Cape tradition" would of itself, without the means of

[1] Rogers, *Native Administration*, pp. 31–5.

making it felt which the native franchise provides in this way, have preserved such advantages as the Cape natives still enjoy over their fellows in the other Provinces, is more than doubtful. This safeguard they now seem to be about to lose.[1]

This situation throws some light on the general question of the value of the franchise as a safeguard for native interests, an issue sometimes confused by fallacious or irrelevant arguments. Doctrinaire "democrats" believe that representative government is the only political system which allows for the free expression of every point of view and gives a fair hearing to all. They forget how far from equal in practice is the amount of hearing given to different types of opinion. They assume that any other form of political organization involves the type of repression of all criticism of the regime in power which we see in many countries of modern Europe. It is that assumption which has led to the introduction of popularly elected organs of local government among native societies, of whom no one 'ever troubled to ask what means for the expression of public opinion existed under their own political system. If the argument be accepted that the efficacy of a political system must be evaluated in relation to the circumstances in which it functions, that assumption will not in itself be sufficient to justify the introduction of the ballot-box to native societies.

As soon, however, as a local European population, whose demands upon such societies are necessarily not based primarily on consideration for their interests, begins to have any control over their destinies, the question arises of devising some means whereby native interests may be enabled not only to make themselves heard, but to make themselves felt with comparable effectiveness to those of the Europeans. The grant of the franchise on a sufficiently broad basis to produce this result, in the present state of native education, would merely intensify the problem that faces all modern democracies, of the demand of ignorant self-interest to decide issues that it is incapable of understanding.

What alternatives are there? The obligation to refer legislation affecting natives to the impartial authority of the home

[1] The measure was passed with minor amendments in March 1936.

Parliament, though it has by no means always preserved native interests from serious damage, allows for the possibility of decision by a government not directly dependent upon the support of the local European population. Where the Imperial Government remains the final arbiter, and takes this responsibility seriously, local assemblies can do no more than express points of view; the weight of numbers on one side or the other is not all-important, and the arguments of the Hilton Young Commission for the communal roll as better suited to an electorate which is not homogeneous have considerable force. But in a state where the European population has full responsible government—where a government with complete control over native policy maintains itself in power by commanding a majority of votes in the House—what hope is there that any serious consideration will be given to a point of view whose representatives, however elected, are always to be in a minority?

The failure of General Hertzog's first Natives Representation Bill to pass its third reading shows that where European interests are not *directly* affected those of the natives will receive some consideration even from the elected representatives of European constituencies. Liberal European opinion has been strong enough to secure amendments in measures such as the Native Service Contract Act. It has been able, that is to say, to palliate measures designed to serve European interests without regard for those of the native; but it has not modified the general trend of a policy which inevitably places European interests first. Nor is it easy to say how that trend can be reversed so long as the native point of view is irrelevant to the maintenance of a government in power.

There is no easy remedy. A more even balance of representation could be achieved by imposing an educational qualification high enough to exclude a large number of Europeans who are now voters, and making better provision for the education of natives; but such a step is not practical politics, in the sense that one cannot conceive of its serious consideration by any possible South African government. Perhaps we must be content with learning from South Africa how utterly incompatible is the grant of responsible government to a

51

colonial community with any consideration for the "well-being or development" of the native populations upon whom their economic position depends.

Racial Differentiation in Education.—In educational policy the Cape theory of the potential equality of black and white, and the Transvaal conception of the inherent inferiority of the native, are reflected in the relative stress given to literary and manual training, and to instruction in English and the vernacular. In both systems little attention has been given to the relation between the subjects taught and the native environment, and the curriculum has been planned on the assumption that a complete course includes attendance both at elementary and secondary schools, regardless of the fact that only 3 per cent of the total school-going population passes beyond the elementary stage. For this small percentage the Cape provides higher education up to university standard, the examinations taken at Fort Hare Native College being those of the University of Cape Town. Thus we have in effect the same concentration upon the education of the *élite* that characterizes the French colonies, without the opportunities of advancement that the French *élite* are accorded, and without the complement of a comprehensive programme designed to enable the majority to make the best of their short school period. Their education comprises merely an introduction which has little meaning apart from the further study to which it is proposed to lead. Despite the obvious additional difficulty of learning unfamiliar subjects when these are presented in a foreign language, which was commented on by Dr. Loram in 1917 as one of the main hindrances to the progress of native pupils, the Cape continues to lay stress on the use of the English language. This has now become associated in the native and in many European minds with native advancement, and any proposal to extend the use of the vernacular is suspect as an instrument of racial differentiation.

While the insistence on such racial differentiation is undoubtedly the motive which leads to the wider use of the vernacular in schools outside the Cape, from the educationist's point of view there seems no doubt that this produces more

satisfactory results, especially where education is not to go
beyond the elementary stage. The generally expressed desire
of the European population in the Orange Free State and
Transvaal is that the native should be educated enough to
make him industrious but not enough to enable him to compete
for skilled employment; and the fact being that he is to be as
far as possible debarred from entering such employment, an
intelligent system of education must aim at enabling him to make
the best use of that life which is to be open to him. In Natal,
in particular, much attention has been devoted to instruction
in practical activities which will improve the standard of native
home life, such as agriculture for boys, cooking and needlework
for girls.

The best efforts of educationists, however, are bound sooner
or later to be brought up against a political system which does
not aim at enabling the native to take advantage of European
knowledge, but only at making him a docile servant of European
masters. One type of training after another becomes futile
as restrictions debar the native from taking advantage of it.
Even the Natal method meets with the difficulty, in justify-
ing itself to the native parent or pupil, that, while it creates
a desire for a higher material standard of living, it does
not enable its products to command a wage that will enable
that standard to be maintained in an economic organization
where cheapness is valued far more highly than intelligence
or efficiency.

Indifference or hostility to the education of the native
manifests itself in other ways. The permission of European
landowners is required before schools can be opened on their
land, and while a few have actually built schools for natives,
this consent is frequently refused, a factor of some significance
where such a large native population is living on European
land. Some farmers object even to children crossing their land
on the way to school; others, while they allow schools, demand
labour from the pupils. More serious still is the failure to
make budgetary provision on anything like the scale necessary
for an efficient system of native education. Native education
is financed from a Native Development Fund provided by a

fixed annual contribution from Union funds, calculated on the basis of the amount spent for this purpose by the Provinces in 1921–22—*i.e.* £340,000—along with one-fifth of the proceeds of the native poll-tax. The share of this fund devoted to education averages £530,000 annually.[1] The *per capita* expenditure is £2, 3s. 6d. for the native as against £17 to £20 (in different Provinces) for the European population. This disparity is far too great to be accounted for merely by the lower cost of buildings and rate of salaries in the case of native schools. It has meant not only a far lower proportion of schools for the total native population but perpetual difficulty in securing teachers of sufficiently high standard, since the wages which can be offered them are lower than those ruling in towns even in the occupations from which natives are not barred. This difficulty has to some extent been countered in Natal by the introduction of a Cost of Living Allowance for teachers in urban areas.

The Three Native Territories.—When in 1909 South Africa attained full responsible government as a federation, liberal opinion in Great Britain was somewhat exercised at the prospects for the development of native policy under an independent State where the Cape point of view was likely to be outweighed by that of the Provinces whose whole *raison d'être* lay in revolt against the Cape tradition. The attempt to extend the Cape policy in the matter of franchise succeeded only in imposing special safeguards against alterations in the Cape itself. Imperial solicitude for native interests resulted, however, in the retention through the High Commissioner of British control over the three native Protectorates of Basutoland, Bechuanaland and Swaziland. It was understood that they should eventually pass to the Union, but no time-limit was agreed upon, and it was equally clearly understood, at any rate on the British side, that the transfer should not be made unless Great Britain was satisfied that the interests of the native inhabitants would not

---

[1] Evans, *Native Policy in Southern Africa*, p. 42. As long ago as 1930 the Chief Inspector of Native Education stated that the limit of its resources had been reached (Annual Report of the Superintendent of Education, Natal, p. 45). But no increase in the provision for native education has been made.

suffer as a result.[1] There is an insistent and growing demand
in South Africa for the transference of the Protectorates at an
early date. The demand is based on the argument that policy
should be co-ordinated over as wide an area as possible, on the
claim that the Union is unfairly accused of being incapable
of dealing justly with native populations, and, if that is denied,
on the assertion that the condition of the Protectorates could
not be worse than it is at present. Among the motives alleged
to be behind it are the desire to utilize the unalienated Crown
lands of Bechuanaland to make up the shortage of native land
in the Union, and the insatiable demand for fresh sources of
cheap unskilled labour.[2]

Indirect Rule versus the Council System.—To the student
of comparative method the most interesting question that arises
out of the discussion turns on the relative merits of the types
of administration that have been adopted for purely native areas
in the Union and in the Protectorates. The question is particularly interesting because a large section of liberal opinion
in South Africa draws from the Protectorates the conclusion
that the whole system of Indirect Rule is valueless as a means
of adapting native societies to modern conditions. To this
group of thinkers, represented by such authorities as Professor
Edgar Brookes, Professor W. M. Macmillan and Mr. Ballinger,

[1] Definite stipulations to this end were inserted in a Schedule to the
South Africa Act, which prescribed the conditions of transfer. In particular
no native land was to be alienated, existing native assemblies were to be
maintained, revenues derived from the Protectorates were to be expended
on their behalf, and the legislative authority was to be not the Union
Parliament but the Governor-General in Council. Powers of reservation
and disallowance were retained by the Crown.

[2] All the sections of the South Africa Act which provided for reservation
or disallowance by the Crown have now been repealed by the Statute of
Westminster and the South African Status Act of 1934. Consequently
the Imperial Parliament is no longer in a position to intervene in case the
safeguards laid down in the Schedule to the South Africa Act are disregarded. The only way in which it can exercise any influence in this
direction is by refusing to consent to transfer so long as the general native
policy of the Union is not such as to justify a belief that the principles of
the Schedule will be followed in practice. At the time of writing Union
statesmen are demanding an early settlement of the question, while the
Secretary for the Dominions has stated that no transfer will be made
without consulting representatives of native and European opinion, but has
made no specific reference to the probable effect of the transfer upon the
native populations.

Indirect Rule is no more than the perpetuation of an oppressive political system in which they can see no merits, by authorities who are either too apathetic to take an interest in changing it, or deliberately use respect for native institutions as a blind to conceal a determination to prevent the native from attaining to equality of status with the white man.

In order to deal with this argument it is necessary to be quite clear as to what is meant by Indirect Rule, even if for this purpose we must anticipate the argument of the next chapter. Much discussion of this subject is made unprofitable because it proceeds on the assumption that the essentials of the Indirect Rule policy can be deduced from reference to the literal meaning of the words "Indirect Rule"; it is common to oppose the concepts of "direct" and "indirect" administration. But the real opposition between Indirect Rule and other forms of native administration is not one which can be deduced from first principles by reference to the common associations of the words "direct" and "indirect"; it is the difference between a particular system, first worked out in Nigeria and called by that name because some name had to be given to it, and since extended to Tanganyika, and systems whose guiding principles are opposed to those on which it is based.

The system devised by Lord Lugard and Sir Donald Cameron consists in the progressive adaptation of native institutions to modern conditions. It is Indirect Rule not because of some intrinsic quality of indirectness which characterizes it, but because that is what it was called in Nigeria. Its opposite is the type of policy which disregards native institutions in the belief that European methods are inherently superior, and in the confidence that the assimilation of entirely new forms of political and other organizations presents no real difficulties to the native societies which are asked to undertake it. Such a policy could be conventionally styled "direct" rule if writers on the subject agreed to give it such a name; but at present the formulation of the problem in terms of "direct" as opposed to "indirect" rule merely leads to confusion of thought.

Indirect Rule then is not a policy of non-interference. It presupposes respect for existing rights and to a certain extent for vested interests, but only as the foundation for changes whose desirability can be more clearly estimated if for the general belief in the superiority of European culture we substitute a specific inquiry into the adequacy of a given institution for the needs which it is called upon to meet. Because the search for a vehicle of the orders of the European government has to be an important administrative preoccupation, Indirect Rule has sometimes been unintelligently condensed into the phrase "Find the Chief". But this is only the starting-point, not the sum, of what is involved in this policy.

Characteristics of Policy in the Protectorates.—The policy followed in the Protectorates has done little more than respect the claims of traditional authority. Though such claims are in native society almost invariably bound up with rights over recognized areas of land, little attempt to respect such rights has been made. In Swaziland Umbandini in 1888 signed away his whole kingdom, and though he reserved the rights of natives resident in it, this was never taken to engage the concessionnaires or the British Government in any obligation to find out what those rights were. After a long period of confusion the Concessions Partitions Proclamation of 1909 divided the territory in the usual way into Crown land, alienated land and native land, and after a five years' period of grace there was in 1914 a wholesale removal to the reserves of natives living outside them. At present natives own 806,290 morgen (2661 square miles) in thirty-one blocks throughout the Protectorate, while 1,145,000 morgen (3767 square miles) is owned by Europeans, mainly in the southern half of the territory. There are about 500 European owners, some 40 per cent of whom are habitually absent. An area of 1378 square miles, including a high proportion of the best grazing in the country, is owned by Transvaal sheep-farmers, who use it only for winter grazing, while much of the rest is in the hands of speculative companies.

As a consequence one-sixth of the native population (20,000) are squatters on alienated land, paying a rent of £1 a year or six months' labour. The Pim Report [1] estimates at ten thousand the number of young men who "ebb and flow" to sources of

---

[1] Cmd. 4114 (1932), from which the above information is taken.

employment outside the territory, and mentions a district where 8 per cent of the registered taxpayers had been absent from home for more than four years.

Ploughing has, it is true, become popular, but though the plough enables an individual farmer to cover a larger area of ground, the cultivation is not as thorough as by native methods. Improvements recommended by agricultural demonstrators are beyond the natives' means. Dipping preserves stock for which there is no market, and so increases overstocking. Thatching and fencing materials must be paid for if they are taken from European land—hence the dilapidated condition of native huts and the prevalence of the round mud hut condemned as unhygienic by Europeans. Land shortage has affected native society in other less obvious ways. Where the right to allot land to his subjects is an important element in a chief's prestige, those chiefs who have no further land to dispose of will grant areas claimed by their neighbours rather than turn away a new follower, and disputes on such questions are frequent. The claim of every man of royal rank to be chief over an area of land can only be satisfied at the expense of the hereditary rights of commoners to certain areas; and even so it is difficult to find suitable land for the brothers and sons of the reigning king.[1]

What has all this to do with Indirect Rule? The circumstances to which Swazi society is called upon to adapt itself are such as the Indirect Rule policy rejects from the start. In the interests of a foreign community, and not of any conception of the betterment of the people themselves, more than half the land which is the basis both of their subsistence and of their institutions has been taken from them. Consequently a large proportion have been obliged, if not for a mere livelihood, at least for the necessary money to pay the taxes imposed on them, to detach themselves from their own organization and live temporarily or permanently in towns or as squatters. In these circumstances the question which arises is whether any adaptation is possible which will give satisfactory results.

[1] This information has been communicated to me by Dr. Hilda Beemer, who is at present (1935) engaged in anthropological research among the Swazi.

In Bechuanaland Great Britain, after failing to persuade the leading chiefs to accept the administration of the British South Africa Company, handed over to the Company all territory not actually in the occupation of the tribes, as well as a railway strip which the chiefs were persuaded to cede. This left the natives with 102,000 square miles of land allotted in separate reserves to eight different tribes. An area of 7500 square miles has been alienated to Europeans; the remaining 165,000 square miles, that is more than half the Protectorate, remains as Crown land available for alienation but at present almost wholly unoccupied because the terms of alienation have not been decided upon. The railway and almost all the surface water are in the alienated European area.

In most of the reserves the level of production is so low that the natives are often obliged to buy foodstuffs. No attempt has been made to encourage agricultural production for export, even in those reserves where there is sufficient arable land to make this possible, and though of recent years dairying and the preparation of hides have been encouraged, the majority of natives are only able to pay their taxes by selling stock or going out of the reserves to earn wages.[1] Here again the essential condition for Indirect Rule—the participation of the native society in the world economic system on terms which do not involve its disruption—is absent.

In Basutoland alone the whole of the land continues to be occupied by the natives and controlled by the Paramount Chief in accordance with tribal custom. Here Indirect Rule is blamed for the inefficient manner in which the country's natural resources are utilized, and the consequent exodus of more than half the adult male population to earn the amount of their poll-tax outside the territory.[2]

In fact almost the only point in common between the system of administration in force in these territories and Indirect Rule is that the powers of hereditary chiefs have not been curtailed as they have in the Union. In Swaziland the administration of native affairs is in the hands of tribal councils who are still

[1] Cmd. 4368 (1933), from which the above information is taken.
[2] Cf. Hodgson and Ballinger, *Basutoland*, pp. 25-30.

composed for the most part of the older and more conservative natives. In Basutoland the Paramount Chief and the Sub-Chiefs who are his kinsmen retain their traditional authority over their people. In Bechuanaland they have still the right to call out the age-grades or "regiments" for labour on public works.

The criticism brought against them is, in the main, that vested interests militate against economic improvements; that chiefs are jealous of wealthy subjects; that land which is used for individual cultivation in the summer and communal grazing in the winter cannot be fenced, so that fruit-trees, for example, cannot be planted there. Of Bechuanaland it is also pointed out that the tribal levy system is a hopelessly inefficient means of executing those public works for which it is now used. We are asked to contrast the progressive Transkei with stagnant Basutoland.[1]

The question which remains undecided, however, is, What is the real reason for the contrast? Is it simply because local government in the Transkei is in the hands of bodies created *ad hoc* with no reference to existing institutions? Facts are not available which would show whether the evident progress of the Transkei—its roads and bridges, its schools, its agricultural demonstrators—has nowhere created maladjustments in the native social organization. It is established that the Transkei has got no further than the Protectorates in the attempt to wean its natives from that attachment to the possession of cattle which has become so inconvenient now that no land is left them for grazing.

It is worth considering whether the contrast, instead of proving the inherent futility of maintaining native institutions, does not merely underline the patent necessity of European advice for all native tribes during the transitions which are being forced upon them. In the Transkei advice has been liberally given; the lines it has followed have been determined solely by European criteria. In the Protectorates little advice appears to have been given at all, and the principle that innovations cannot be made without the chief's consent seems

[1] Cf. Brookes in Schapera, *Western Civilization and the Bantu*, p. 249.

60

to have excused officials from the necessity of making serious attempts to secure that consent. In other Indirect Rule territories such a formalistic interpretation of respect for native rights has not been followed; other rights than those of the chief have been considered, and where his have been thought to require curtailment his consent has not been asked. Yet where his position in relation to his subjects has been intelligently envisaged this has not alienated him from co-operation with the government in introducing necessary reforms.

It is of the essence of Indirect Rule that the whole complex of relationships in which the chief exercises his power must be taken into account, and allowance made in particular for those changed circumstances that may make a customary obligation, once freely accepted, into a burden that can now only be exacted because British authority is behind the chief. But it is equally essential to avoid the contrary error of assuming, as certain of the Protectorate administrations do, that there is no half-way house between complete maintenance of native institutions and their complete abolition. Only if it could be demonstrated that chieftainship had no value in the organization of native life would it be justifiable to regard it as a doomed institution; and if that point was reached it would be equally justifiable to abolish it by direct action.

There are actually in each of the Protectorates institutions which could be used by the European administration for the imparting of that advice which is surely no less authoritative there than in other colonies—and rightly so if the course which it advocates has been decided on with a full understanding of the necessities of the case. In all three Protectorates a council of chiefs from all over the area meets the Resident Commissioner at stated intervals. In Basutoland and Bechuanaland the meeting takes place annually. In Bechuanaland, since its main business is the administration of a Native Development Fund financed by a special tax on the natives of the reserves, it could surely be made into a potent instrument for progressive development. The first step in this direction has been taken by the Native Administration and Native Tribunals Proclamations

61

(74 and 75 of 1934), which came into force on January 1, 1935. These follow the general lines adopted in "Indirect Rule" territories. Provisions special to Bechuanaland include the power given to chiefs to nominate councillors other than those qualified by birth for membership of their Councils, intended to make possible the inclusion of the educated young men, the prohibition of the raising of levies without the approval of the Tribal Council and the consent in writing of the High Commissioner, and the rule that the tribe cannot be held responsible for the personal obligations of the chiefs.[1]

In Swaziland as in Basutoland the younger educated natives have formed Progressive Associations, which not only voice the opinions of the section of the community upon whom tribal obligations press heavily, but criticize the whole system of administration in a not too intelligent way. In Swaziland the practice has recently been instituted of holding meetings every six months at which the Resident Commissioner and Paramount Chief meet the Progressive Association. It is hoped eventually here too so to modify the constitution of the Tribal Council as to give this element a share of responsibility.

An effective Indirect Rule policy might, by an intelligent appreciation of the needs of the situation, by constant advice and persuasion and by the constructive education of the generation destined to succeed to authority—for the Protectorates have now been under British administration for fifty years—have been able to forestall the development of these Progressive Associations. Their existence is no proof of the inevitable craving of the awakening intelligence for European institutions (among which there is, after all, considerable diversity); it is rather a reflex of a not very intelligent system of education coupled with an impossible economic situation. The answer to it is not to push on with the destruction of such elements of cohesion as remain in the native societies in question but rather, along the lines which have already been adopted, to attempt, after a thorough discussion of the points of view of both sides, to give satisfaction to "progressive" demands without further complicating the problems of adaptation by

[1] Evans, *Native Policy in Southern Africa*, p. 98.

introducing novelties not directly called for by the situation under consideration.

II. SOUTHERN RHODESIA

Rhodesia was from 1889 till 1924 administered under a charter by Cecil Rhodes' British South Africa Company. On the termination of the Charter Southern Rhodesia, which then counted a European population of 34,000, by a popular vote rejected amalgamation with the Union of South Africa and chose responsible government as an independent entity, while the relatively undeveloped Northern Rhodesia became a Crown Colony. Southern Rhodesia's independence is limited by the provision that legislation on certain subjects, of which the most important are matters affecting the native population and the disposal of land not yet alienated, remains subject to disallowance by the Crown. The general attitude of the European population of the Rhodesias towards native policy differs little, if at all, from that of the Union. It is comfortably stayed on the theory of the inherent inferiority of the native; and the White Paper of 1930, which asserted the paramountcy of native interests, was received in both territories with a storm of indignation. Official policy, however, has differed to a certain extent. Sir James Maxwell, the Governor at the time of Northern Rhodesia, upheld the principle of paramountcy in the Legislative Council as mere political common sense, but no such voice was heard in the Southern territory. There it is regarded as axiomatic that such a principle cannot be applied to an area with a considerable European population, and that although the White Paper, and the Hilton Young Report on which it was based, had precisely such areas in view.

Liberalism in a White Man's Country.—The policy adumbrated by the present Premier, Mr. Huggins, is one dictated primarily by the desire to prevent the creation of a "Poor White" class through the economic competition of the native with the less efficient white population. In an address delivered in London in July 1934 he appeared to advocate its extension beyond the confines of Southern Rhodesia in the form of a final division of all British Africa into "white paramountcy" and "native paramountcy" areas. In the latter, the native population was to "advance right up to the top socially and politically" and "build up native civilization on the model of the European". In the former they "would have practically no political rights", but would be entitled to work for wages.[1] The Imperial Government has as yet shown no eagerness to accept his suggestion. In effect its professions represent the political complement to the Kenya dual policy [2] in the economic sphere; the results of its application do not appear to the overseas observer to differ so widely from those of Union policy as is claimed by its adherents.

The Delimitation of Reserves.—The principle of territorial segregation has been followed in Southern Rhodesia with the same modifications in the interest of the labour supply as are found in the Union, but not in the face of such impossible pre-existing conditions. The first delimitation was made in 1894 when the death of Lobengula "solved the difficult question of how to dispose of him",[3] and the Company arrogated to itself his former sovereign rights over the native population. The Matabeleland Order in Council which sanctioned the new state of affairs provided, as did the Southern Rhodesia Order in Council of 1898, that sufficient land be assigned for native occupation before the alienation to Europeans, which was the Company's main object, began. A Commission appointed under the earlier Order set aside two large reserves, one for Matabeleland and one for Mashonaland. Neither was selected with any consideration of existing native rights; the aim was rather that the native population should eventually be transferred to the reserves as the land on which they were living was taken up by the Europeans.[4] The former was not even inspected by the Commission. It proved to be waterless, and the greater part of it was never inhabited by the natives.

After the Matabele Rebellion these reserves were extended to an amount which the Surveyor-General, in evidence before a Native Affairs Commission of 1910, characterized as excessive,

---

[1] *East Africa*, July 1934.
[2] See below, p. 77.
[3] Hole, *The Making of Rhodesia*, p. 331.
[4] Hole, *ibid.*, p. 335.

while representatives of the Native Department before the same Commission stated that the soil was poor, water supplies deficient and certain parts of them "unsuitable for human occupation".[1] That Commission already advocated the South African method of a final partition of the land between native and European areas and the transference to reserves of all natives resident outside them.

A Native Reserves Commission which reported in 1918 recommended the exchange of certain small native areas surrounded by European farms for land adjoining the larger reserves, and boundaries were gazetted in accordance with its recommendations in 1921. A plea for the recognition of native rights in land not yet alienated was put forward by the Aborigines Protection Society, in the course of litigation between the B.S.A. Company and the Rhodesian Government regarding the ownership of this land, which eventually reached the Privy Council. Their Lordships found principles of law to justify the extinction of native rights on each of several hypotheses as to their nature. Their decision on this point probably had no influence on the course of events, but it is remarkable as an example of complacent disregard of the existence of rights which cannot be forced into any formal category of European law.[2] The reserves were of course delimited without any consideration of native claims.

The Ordinance of 1920 allowed four years' grace for natives to move to the reserves from areas "which by that Order ceased to be reserved and reverted to the Crown", and from that date onwards successive Chief Native Commissioners' Reports mention the movement towards the reserves at the same time as they stress the necessity of making contiguous land available for future expansion.

The Land Commission of 1925.—This was dealt with by a Land Commission appointed in 1925, after a delegation of European settlers had approached the Secretary of State with the demand that the whole territory be divided into areas

---

[1] Native Affairs Commission, 1910, p. 11.
[2] A.C. 1919 *in re* Southern Rhodesia. The most striking of the relevant passages are quoted in Buell, *The Native Problem in Africa*, vol. I, pp. 210–11.

reserved exclusively for the occupation of natives and Europeans respectively. This involved a departure from the provisions against differential legislation laid down in the 1898 Order in Council and repeated in the Letters Patent of 1923,[1] but Mr. Winston Churchill agreed that such a step might be considered should it prove after full inquiry to be desirable.

The Commission interpreted its task as requiring a speedy settlement of the land question in order that the alienation of those areas assigned for European occupation need not be delayed. It did recommend complete possessory segregation, but opposed the creation of large blocks of contiguous native territories on the ground that this would involve too great disturbance of existing rights and too much shifting of the native population. Also

"it would reduce the points of contact between the races to too great an extent and would not only prevent the native from profiting by example but would be detrimental both to him and to the European, in that the families of native farmers and small holders would be discouraged by distance from offering their services as labourers to European farmers."[2]

The Commission found that, of a total area of 96,250,000 acres, 21,000,000 were gazetted reserves while 45,000 acres had been acquired by native purchase. The area alienated to Europeans was 31,000,000 acres, leaving 43,000,000 acres unalienated Crown land. It recommended the expropriation of some 426,000 acres of land held by Europeans in predominantly native areas, and further fixed as "semi-neutral areas" 80,000 acres of European enclaves, in which purchase should be open to both races until the land fell into native hands, when Europeans should not be allowed to repurchase it.

In approaching the main part of its task, the delimitation of the areas for future native and European expansion, the Commission recognized that the native population deserved some *quid pro quo* for its loss of the unrestricted right of purchase.

[1] S. Rhodesia Order in Council, 1898, Sec. 80, Letters Patent, 1923, Sec. 42.
[2] Land Commission Report, p. 11.

The actual distribution therefore occasioned a good deal of surprise. Seven million acres were assigned forthwith for native purchase, leaving 34,000,000 available for the future development of both races. An allotment of half this land to each would not, it might be supposed, have been unduly liberal to the native 95 per cent. of the population. What happened was that half of it was thrown open at once for European purchase and the other half reserved for future determination, with a view to the possibility of rectifying in the future disproportions in the division between the two races. Nothing is said about the way in which this is to be done; presumably portions of the undetermined land are to be released as the Government becomes convinced that one or other of the two races is bursting its bounds. Which will first make its claims felt, it is perhaps not hard to conjecture. The Assistant Director of Native Lands points out that as a good deal of the undetermined area is either tsetse country or below the 3000 feet level, there is not likely to be much demand for it.[1]

The recommendations of the Commission were made operative by the Land Apportionment Act of 1930, which established a Land Board for the administration of the native area. This is a body of five nominated persons, the Chairman being the Chief Native Commissioner. Members of the Legislative Council are not eligible to sit on the Board.

Squatting and the Labour Supply.—The demand for agricultural labour has expressed itself in Southern Rhodesia in very much the manner that has already been described in the Union. It has not met, however, with such a ready response. Owing to the manner in which the original reserves were selected it is not surprising that a large number of natives should have remained on the Company's or on an alienated land. A Private Locations Ordinance of 1908 limited the number of rent-paying tenants on a single European farm to forty, while allowing natives in excess of this number to live on the land provided no burden was imposed on them. The customary

[1] Jennings, " Land Apportionment in Southern Rhodesia ", *Journal of the African Society*, 1935, p. 297. Cf. Report of the Native Land Board, 1933, p. 4, which names the only two tsetse-free districts in the unassigned areas.

rent charged was £1 on unalienated Company land and on private farms 10–40 shillings, sometimes with an additional charge of 10 shillings for each polygamous wife. The Native Affairs Commission of 1910 already advocated the substitution of labour for cash rent tenancy, with other measures familiar in the Union—that natives should not be allowed to acquire land outside the reserves, that no native should reside outside the reserves unless he could show that he was in European employment for a definite period in the year, but that natives should not be removed from Crown lands because "their services may be of great value to European occupants".[1]

The Land Commission of 1925 accepted the farming community's contention that squatting was "quite unnecessary in connection with the question of the labour supply and [tended] to keep labour out of the market". It was accordingly provided that all private locations should be dispersed within a limited period from the adoption of the Commission's proposals for separate areas, existing agreements being allowed to continue for six years, but no new ones to be made. Exceptions were made for the Melsetter district "where the farmers would feel the loss of revenue", and that part of Matabeleland where the majority of the native population live on private farms. As regards labour tenancy agreements, it was held that they should be allowed to continue "where no burden is imposed on the native", and that it might be made legal for the landlord to require the squatter's wife and children to work for him. Those natives already in occupation of unalienated Crown land might remain until it was required for alienation, but no fresh permits were to be given. In the areas reserved for future determination, they might continue to live without payment of rent, and their interests must be safeguarded when applications were made for occupation within those areas.

It was proposed also that natives who could not afford to buy land outright might lease it in native purchase areas, and a system was introduced in 1932 whereby it could be leased for the ordinary Crown land rent of £1 per annum plus an additional sum representing an instalment of the purchase price.

[1] Commission on Native Affairs, 1910, p. 10.

These provisions are far more liberal than those of the Union land legislation. The area allotted for native expansion, even if it is inadequate and even if there seems no good reason why such a large proportion should be held back for a hypothetical future, is still larger than the total Beaumont Commission scheduled areas for a much smaller native population (about 1,000,000 as against nearly 6,000,000 in the Union).

A certain amount of time is allowed for the native population to withdraw within the boundaries allotted to it, and it is conceivable that the permission accorded to natives to occupy temporarily the undetermined area may constitute a claim when its allocation is eventually decided.

Yet this comparison only serves to show the situation in the Union in a more depressing light, rather than to bear out the view of the *Round Table's* correspondent that "Local native policy is probably the best in Africa".[1] Reports that the reserves are already overcrowded begin to be recorded in 1925, and the number of districts in which this is the case increases from year to year. The average density of population is estimated at twenty to the square mile.[2]

In 1932 it was stated that about 65 per cent. of the native population was in the reserves and that erosion was beginning to be noticeable.[3] The remedy proposed is an extension of water supplies and development within the reserves such as to "avoid, as far as possible, the necessity for the acquisition of more land for native occupation". This is to be done by the most efficient possible distribution of the land between grazing and arable. A survey has been begun with that aim in view, and agricultural demonstrators have been posted in the reserves whose duties include the encouragement of the concentration of cultivated areas.

An area of 32,000 morgen or about 64,300 acres has been purchased by the Government for native use in Matabeleland and a few smaller areas elsewhere.[4] But it will be noticed

---

[1] "The Situation in Southern Rhodesia", *The Round Table*, December 1932.
[2] Jennings, *loc. cit.*, p. 303.
[3] Chief Native Commissioner's Report, 1932, pp. 1–2.
[4] *Ibid.*, 1932, p. 2.

that there is no question of encroaching on the undetermined area. The number of applications by natives to purchase land dealt with each year varies between 150 and 200. In 1931-2 the majority were said to be for farms of 50 to 500 acres; in the following year the decision was announced that in principle allotments should be from 300-400 acres.[1]

By 1933 there still remained 132,414 natives who ought, strictly speaking, to transfer to the reserves before the end of March 1937. The Chief Native Commissioner in that year proposed asking Parliament to extend the period of grace. His report states that "there seems to be some doubt as to whether it will be possible to accommodate the whole of the above-mentioned population in the Reserves and native areas as they exist today".[2] In 1934 the Premier stated: "It is quite impossible to get them back by 1936", and at the end of that year there were still 100,000 due to be transplanted.[3]

Here as elsewhere the crucial problem is that of an over-stocking due to the native's "uneconomic" attachment to cattle as an indispensable element in the making of ceremonial contracts. Here as elsewhere everything possible is done to encourage the native to slaughter and sell his surplus stock, and he does sell those which, according to his standards, are surplus. But the Government prefers to put the onus on him of adopting a more "economic" mode of existence rather than allow him to occupy further areas which, it is argued with some truth, will simply become eroded in their turn. It teaches improved methods of cultivation with considerable success, but it refuses to recognize that the attachment of a people to its social institutions is something which will not be overcome by rational argument. Yet this is as hard a fact as the conviction of the European that his superior efficiency entitles him to occupy any land which he is able to make productive. The invincible force has come up against the immovable obstacle.

The Exodus to Labour Centres.—The demand that the natives should be urged out to work has been less acute in Southern

---

[1] Native Land Board Reports, 1931-3.
[2] Chief Native Commissioner's Report, 1933, pp. 1-2.
[3] *East Africa*, July 1934. Jennings, *loc. cit.*, p. 308.

Rhodesia than elsewhere, since a large proportion of the labour supply has been recruited from Northern Rhodesia and Portuguese East Africa by the Rhodesia Native Labour Bureau. It was heard in 1921, when the South African device, at one time adopted in Nyasaland, of a tax rebate for natives proportionate to the period during which they had worked was rejected by a Native Labour Committee on the ground that "it would seem difficult to draw the line as to what constituted work, whether work for a European or on his own fields". This Committee reported that "the solution seems to lie in offering higher wages".[1] Taxation and the limitation of land for native cultivation have not been deliberately used in Southern Rhodesia as a means of procuring labour, though they inevitably have this effect; and the Chief Native Commissioner reports without regret that natives who can find a market for their produce in European areas will not engage to work for wages.[2] For the majority of the native population, however, this alternative method of meeting their money obligations is not open. By 1926 we find the same reports quoting figures to demonstrate that migration from the reserves in search of labour is having serious results. In this year the average number of able-bodied native men employed on farms was 72,000—and in the reserves only a quarter of the cultivable acreage was tilled. "The indefinite expansion of such numbers," he writes, "cannot be seriously contemplated." [3]

The number had risen in 1933 to 75,000. The latter figure represents 75 per cent. of the total labour supply of the Colony; but before the present depression began the local labour force never amounted to much more than half the total. The largest average number of natives employed in any year is 90,000 in 1926. The number employed in mining in 1933, 15,000, was considerably larger than in any preceding year.

The interests of the employer are protected, as in the Union, by pass laws which provide that every male native must have a pass or a certificate of contract. Oral contracts may be made

---

[1] Native Labour Committee, 1921, Report, p. 10.
[2] See Chief Native Commissioner's Reports from 1920 onwards.
[3] *Ibid.*, 1926, p. 6.

for a maximum period of one year, written contracts for three. The certificate is delivered by the Registrar of Natives, whose duty it is to see that the native understands the contract, and while he is in employment the employer retains the pass. It is illegal for him to enter on further employment until the employer has given him a written discharge. Failure to produce the pass is a penal offence. Employers can be prosecuted, among other offences, for withholding the pass or refusing to certify discharge.[1]

The Land Apportionment Act of 1930, following the recommendations of the Land Commission, provided for the establishment of Village Settlements near urban centres, where natives in employment might be allotted holdings to live on with their families. The Act makes no provision for the administration of such settlements. By 1933 land had been made available for their construction near Bulawayo and Salisbury, and it had been decided to establish a third such village near Umtali.[2] The whole policy was criticized recently in the Legislative Council on the ground that natives who had learnt crafts in these villages would compete with Europeans.[3]

Education as Native Development.—Of recent years the improvement of economic life in the reserves has received a certain measure of attention. Since 1929 it has been regarded as the most important function of education. The origin of this development is to be found in a Report by the Director of Education, Mr. Keigwin, in 1919. This, for the first time, proposed a system of education which should aim, not at removing a favoured few from the village environment, but at applying European knowledge to the improvement of material conditions for the majority remaining in the villages. His plan, stated in his own words, was to "deal first with the simplest and humblest vocations of the people, building upon them among the people in their own villages".[4] The subjects to which attention were to be given were the manipulation of hides and skins, food production, rope and mat making, basket

[1] See Orde-Browne, *The African Labourer*, p. 166.
[2] Native Land Board Reports, 1932–3, p. 5 ; 1933–4, p. 5.
[3] Debates, March 20, 1935.
[4] Quoted in Report of Native Education Commission, 1924, p. 15.

and chair making, pottery and tiling, carpentry and wagon work and smithing.

Two schools which proposed to follow this programme were opened in 1920, at Domboshawa for Mashonaland and Tjolotjo for Matabeleland. The financial grants provided were insufficient to allow of the introduction of the proposed new subjects, and since it was argued that there was no demand in the reserves for the products of skilled craftsmen, the schools for the time fell back on teaching agriculture, with building and carpentry of a type for which there was a European demand. By 1924 the inevitable protests against training the native to compete with the European had begun to be heard. In that year a Commission was appointed to inquire into the whole educational system, and its findings showed little sympathy with the new industrial schools.

Nevertheless, they were continued in existence, and in 1929, when a separate Department of Native Development was established to organize native education in the widest sense of the word, including agricultural and other demonstrations in the reserves, their aim was recognized as the guiding principle of the new system. Mr. Harold Jowitt, who became Director of Native Development, writes in his first Report: "One of the chief functions of the Department must be the forging of links between school and home rather than the widening of the rupture between them by the throwing of undue weight in the detribalizing scale." The whole syllabus which he has worked out aims at making literary instruction directly relevant to the practical needs of life, while agriculture, hygiene, child welfare and the like are taught not as "school" subjects but with constant stress on the application at home of what is learnt at school. Every care is taken not to teach methods which will prove inapplicable in the village for lack of European implements. Girls learn to cook native foods in new ways, but in native ovens. Agricultural methods, aiming at more intensive utilization of the limited native lands, have been carefully studied in relation to the possibilities of the local soil, and in 1932 it was reported that five different crop rotations had been worked out, adapted to local conditions. The school

is envisaged as the centre of the community rather than as a
isolated institution. The extension of the ideas taught there t
the village is carried out by the Jeanes School method recom
mended by the Phelps-Stokes Commission, whereby nativ
teachers and their wives spend periods of training in an in
stitution which combines practice in class-room teaching witl
instruction in building, agriculture, maternity and child welfar
work of a type which can subsequently be demonstrated in th
village.

Recently, however, the Jeanes teachers have been supersede
by "community demonstrators" whose work is to be carrie
on entirely with the adult population, so that the link betwee
school education and the improvement of village life, whicl
is an essential element in the Jeanes system, is broken. Th
new demonstrators are responsible to Government, not, a
are the Jeanes teachers, to the missions, and their introductio
is perhaps a sign of the increased interest in native educatio
which has caused the Native Development Department to b
amalgamated with the Native Affairs Department, so tha
native education is now one of the responsibilities of every
administrator. Their efficacy in practice has not yet bee
tested.

The native industrial schools are criticized on the groun
that they "only teach the native to grow maize for sale", an
the Director of Native Development has been constrained t
reply that "We have not deviated in any manner from ou
original scheme, which is one of conservation of the natura
resources in Native Reserves." [1] The controversy raises th
whole question of the function of native education. Libera
champions of native interests condemn any system whic
appears to relegate the native's future to a separate world; the
regard as false friends those who, as they hold, make hi
educational training subservient to the theory of his unsuit
ability for occupations calling for skill, or careers which deman
responsibility or leadership, within the framework of the
European society. Some of them might be less suspicious o
Mr. Jowitt's conception of education if they realized how widely

[1] Report, 1931, p. 15.

74

is beginning to be felt in Europe that a school syllabus
divorced from the realities of life has little real value as a
training for adult citizenship.

To the rest one might perhaps answer that the educationist,
with his experience of native adaptability and intelligence, is
no doubt on stronger ground than anyone else in criticizing,
as a private person, a social system which prevents the African
from exercising his powers in competition with Europeans,
and that most of them would join with the other friends of
the native in pressing for its alteration. But while that system
exists, he is failing in his task as an educationist if he gives to
his native pupils a training which fits them primarily for a life
that only a small minority can hope to live, and leaves them
in no way better adapted for the existence which in fact awaits
them. It is simply sacrificing the native population to an
ideal which that particular form of sacrifice can do nothing to
realize. Even were the colour bar broken down, the number
of the native population who could profit by its absence in
entering on skilled work or professional careers would remain
a small minority of the total—a fact which the French have
recognized in their dual system of education for the *élite* and
the masses.

On the other hand it is perfectly clear that the native reserves
cannot be developed as a self-contained economic system.
Such a system at the present day would be a ridiculous museum
specimen. Even were it to be regarded as the principal aim
in the development of native agriculture to keep up the food
supply, the improvements in the standard of housing, hygiene
and cleanliness presuppose the purchase of European goods—
not to mention the fact that it did not need any Jeanes schools
to create a general demand among natives for such goods.
These can be obtained for cash earned either in wages or by
the sale of agricultural produce, and if it is accepted that the
drain of men from the reserves to centres of European employment is detrimental to the food supply itself as well as to the
whole social system, then it must necessarily be an aim of
development within the reserves to enable them to obtain
their cash requirements without it. This aim has been tacitly

75

neglected in the White Man's countries; none of them would accept the view that production in the reserves should be more than complementary to wage-labour, and many fear the result of its encouragement on the labour supply. Only in Southern Rhodesia has the fear been also expressed that the native may compete successfully with the European in the same lines of production. This it is proposed to prevent by the "Organization of Native Marketing" so that the native "does not drive out the White Settler by under-selling in the local White market". "This does not," we are assured, "mean exclusion from the White market."

Native Administration.—Native administration has been based on the theory that the "tribal system" is crumbling, and something more modern must be put in its place. Apart from the fact that with the death of Lobengula the centralized political organization of the Matabele went to pieces, there is little positive evidence for or against this contention beyond the statement that "the authority of native chiefs is rapidly declining", which is repeated annually, with slight variations, by the Chief Native Commissioner. Government has largely disregarded the existence of native authorities, but as to the degree of importance that they may still hold among their own people not many questions have been asked. The Native Affairs Act of 1927 is regarded as an advance in that it gives to native chiefs a status in the administrative system, but their officially recognized authority is confined to police powers. Native civil cases are heard by the Native Commissioners; native criminal cases are divided between them and the magistrates. The Native Commissioner has had, since the original grant of the Charter, the right to assign grazing lands, settle disputes concerning access to water, determine the site of a new kraal; he may fix the number of adult males comprising a kraal and must give his consent before any native moves from one kraal to another. In practice many Commissioners have exercised their powers with the utmost respect for native custom; but it is obvious that under this system the degree of such respect is determined solely by personal inclination.

While the Native Commissioner is only expected to exercise

his powers in case of an appeal against the Chief's decision, the mere existence of such an appeal considerably diminishes the Chief's authority. In those areas where the land is being surveyed with a view to more economic use his right to distribute the land is set aside altogether. The Chief may still nominate his own headmen, subject to Government approval, but his official duties are reduced to keeping the peace, arresting criminals, making census returns and giving other types of information, and promulgating Government orders. Whether there is any particular advantage in entrusting such duties to an hereditary chief rather than to a native clerk is doubtful.

Development in the reserves has since 1924 been carried out through a Native Reserves Trust Fund administered by a Board of three Europeans. Its revenues are derived from rents for trading sites in the reserves "and other purely native sources".[1] At the same time the chiefs and headmen are regarded as representatives of their people, and from 1924 onwards periodical meetings of groups of chiefs and headmen with the Native Commissioners have been held for the discussion of matters of native interest. In 1930 the system was crystallized by the establishment by legislation of a system of local Native Boards consisting of chiefs and headmen with an equal number of elected members.[2]

III. KENYA

Kenya is ostensibly committed to the "dual policy" of "increasing native production in the reserves *pari passu* with the development of European enterprise".[3] The relative weight to be given to the two aspects of this policy, particularly where they may seem to be mutually incompatible, is in theory governed by the statement in the Devonshire White Paper of 1923 [4] that "the interests of the African Natives must be paramount", and that "if and when those interests and the interests of the immigrant races should conflict, the former

[1] Chief Native Commissioner's Report, 1925, p. 9.
[2] Evans, *Native Policy in Southern Africa*, p. 128.
[3] Report of East Africa Commission, 1925 (Cmd. 2387), p. 181.
[4] Cmd. 1922 (1923), p. 10.

should prevail". Local Europeans accept no interpretation of the policy which involves any retardation in the alienation of land to settlers, and are content to believe that it is possible to aim at a maximum development in both directions at one and the same time.

The present European population number some 11,000, as against 2,250,000 natives. They elect the unofficial members of the Legislative Council, and press continually for an elected majority as the first step towards full responsible government. Kenya politicians aim at the encouragement of settlement in order to ensure the predominance of European interests, and at the self-government without which they feel that these interests will never be adequately safeguarded.

Settler Influence on Policy.—In the meantime the settler population has attained to a degree of influence on policy which is remarkable in a Colony without responsible government. Since 1910 a Convention of Associations, representing bodies of farmers in all districts, has held regular meetings at which Government policy is discussed, proposals made, and officials frequently censured. While the more extravagant statements of this body have been disregarded, it has been the practice of successive Governors to keep in close touch with it and be prepared to offer sympathetic consideration to its views. It has indeed been described as "the unofficial parliament recognized by Government as the organ of general settler opinion".[1] Its moving spirit, Lord Delamere, was responsible for the meeting, in 1926, of the first "Unofficial Conference", representing settler interests in Kenya, Uganda, Northern Rhodesia and Nyasaland. This body has seen itself as the forerunner of the elected Parliament of a future self-governing Dominion of East Africa, and now that its hopes in this direction are, at least temporarily, disappointed, proposes that its Conference should be given a recognized advisory status in connection with the periodical Governors' Conferences held in Kenya, Uganda, and Tanganyika.

In other ways also non-official Europeans have an important influence on administration. The Select Committee on

[1] Huxley, *White Man's Country*, vol. I, p. 262.

Estimates has a large unofficial majority, and Lord Moyne, when he proposed the establishment of a Native Betterment Fund, found it necessary to recommend that the administration of this fund should not come under review by that Committee. The Board of Agriculture, established as a result of Sir Daniel Hall's recommendations in 1929, to advise on the furtherance, of agricultural development in all areas, consists of representatives of different European interests, along with the Chief Native Commissioner and one Provincial Commissioner. The settler representatives before the Joint Select Committee on Closer Union complained that this Board was unpopular with the administration, who did not bring matters connected with native interests before it.[1]   The settler community is represented on all the bodies recently established to safeguard native rights in land.   From the outset it was a frequent practice to appoint a majority of settler members to official Commissions.

History of Land Alienation.—In Kenya European settlement has been much more a matter of deliberate policy than in South Africa.   To Sir Charles Eliot, who was appointed as High Commissioner in 1900, the central problem of policy was "to make the railway pay"; and the solution "to fill up the empty spaces with settlers".   Consequently, where South African Governments found themselves called upon to delimit boundaries already in dispute between advancing colonists and native populations, Kenya procedure was to take time by the forelock and declare given areas available for settlement, if necessary removing from them the native inhabitants.[2]   Since the Crown Lands Ordinance of 1912, which was introduced to provide for European settlement, respect for native *rights* has not been a principle of policy, though native *needs* were ostensibly considered and land actually in native occupation was in theory left undisturbed.   But a large proportion of the Kenya tribes are nomadic pastoralists, and it has been a constant practice to take part of their grazing grounds for alienation, either ordering them to take their herds elsewhere, or, if the

---

[1] Evidence, p. 639.
[2] See Huxley, *op. cit.*, vol. I, pp. 77-9.

land taken was temporarily unoccupied, forbidding them to return to it. Where land thus removed from native ownership has not been settled this prohibition causes acute discontent; where it has, the tribes accustomed to find grazing there are constrained to return as squatters. The evidence heard by the Carter Land Commission of 1932 presents a picture of constant conflict between a Land Office only concerned to make as much land as possible available for alienation, and local administrative officers, aware of the grievances of the natives affected, protesting sometimes successfully, constrained sometimes to move the same tribes repeatedly from grazing grounds to which they persistently return.

From the outset the whole area of the Colony has been held to be Crown land, and even the Native Lands Trust Ordinance of 1930 does not depart from that position. As the famous Barth Judgement of 1921 has it, "Natives are tenants at will of the Crown"; and it is as an act of grace rather than a belated restitution that certain areas have now been set aside for the use and benefit of the native tribes "for ever". The Crown Lands Ordinance of 1915 empowered the Governor in Council to reserve from sale, lease or other disposal "land required for the support of native tribes", and also to reduce native areas if they were found to be unnecessarily large. Action of the latter type required the consent of the Secretary of State, but in practice it was sometimes taken without his consent.[1] Land might be taken from such reserves for public purposes, and there was no obligation to provide alternative land unless it was held that the remaining area was insufficient for the needs of the tribe, and then only if there was unalienated Crown land available adjacent to the reserve.

The principle followed in the original delimitation was that natives must be taught, by the restriction of the land available to them, to use it more economically.[2] The allocation of

[1] Cmd. 2387 (1925), p. 29.
[2] "Tribes like the Kikuyu require showing that their just and ample requirements can be met by their being restricted to much more limited areas."—Mr. J. Ainsworth, then Sub-Commissioner, Ukamba. "I deprecate in the strongest possible way the suggestion that the natives' pernicious pastoral proclivities should be encouraged by the grant of any land for grazing purposes."—Sir H. Belfield to the Secretary of State, 3.4.14.

reserves followed the decision to throw open areas in their vicinity to European settlement, and in most cases alienation was well advanced before any delimitation of reserves was made. With the exception of the soldier settlement schemes at the close of the War, all the alienations of large blocks of land took place before 1915.

These began in 1902, as soon as the policy of settlement had been finally decided upon and the former Eastern Province of Uganda had been included in Kenya.[1] The first alienations to be made were in the Kikuyu country to the north-east of Nairobi. By 1906 they had extended to a number of districts in the Masai country. In 1904-5 the Elgeyo were moved from an area on the Escarpment which was granted to Major E. S. Grogan as a forest concession. In 1907 settlement began in the Mua and Lukenia Hills, and the Akamba who had previously been in occupation there were moved into Crown land to the north and east. In this year the Londiani area and 138,000 acres in the Sotik district were thrown open for settlement. In 1915 and onwards 4560 square miles were allotted in soldier settlement farms in a number of different districts. Some of these proved quite unsuitable for settlement, and in order to compensate disappointed applicants 82,000 acres at Kipkarren were excised from the Nandi Reserve. Half of this was returned in the following year owing to the intervention of Mr. G. V. Maxwell, then newly appointed Chief Native Commissioner.[2] Although no further large-scale alienations have been made, Sir Edward Grigg in 1922 fixed as the boundary of the Samburu tribe a line which left 1,500,000 acres open for European settlement.

The Delimitation of Reserves.—The first reserves to be declared were the Kikuyu and Masai. The Kikuyu area amounted to 1285 square miles of land actually in occupation; to these were added 74 square miles in 1913 and a further 20 in 1927. The Masai, being a pastoral tribe, were invited to leave the northern Rift Valley for an area of land in the Laikipia

---

[1] See Memorandum by the Commission of Lands in Kenya Land Commission Evidence, pp. 44 ff.
[2] Ross, *Kenya from Within*, p. 82.

district which was guaranteed them by a treaty. They were also allowed to remain in the southern portion of the Rift Valley. In 1910 a demand was made for the alienation of farms in Laikipia, and after protracted negotiations with Masai chiefs on the one hand, and the Secretary of State on the other, the population of the northern reserve were moved to this southern area, which was increased by 150 square miles in order to receive them.

The Akamba move has already been mentioned. They were allotted two areas at Machakos and Kitui, and allowed to graze their stock, on payment of a fee, in an area of unalienated Crown land known as the Yatta. The Nandi Reserve was demarcated in 1907 at the close of a punitive expedition, and increased by 70 square miles in 1910. In 1909 the Lumbwa, Kipsigis, Sotik, Buret and Kamasia had limits set to the areas in which they might graze their cattle—limits which in nearly every case deprived them of pasture essential to the maintenance of their herds, and usually left watering-places and salt-licks under European control, and which have been progressively drawn further back. In some cases also movements of the native population have involved the settlement of one tribe on areas claimed by another. This has happened even in Kavirondo, where there has been practically no alienation of land. When the Ormsby-Gore Commission visited Kenya in 1924 fifty areas had been proclaimed as native reserves, though only two, Kikuyu and Nyika, had had their boundaries gazetted.[1]

Official memoranda communicated to the Carter Commission are unanimous in protest against the exclusion of the pastoral tribes from all the land of any value to them, and reveal a history of attempts to secure redress by exchanges or by the return to the reserves of unoccupied land. The Government position has been in the main that land once alienated is alienated for good, and that the expense involved in any measures to ease the position of the natives must be borne by themselves. Thus the restoration of a salt-lick to the Lumbwa is described by the D.C. Kericho as "a mixed blessing since the natives will have

[1] Cmd. 2387 (1925), p. 29.

to erect and maintain the fence at considerable expense",[1] while the proposal for the return of another area to them was found to be impracticable because the total sum standing to their credit in the Native Trust Fund was only half the purchase price.[2] Meantime, the natives return as often as they can to their old grazing, and district officials from time to time reluctantly carry out evictions in which as much as 33 per cent. of their stock may be lost.[3]

The demand of the settlers is consistently for more and yet more land. While some are genuinely convinced that the native population has ample land of which it makes insufficient use, and some believe that to throw open land to native occupation is merely to hasten the process of erosion, to others native rights, claims or needs appear to be indifferent, and one is sometimes driven to wonder if the very conception of native reserves is something outside the range of their ideas. Proposals for further settlement complacently ignore their existence. An Economic Commission appointed by the local Government in 1917, whose findings were repudiated by the British Government, recommended the "interpenetration" of the natives in the interests of their own development.[4] Two Land Settlement Committees, in 1917 and 1918, recommended the excision of large areas from the Kikuyu Reserve,[5] and in 1921 6000 acres were actually surveyed in Embu district to compensate a settler who found that the farm he had chosen had been allotted to someone else.[6] That land once declared suitable for European settlement shall never return to native occupation is a cardinal point of their policy; hence the persistent opposition to the occupation of the north-eastern corner of the old Masai Reserve by the Samburu, a branch of the tribe which had been driven

[1] Carter Commission Evidence, p. 2459.
[2] Ibid., pp. 2411–2. In the case of the Kamasia, of whom the P.C. Kerio writes " all the good land, all the water, most of the grazing, was taken for European occupation ; all barren, rocky, waterless land was left for the natives ", Government refused to buy back land which its owners were ready to sell, and could only suggest that the natives themselves buy it back. Ibid., pp. 1786–7. In the Sotik area the bulk of the alienated land is not even suitable for cultivation, and on 5000-acre farms an average of about 300 acres is actually being developed.
[3] Ibid., p. 1456.   [4] Ross, Kenya from Within, p. 101.
[5] Carter Commission Evidence, p. 3372.   [6] Ibid., p. 3376.

out by the main tribe and returned after the move, and the indignation which has greeted the Carter Commission's recommendations to leave them there.

The "White Highlands".—Hence, too, the insistence on the "principle of the 'White Highlands'"—that a certain area, as to whose limits there is still controversy, shall be available only for European occupation. The "principle" was enunciated in connection with the controversy between Indians and Europeans for land grants, when the subtle distinction between legal restrictions, to which His Majesty's Government were opposed, and administrative convenience was invoked to allow of the refusal to Indians of land in the Highlands. It has now become significant in connection with the distribution of land as between natives and Europeans, for the Carter Commission, invited to define the area known as the White Highlands, has proposed that an area of 16,700 square miles [1] should be reserved by Order in Council for European occupation, and be subject to the same safeguards as native lands, and the recently formed Kenya Vigilance Committee is demanding that this shall be done at once.

The Native Lands Trust Ordinance.—This being the prevalent European attitude towards land distribution, supported by the highest executive authority, though not by officials in direct contact with the native population, it is not surprising that the Ormsby-Gore Commission was impressed by the general feeling of insecurity among the natives as regards the possession of their land.[2] That Commission discussed with the then Governor, Sir Robert Coryndon, the provision of such safeguards as would remove this uncertainty. They recommended the final demarcation of the reserves, and the establishment of a Trust Board in which all native lands should be vested; they also dissented from the proposal that alienation of land from gazetted reserves should be permitted with the approval of the Governor in Council or Secretary of State, holding that it would always be sufficient to grant a lease which did not

[1] The area proposed by Sir Edward Grigg in 1929 was three times as large.
[2] Cmd. 2387 (1925), p. 28.

involve the excision of land from the reserve. As a result of their recommendations the reserve boundaries were gazetted in 1926, and at the same time an amendment to the Crown Lands Ordinance of 1915 empowered the Governor to declare such areas to be "Native Reserves" "for the benefit of the native tribes of the Colony". Leasing of such land was only to be allowed for purposes beneficial to the inhabitants; but the right to cut down the area of reserves remained. The settler population understood the gazetting of boundaries to mean that all the land outside them would at once be offered for settlement, and from time to time express indignation at the delays caused by such inquiries as those of the Hilton Young and Carter Commissions.

A Native Lands Trust Ordinance on the lines which had been proposed by Sir Robert Coryndon was introduced into the Legislative Council in 1928. Under this Ordinance the control of all native lands was to be entrusted to a Native Land Board consisting of the Governor, five official and four nominated unofficial members, and acting in consultation with Local Advisory Boards, consisting of two officials, a nominated unofficial European, and an African member, in each administrative district in which there were native reserves. Permanent excisions from the reserves were no longer contemplated; but provision was made for the granting of 99-year leases for purposes beneficial to the native population, including the execution of public works requiring capital on a large scale and "private enterprise in the ordinary form", which would be able to develop undeveloped parts of the reserves while enabling the native population to use the rents received in improving the remaining area.[1] Reference to the Secretary of State was only to be made if the native member of the Advisory Board concerned opposed the proposal.

The Hilton Young Commission, who upon their arrival in Kenya had urged that the passing of any such measure should be suspended until the Government had considered the report which they were asked to make on principles of native policy, accompanied that report with severe criticism of the proposed

[1] Speech by Sir Edward Grigg to Legislative Council, 12.5.28.

Ordinance. In particular they disputed the necessity in native interests of introducing private enterprise into the reserves, and stressed their opinion that the lease of large areas in reserves to Europeans should be regarded as an exceptional measure requiring in all cases the prior approval of the Secretary of State.

The Ordinance as finally passed in 1930 contained much fuller safeguards than those proposed in 1928. The period of leases was restricted to 33 years, with extension to 99 only in special cases and with the prior consent of the Secretary of State, and it was provided that no land should be even temporarily excluded from a reserve without consultation with both the Local Land Board and the Local Native Council, and without an area of equivalent value being added elsewhere. The composition of the Central Board remained as originally proposed, almost identical with that of the Executive Council, with whom it largely corresponds in personnel. Witnesses before the Carter Land Commission pointed out that since the duties of membership represented a further call on the time of people already burdened with the work of the Executive Council, the Board was apt to be content with a perfunctory examination of cases put before it.

The Kakamega Goldfield.—Hardly was this Ordinance on the Statute Book than gold was discovered at Kakamega in the Kavirondo Reserve, whose boundaries had up till then suffered no encroachment. Prospectors began to flock into the country and the suspicions of the native population were aroused. Sir Joseph Byrne, the Governor, addressed a large meeting of natives and assured them that their rights would be respected, though when asked to swear in native fashion he refused to perform the rather barbarous ritual which this involved. By the end of 1931 there were 300 prospectors in Kavirondo, in an area where the native population averaged 157 to the square mile. By July 1932 the Secretary of State had agreed in principle to an amendment of the Native Lands Trust Ordinance whereby, in the case of mining leases, compensation might be given in cash and not in land, and the consent of the local Native Council need no longer be asked before land was excluded from the reserve. This amendment was passed in December 1932.

If, as it appears, there is not in fact much gold in Kakamega, the advantage gained by the amendment consists in the provision of temporary occupations for a number of Europeans who had been thrown out of employment by the slump. The disadvantage was described in advance by the Hilton Young Commission as "a blow to the confidence of the natives in the justice of British rule from which it might never be able to recover".[1] The obligation to give land for land was certainly irksome; before it became law many people, including Sir Edward Grigg, declared that it was impracticable, and after it was repudiated it was explained that equivalent land a long way from their houses was no use to the natives in any case. But the possible alternative of leaving the natives undisturbed seems to have occurred to no one; still less the consideration, which in relationships between Europeans is axiomatic, that the possibilities of dealing with a given situation are limited by obligations previously undertaken. That the obligation was imposed with the very object of making it difficult to encroach upon native reserves must surely be known to the defenders of the amendment, but they discreetly refrain from admitting it.

The Carter Land Commission.—Meantime a Commission had arrived in Kenya, under the chairmanship of Sir Morris Carter, who had previously been Chairman of the Southern Rhodesia Land Commission, to inquire into native claims over alienated land, make a final settlement of these claims, consider the needs of native tribes and the desirability and practicability of setting aside further areas for their occupation, define the European Highlands, and suggest improvements in the Native Lands Trust Ordinance.

This Committee recommended the addition of about 1474 square miles to all native reserves in satisfaction of claims of right, 896 square miles on ground of economic need, and 259 square miles as "Temporary Reserves". The most important of the grants made are an addition of 383 square miles to the Kikuyu and 300 square miles to the Akamba Reserves, both on

[1] Cmd. 2324 (1929), p. 350.

the Yatta Plateau, 100 square miles to the Njemps and 74 square miles to the Kamasia. The Lumbwa receive as of right the area of 148½ square miles in the Chepalungu forest, which it had previously been proposed they should buy. Two Temporary Reserves "to be held on lease terminable by the Government" are allocated to the East Suk (130–160 square miles) and the Teita (119 square miles). The principle underlying these temporary grants is apparently that they are made subject to conditions, in the one case that stock be reduced so as not to destroy the land, in the other that the tribes themselves clear their land of tsetse fly. An area of 931 square miles is recommended to be open for leasing by natives. The remainder of the territory is to be open for acquisition on equal terms by all races. This settlement is to extinguish all such rights of natives to reside in alienated land as were created by the Crown Lands Ordinance of 1915, which provided that where an area alienated included land in native occupation such land was excluded from the lease so long as the occupation continued. Thus here, as in South Africa and Southern Rhodesia, natives cannot now legally reside on European land except as squatters.

By these provisions the native share of the territory is fixed at 53,000 square miles, plus such share as they may obtain of the 99,000 square miles open to all races, much of which must be desert, as against the 16,700 square miles of Highlands reserved for the Europeans. The native areas are increased by 5 per cent., the European by 60 per cent. The Commission envisages the overstocking and erosion of the reserves as inevitable, though not so closely imminent as in South Africa, unless a change occurs in the native attitude towards stock. In evidence before the Joint Select Committee on Closer Union the settlers' delegates stated that 80 per cent. of the land already alienated was not cultivable.[1] Only 12½ per cent. is under cultivation and many of the farmers who are developing their land are only enabled to do so by loans from Government.[2]

---

[1] Questions 8240–51.

[2] "Today we see 24,424 head of native stock on Sotik farms and £22,500 advanced to settlers." Memorandum by C. Tomlinson, D.C. Kericho, to Carter Commission.

But interpenetration by natives cannot be allowed, because it would depreciate the value of the land.

As regards the legal status of native lands the Carter Commission make proposals intended to increase the security of native tenure in the existing reserves. It is recommended that the reserves, with those areas which have been added to them "as of right", should cease to be Crown Land and be styled Native Lands, to be administered by Government as part of general native administration, subject to the safeguard against encroachment provided by the control over alienations of the Native Lands Trust Board. This provision is to be secured by Order in Council. It is proposed to replace the existing Local Boards by bodies of natives under the chairmanship of the District Commissioner, and thus make unnecessary the consultation of the Local Native Council, which has been found to involve a cumbrous double procedure. The dissociation of the Lands Trust Board from local politics was to be secured by establishing it in London and giving it full powers to obtain information if necessary by sending representatives to the Colony. The desirability of this provision was particularly stressed by Mr. Hemsted, who as an administrative official had first-hand experience of the tug of war of Kenya politics. Sir Philip Cunliffe-Lister, in signifying his general approval of the Commission's recommendations, rejected this proposal as impracticable. It is inconceivable that any organ for the control of land settlement can be set up in Kenya in which the elected members are not represented, so that the new safeguards are reduced to the difficulty of amending an Order in Council.

Control over the Movements of Natives.—While the South African pass system is not in force in Kenya, every adult male native is obliged to carry a certificate, and his finger-prints are registered with an official department of Government created for the purpose. Failure to produce the certificate is a criminal offence. Its main purpose is to facilitate the tracing of deserters from employment under contract, though it is also said to protect industrious natives from being "sent off again by their Chiefs as soon as they come home for a rest".[1] It is also used

---

[1] Huxley, *White Man's Country*, vol. I, p. 275.

by employers, who record on the *kipandi* the wages paid by them and sometimes particulars of the native's character. While it was maintained before the Joint Select Committee on Closer Union that these records enabled the native to demand a higher wage from each new employer, it is also widely held that they are a means of keeping down wages.[1] Moreover, there is no check on the accuracy of the statements made by the employer. Since 1925 the Registration Ordinance has been amended so that desertion is no longer an offence cognizable by the police; a deserter cannot be arrested unless his employer has charged him. In this respect, and in the fact that it is not an offence to be outside his reserve without being in employment, the Kenya native is more fortunate than the South African.

The Squatter in Kenya.—The demand for cheap labour has been as insistent in Kenya as elsewhere, and has been expressed at times in even more crudely brutal terms than are on record in South Africa.[2] In the circumstances resulting from the land policy that has just been described a certain amount of squatter labour is available. As in South Africa, labour tenancy is the only form of squatter contract which is legal. The contract may be made for a period of up to three years and must involve an agreement to give not less than 180 days' work for wages in each year. An ordinance of 1924 which empowered the Governor at discretion to direct that remuneration in money might be "waived in the public interest" was disallowed by the Secretary of State. The same Ordinance would have made the son of a squatter, on attaining the age of sixteen, automatically subject to contract on the same terms as his father. Existing legislation offers him the choice between entering into such a contract, finding employment elsewhere and returning to the reserve allotted to his tribe.

How to Stimulate the Flow of Labour.—Squatter labour does not satisfy the whole demand, however, and since the chief incentive to the native to make a squatter contract lies in the

[1] Evidence, pp. 849–50.
[2] Quotations from evidence before the Labour Commission of 1903 in Ross, *Kenya from Within*, pp. 93–4.

need of grazing for his stock, it is not a suitable arrangement for agricultural estates. To encourage natives to engage in employment there, all the time-honoured methods of pressure, direct and indirect, have been proposed and most of them have been employed. It is seldom safe to assert that such negative action as neglecting entirely the development of agriculture in the reserves are deliberately designed to make the native dependent on wage-labour; but what is certainly true is that protests are raised at once against any proposal that is expected to "decrease the flow of labour", and that given the limitations of time, money and human energy, the more of all these are devoted to supplying with labour the settler who has been encouraged to come to Kenya on the understanding that labour is available, the less can be directed to any other ends. The mere indifference of the settler community to native development, along with their keen awareness of their own necessities, accounts as much as deliberate hostility for the policy which they pursue. The success which that policy has achieved under a constitutional regime which provides the local administration with considerable support against it is largely a matter of unfortunate personalities.

The inadequacy of the land reserved for native occupation is a direct outcome of the European demand for land and not a deliberate device to reduce the natives' means of support, though the connection between the area reserved and the labour supply was explicitly recognized by the recommendations of a Labour Inquiry Board.[1] Progressive increases in native taxation, again, have not had this avowed object in responsible quarters, though the local press attributes this aim to them.[2] Opposition to the cultivation of coffee by natives is actuated primarily by a genuine fear that native plantations will spread disease, and that the native owner will steal his European neighbours' produce and pass it off as his own. The weighting of railway charges in the interests of European produce is due to mere disregard of the fact that the loss involved in subsidizing the European cultivator has to be made up somehow.

In two ways, however, Government has at different times

[1] Ross, *Kenya from Within*, p. 42. [2] *Ibid.*, p. 149.

made it a deliberate aim of policy to "encourage" natives to come out to work. One method has been that of instructing officials to assist Europeans in obtaining labour. The settler community has always held this to be one of the functions of Government, and their view was officially upheld by the famous Labour Circular No. 1 of 1919, which instructed European officials and native chiefs and headmen to use "every possible lawful influence" to this end, and required a record to be kept of native officials who are "helpful" and "not helpful". In particular District Commissioners were invited to hold meetings at which employers and their agents should be present, for the purpose of explaining where openings for employment presented themselves. The other positive step was taken by an amendment to the Native Authority Ordinance in 1922, which rendered every male native liable to be called up for 60 days' paid labour on work of public urgency. Exemption from the obligation is granted in the case of natives who have worked for three months in the previous year. By a ruling of Lord Milner this exemption applies to work done in the reserve, a point which similar legislation elsewhere has never made clear. If this, as McGregor Ross suggests,[1] has largely reduced the efficacy of the Ordinance as a stimulus to labour it remains true that the labour required for public works is of course only sought in the reserves, and that natives may be inspired to evade the obligation by seeking employment of a more congenial type. Since the numbers called up in this way have steadily declined from 1500 in 1925 to 700 in 1932, the influence of this measure on the supply of labour may also be said to be decreasing.

A White Paper of 1921 issued by Mr. Winston Churchill definitely condemned the association of Government officials with the procuring of labour for private enterprise,[2] and the East African Commission of 1924 declared its view that

"no individual has an inherent right to obtain labour and the hazard whether he can or cannot obtain labour . . . is one of the chances which must be taken into consideration by

---

[1] *Ibid.*, p. 109. [2] Cmd. 1509 (1921).

the non-native when embarking on any particular form of capital investment." [1]

Since that time the demand for assistance, direct or indirect, in the supply of labour has decreased. Sheer necessity, in terms of a higher material standard, has caused the greater number of young men in such tribes as the Kavirondo and Kikuyu to regard a periodical absence at work as part of their normal existence, and the visitations of drought and locusts in the years preceding the present world depression increased that necessity to a point where little shortage of labour was complained of. The basis on which the available labour supply is calculated is four-fifths of the adult male population; [2] in 1927 the proportion actually in employment at any given time was estimated as about 39 per cent., while in the case of the Kavirondo it was as high as 62 per cent. [3]

On the other hand European opinion has to a certain extent accepted defeat in the sense of recognizing that the labour supply will not be sufficient for a rapid extension of plantations throughout the European area, and attention is being turned to stock-farming, which requires much less labour. Sir Daniel Hall's Commission on Agriculture recommended encouraging the immigration of farmers from eastern Europe who would be prepared to undertake a greater proportion of their own manual labour than the present type of settler.

Meantime here as elsewhere the problem of labour shortage has suddenly given way to the problem of unemployment. The average number of natives in employment fell from 180,000 in 1929 to 132,000 in 1932, rising in 1933 to 141,000 with the expansion of the mining industry. [4] The Native Affairs Department Report for 1931 describes "bands of labourers wandering from farm to farm looking for work", a drift of the unemployed to the urban areas and an increase of crime in those areas. No measures proposed for dealing with this situation are yet on record.

[1] Cmd. 2387 (1925), p. 45.
[2] Compare the Belgian view of the available percentage, below, p. 233.
[3] Labour Commission, 1927, p. 17.
[4] Native Affairs Department Report, 1933, p. 122.

The "dual development" theory represents an attempt to formulate a common policy for a territory committed to the furtherance of white settlement, a mandated area in which white settlement has been permitted with strict regard for native interests, and one where, owing to climatic conditions, it is impossible, and economic development has rested mainly on native peasant production. As applied to Kenya, the dual policy, in the words of Lord Delamere,

"sets out to keep the native in close and continuous touch with the work of the world; to break down those tribal customs which make for reversal to barbarism and to provide innumerable unpaid teachers of civilization who themselves have to meet and overcome the problems of African life and economics." [1]

In those of Mr. McGregor Ross, it means

"that the native is to be allowed to do the impossible—feed himself and all dependants, produce crops for export, and at the same time keep all the European estates going to the satisfaction of their owners." [2]

In terms of concrete administrative measures the "dual policy" means in Kenya that since 1924 Government has interested itself in native education. Since 1923 rather more serious efforts have been made to improve agriculture in the reserves, and since 1924 Local Native Councils have been created which have power to levy rates for public works in their areas. In this connection, it is pointed out in the Native Affairs Department Report for 1927 (p. 25) that the levying of rates is not without its influence on the labour supply.

Native Local Government.—There were in 1930 twenty-four Native Councils "on which all native interests are represented".[3] These bodies are constituted without regard to

---

[1] Huxley, *White Man's Country*, vol. II, p. 205.
[2] *Kenya from Within*, p. 445. The terms of a Government Circular on the subject of the "Dual Policy", in which officials are instructed to impress on natives the loss which will result to the whole country, themselves included, if insufficient labour is available in the planting season, tend to confirm this interpretation. See Circ. 5, 1927.
[3] Description in Native Affairs Department Report, 1927, p. 25.

existing native institutions, and meet under the presidency of a European official. They receive such share as may be due to them from the Native Trust Fund established in 1921, into which were paid moneys due to the relatives of native porters who died in the War and sums exacted from various tribes as collective fines. Rents and licences paid within the reserves are credited to them. As has been mentioned, they have power to levy rates. They receive no share of the general revenue. The aim of these Councils, as envisaged by Sir Robert Coryndon, in whose Governorship they were introduced, and Lord Delamere, who seconded the Bill establishing them, is to provide a basis for the ultimate development of a Central Native Council. Sir Donald Cameron looked towards a similar goal for the native authorities whom he established in Tanganyika, but with the significant difference that he refused to consider the grant of political rights to the European population before this goal should have been reached. Despite the fact that these Councils have no traditional authority, they seem to have been able to carry through a good deal of constructive work in such matters as fly clearance, re-afforestation and the reconditioning of eroded land. They have raised large sums of money for the establishment of schools. Their main function seems to be regarded as the raising of revenue for local purposes rather than the exercise of general administrative responsibility. The Kikuyu Councils have passed resolutions dealing with female circumcision, and the Akamba Council has considered the substitution of cash for goats in the payment of bride-price, but the issuing of general orders does not appear to be considered as an important duty of these bodies. They are described in an official report as useful "media for making known the policy of the Government".[1]

Native Tribunals.—Native Tribunals have been provided for ever since the Courts Ordinance of 1907. Theoretically they are constituted in accordance with native law and custom, but in practice this does not seem to have been strictly followed. It is reported that in North Kavirondo some propaganda was necessary to induce the people to come before a Tribunal

[1] Native Affairs Department Report, 1932, pp. 47, 53.

without the chief at its head; and a few pages later in the same report we read that "it is hoped that these Tribunals will exercise their jurisdiction in support of local authority".[1] The connection between the two points appears not to have been noticed. Although large numbers of cases are dealt with by these Tribunals, it is also recorded that too great insistence on European methods, in some regions, drives the natives to seek the settlement of their claims elsewhere. The Digo are said to avoid the Tribunals because of the insistence that fines must be paid in cash and not in stock,[2] and the refusal reported from North Kavirondo to have anything to do with the inconvenient practice current in some districts of requiring the identical animal in cases where return of bride-price is claimed,[3] cannot, one feels, have made the courts of the district popular. A still further departure from native custom is the reorganization begun in 1933 of the Central Province (formerly Kikuyu and Ukamba), which aims at "the gradual elimination of chiefs and other natives connected with the executive from judicial work ".

The Awakening of Native Nationalism.—The process of imparting the benefits of civilization has produced a reaction among the tribes most affected which is remarkably interesting. It has not proved to be the case that an enlightened younger generation would repudiate the out-of-date methods of its elders; on the contrary, the younger educated natives are showing as much determination as any mythical "old woman of the tribe" to defend their own institutions, while demanding what seem to them to be the advantages of European ways.

The most sensational instance of this native "nationalism" occurred in the contest between the Church of Scotland Mission and the Kikuyu on the subject of female circumcision. The mission having instituted an active campaign against the custom by refusing to allow any native to teach in their schools who did not explicitly abjure it, the entire population boycotted the schools. In this move it was definitely the younger men who were the leaders, as it was a group of them who manifested

[1] Native Affairs Department Report, 1932, pp. 47, 53.
[2] *Ibid.*, 1932, p. 51.   [3] *Ibid.*, 1930, p. 33.

their indignation by murdering a lady missionary and performing the operation upon her body.

But this is only a particularly striking symptom of an attitude which is reflected in a constant determination to resist European interference whenever possible. The insistence of the Kikuyu Native Councils on the right to control themselves the schools maintained by their revenues is held by the local authorities to have been strengthened, but certainly not created, by their quarrel with the Mission. The same insistence is found in Kavirondo, where there has been no such breach with any missionary body.[1] After some hesitation Government has yielded to the demand, and in 1932 and 1933 secular Native Council Schools were opened at Nyeri for the three Kikuyu Districts and at Kakamega for the Kavirondo. Native schools which are prepared to dispense with Government assistance in order to escape Government supervision are also said to be increasing in numbers.[2]

Among the mixed tribes of the Kavirondo there is also a growing reluctance to recognize the authority of chiefs or headmen set over groups of which they are not members, and a demand for territorial reunion among tribes whose members have been scattered. This point of view has not received much sympathetic consideration from the Government, though its existence is mentioned in successive reports.[3]

It is arguable that this rejection of alien influences is the product of simple hostility to European economic encroachment, and that traditional institutions are defended less for their own sake than as a focus of opposition to unpopular authority. Those who hold this view would support it by pointing to the demand for education as proof that the African does desire civilization, and is even suspicious that authority may put obstacles in the way of his attaining it. The answer is only to be found in the future. But it seems at least possible that we have here a phenomenon rather different from the nationalism of the Gold Coast that is voiced by educated

[1] See Native Affairs Department Reports from 1928 onwards.
[2] See Education Department Report, 1932, p. 188, and Native Affairs Department Report, 1932, p. 11.
[3] Native Affairs Department Report, 1932, pp. 8, foll.

Africans engaged in professional work in towns organized on
European lines; that this movement, which comes not from
groups detached from their tribal backgrounds, but from
within the tribe itself, represents in an organized form that
desire to attain to European knowledge and mastery of the
material world, without being forced to accept the entire outfit
of European institutions and moral values, which is familiar to
most anthropologists as the attitude of the individual village
native. In this attitude lies the fundamental justification for
that respect for native ways inherent in the theory of Indirect
Rule, as opposed to the light-hearted attempts to alter them
with a stroke of the pen which have characterized Kenya
administration in many fields.

The Dual Policy through Impartial Eyes.—As to the real
duality of the dual policy impartial opinion has pronounced
on two occasions. The Hilton Young Commission, appointed
in 1927 to inquire into the possibilities of co-ordinating the
policy of the various Governments of Central and Eastern
Africa, was required by one of its terms of reference to suggest
the best methods of application of the dual policy, and reported
that the basis of any co-ordination must be the acceptance of
agreed principles of native administration. Its criticisms of
Kenya policy are in the main left implicit in the contrast
between facts in that territory and the principles which it lays
down, though it does refer specifically to the divergence between
the Belgian Congo and Kenya methods of estimating the
available labour supply, to the relative rates charged on the
railway for European maize and native coffee, to the obstacles
put in the way of coffee cultivation by natives, to the lack of
agricultural work in the reserves, and to the Registration
Ordinance.

The principles which it adopts subordinate the dual policy
to the paramountcy of native interests

"interpreted in the sense that the creation and preservation
of a field for the full development of native life is a first
charge on any territory, and that the Government having
created this field has the duty to devote all available resources
to assisting the natives to develop within it. But if, after

having secured what is necessary for the above purpose, there appears to be room for immigrant settlers . . . then immigration can be permitted and even encouraged."

They recommend

"a policy which would make available for every native, for his own cultivation, sufficient land to maintain himself and his family and to provide him with the cash required for the taxes which he has to pay."

They state that

"the available labour supply must not be estimated solely with a view to the requirements of non-native enterprise. If effect is to be given to the Dual Policy, the labour needs of the reserves must equally be taken into account." [1]

Finally they make it a cardinal point of their recommendations that any increase in the powers of self-government granted to the local European communities must be balanced by the establishment of a powerful arbitral authority which shall have the last word in matters where native or non-native interests may come into conflict.

Closer Union on those terms proved utterly inacceptable to those sections of the community who had envisaged a self-governing East African Dominion in which local bureaucracy and Downing Street Utopianism should no longer impede the attainment of their ideals. Official and native witnesses from Uganda and Tanganyika were unanimously opposed to any form of Closer Union which might involve an extension of Kenya policy, and the Select Committee reported that "the time is not yet ripe".

The second occasion for impartial scrutiny was in 1932, when a series of inquiries were held into the financial position of territories particularly hard hit by the economic depression. The Commissioner appointed to Kenya was Lord Moyne, who is by no means out of sympathy with settler aspirations, and defended the Government when it was attacked on the amendment of the Native Lands Trust Ordinance. As a result of his

[1] Cmd. 2324 (1929), pp. 40, 65, 69.

inquiries he came to the conclusion that the native population could only be assured of a due return for the taxation paid by them, and protected against constant economies at the expense of native services, if a certain proportion of this taxation was paid into a Native Betterment Fund which should be earmarked for native interests, and whose administration should not be subject to review by the Select Committee on Estimates.[1] The sum which was recommended was half the average yield of native taxation during the preceding six years. Meetings of settlers protested. The Trans-Nzoia Press published a pamphlet complaining of "a definite bias towards the conclusion that the non-native is the more favoured community", and demanding a European Betterment Fund in accordance with "the principle of no racial discrimination". A Select Committee was appointed by Government to devise means for carrying Lord Moyne's recommendations into effect, and proposed that this should be done by applying the revenues from the Native Betterment Fund to agricultural and medical work in the reserves, these being services where it is possible to differentiate clearly between work done for natives and non-natives. The statistics published in 1933 of a Health Scheme for Native Reserves presumably represent a step in the application of this fund.[2]

IV. NORTHERN RHODESIA AND NYASALAND

Indirect Rule with European Settlement.—In Northern Rhodesia and Nyasaland official policy has been marked by a reaction against the ideals of early expansion, cherished by the British South Africa Company, towards those more generally associated with Indirect Rule—the maintenance as far as possible of the native population on their tribal lands, and the development of indigenous institutions. In both territories, however, the degree of land alienation and European settlement that had taken place before the reaction began has been too great to allow of anything like a complete realization of these ideals,

[1] Cmd. 4093 (1932), pp. 37–55.
[2] Native Affairs Department Report, 1933, pp. 117–8.

and in Northern Rhodesia there is a European population sufficiently large to be vocal in advocating the use of repressive measures in their own interests.

Northern Rhodesia.—In Northern Rhodesia a further consideration operates against the full application of the Indirect Rule policy. In that part of it which remains predominantly native the soil is so poor that economic development by means of native production is out of the question. Even crops grown for the local market do not bring in anything like the return that can be obtained in the same time by a man working in the copper mines, so that it is almost impossible to maintain that village life which further north is regarded as the essential basis of Indirect Rule. The territory can be divided into three markedly different areas. Barotseland in the west is a reserve having the status almost of a protectorate, in virtue of agreements made with Chief Lewanika by the B.S.A. Company. Its people are pastoral and are largely able to meet their economic needs without wage-labour. East of this comes an area in which intensive settlement has taken place. The railway zone had already been thickly settled by Europeans, with considerable disturbance of native rights, under the Chartered Company's administration. The copper-belt begins to the north-east of this area and extends across the Belgian Congo border. Indeed the peculiar shape of the colony is accounted for by the copper-belt, for Belgium secured her share of it by a frontier which extends like a peninsula between North-Western and North-Eastern Rhodesia. East of the "Congo Pedicle" the land is still predominantly native, though the B.S.A. Company holds a concession there of 2,750,000 acres, and the North Charterland one of 6,000,000. A certain amount of this has been alienated. But the cost of transport militates as much against European as against native production in that region.

A proposal which has been much discussed, and has the approval of the Chairman of the Hilton Young Commission,[1] is that the territory should be divided in two, the eastern part being amalgamated with Nyasaland, which despite a certain amount of European settlement is now regarded as a pre-

[1] Cmd. 2324 (1929), pp. 252-68.

dominantly native area, and the western going to Southern Rhodesia, subject to the maintenance of Barotseland as an inalienable native reserve.

The history of Northern Rhodesia as a Crown Colony is the history of the Ndola copper-mines. The existence of copper in this area had been known since about 1903, but it was only in 1925 that it was found to be of such quality as to have a high commercial value. A construction boom began in that year, and the beginning of effective production coincided with the slump of 1931. Some mines were closed down before they had produced at all. By 1935 there has been considerable recovery and a new production boom is expected. But it would probably be rash to forecast a future of such immense wealth as seemed to be in prospect a few years ago.

Land Distribution.—The policy with regard to land distribution has been to demarcate native reserves in areas where European settlement is expected to take place or has already done so, but elsewhere to leave the native populations undisturbed. The three provinces where no delimitation has yet been considered necessary are Kasempa, Awemba and Mweru-Luapula. Three Commissions were appointed to delimit reserves in East Luangwa, Tanganyika, and Batoka, Kafue and Luangwa respectively. The first two, whose reports are available, took the line that future as well as present needs should be provided for, and inquired in some detail into the nature of existing rights, besides inviting local chiefs to state what part of their lands they themselves would be willing to part with. Even such non-economic considerations as the position of ancestral burial-grounds were taken into account.

Since the two Companies obtained their concessions subject to respect for native rights, the Government was entitled to schedule native reserves within them, and two million acres have been so scheduled in the B.S.A. concession and one million in the North Charterland. They are reserved for the use of the native population "in perpetuity". The boundaries were so drawn as to produce a closer concentration of villages on tribal land, with as little movement of natives as possible, and without requiring any to leave their tribal areas.

The arrangements for moving are very lenient and take into account the native system of cultivation, which in these areas involves moving the village every four years. As the time for a new change comes round, the natives of the villages concerned will be persuaded to move into the reserve, those who remain holding their land at the will of the Companies or the Crown. After a period of grace no new villages may be made outside the reserves, but there is no provision that at the end of this time all natives must have moved within them. On Crown land it was recommended that they should be allowed to remain where they were till it was required for alienation, and the Native Affairs Report of 1932 (p. 11) writes of the Tanganyika Province: "It is unlikely that they will ever have to move from Crown land". On alienated land they are allowed to remain only as labour tenants. The Report of the East Luangwa Commission stated (p. 33) that agreements of this kind were becoming unpopular, but they remain the only legal form of tenancy.

The gazetting of the reserves was accompanied by the development of water-supplies within them, and of facilities for dipping cattle. Their area is two million acres in Eastern Luangwa, giving a population density of 38·7 to the square mile, eight million acres in Tanganyika with 8·5, and just under two million acres in the railway zone, with 6·89. The Barotse Reserve, with an area of 57,530 square miles, has 16 to the square mile in the eastern division and 12 in the western. The total area of land alienated to Europeans is 8,750,000 acres, or about $4\frac{1}{2}$ per cent. of the whole territory.[1] The remainder is unalienated Crown land.

The Governor, Sir James Maxwell, addressing the elected members of the Legislative Council in 1930, said: "In my considered opinion these reserves are far too small," and added "There is land alienated in freehold to Europeans on which no development is taking place and I have no power to make the owners develop." The Native Affairs Report of 1933 (p. 12) mentions the natives' "resentment at being confined to reserves while there is so much undeveloped land around them", but actual shortage is not reported as yet.

[1] Annual Report, 1933, p. 121.

Purchase of land by natives outside the reserves is subject to no restrictions.

Since 1932 small holdings have been surveyed and allotted for leasing by natives on individual tenure in the neighbourhood of most of the large towns.[1]

Native Authorities.—The demarcation of reserves in which the tenure of the tribes should be secured had as its complement the restoration of authority to native chiefs. The adoption of Indirect Rule as the method of development within the reserves is another feature differentiating Northern Rhodesia from the other colonies of European settlement, who have disregarded traditional native authorities in favour of institutions of local self-government of European type. The new system was introduced in 1930 by the Native Authorities and Native Courts Ordinances. At present it rests on the recognition of the judicial functions of the native chiefs, and their endowment with power not only to issue orders for various purposes required by Government, but also to "make rules for the peace, good order and welfare of the natives within their areas". They have no financial powers; court fees go into general revenue and they receive no share of native taxation. It is recognized, however, that Indirect Rule cannot be fully established until Native Authorities administer their own revenues, and that such powers should be given them as soon as they are held to be sufficiently competent. Revenues accruing to the reserves from rents, grazing fees and timber licences are paid into a Reserves Trust Fund which was constituted by Order in Council in 1930, administered by the Treasurer in consultation with the Secretary for Native Affairs. Up till now these revenues have been invested pending decision as to the way in which they should be utilized. Native Authorities have been consulted on the question and are to be given the responsibility for disbursing the sums allotted to them. This fund naturally accounts for only a small proportion of the revenue spent on the reserves, but the success with which they administer their share may be a test of their fitness to undertake greater financial responsibility.

[1] Native Affairs Report, 1933, p. 21.

The failure to provide the native administrations with revenues under their own control at the same time that the chiefs have been forbidden, in accordance with the Geneva Forced Labour Convention, to exact from their subjects the revenues which enabled them to reward their subordinate officials with food and presents, has seriously hampered the efficacy of some native authorities.[1] It leaves a hiatus of a kind which Lord Lugard, when introducing Indirect Rule in Northern Nigeria, was careful not to make: his Political Memoranda stress the necessity of providing the native chiefs with funds which will replace the losses they must sustain through the abolition of slavery. Of some native authorities, however, it is reported that they have readily undertaken their new function, and "what is more important still, are enforcing their rules".[2] In most tribal areas, regular meetings of the chiefs and sub-chiefs are held at which the rules to be issued are discussed. Constant supervision by European officers is recognized as necessary, but this supervision is not given in such a way as to render the chiefs' authority illusory. In their judicial capacity, where their duties are much more closely allied with those which attached to their position in the old days, the chiefs have given general satisfaction here as elsewhere. A wisely tolerant attitude towards non-European methods of procedure records that "in some extraordinary devious way sound judgements are reached in the end".[3]

It is proposed to introduce the general legislation applicable to Native Authorities to Barotseland, where under the present system the Chief and Khotla retain wide powers, including final judicial authority in all but the most serious cases, but are unable to exercise them effectively, since while they have lost their right to appeal to force, the European authority has not made itself responsible for enforcing their decisions. The administration of the Barotse Trust Fund, into which 30 per cent. of the revenue of the area is paid, is not subject to European supervision, and corruption is said to be general. The present

---

[1] See Richards, "Tribal Government in Transition"; Supplement to *Journal of the African Society*, October 1935.
[2] Native Affairs Report, 1932, p. 7.   [3] *Ibid.*, 1930, p. 6.

Chief, however, has agreed that his position should be assimilated to that of other Native Authorities in the Territory, and the change only awaits the approval of the Colonial Office.[1]

Indirect Rule in Northern Rhodesia has a much more difficult task than in areas of predominantly native peasant production. It has meant there not simply the maintenance and progressive development of native institutions in accordance with modern economic ideas, but their reconstruction in the face of destructive influences constantly at work through the periodical migration of a large proportion of the population to and from centres of labour inside and outside the territory. Proposals have been made for the development of native craft within the reserves which might make them independent of such migration, together with such a stabilization of the wage earning population in the mining centres as has been aimed at in the Belgian Congo. But it is very doubtful whether such a development is practicable; if it is not, the maintenance of authority, and of all the tribal institutions with which it is linked, must be always at the mercy of the impact from outside of ideas which may well be subversive and yet not particularly progressive. Superficially in such a situation there might seem to be a strong case for the frank abandonment of any attempt at evolutionary development. But it may be that the arguments brought forward in support of this thesis prove, not that in some circumstances revolutionary change is the only mode of advance, but only that in these circumstances no form of development remains possible in which the cohesion of native society can be preserved.

Labour Policy.—Legislation deliberately designed to force natives into employment has not been introduced in Northern Rhodesia; the necessity of earning money for taxation in areas without local resources has been a sufficient stimulus. A large proportion of the natives who leave their reserves have always found work outside the territory, and the copper boom produced an increase in the total number employed rather than a diversion of these to centres nearer home. In 1930 the average percentage of able-bodied males absent from the reserve

[1] Merle Davis, *Modern Industry and the African*, p. 248.

as 35 to 45 and the period of absence from seven to ten
months.[1]

By 1932, as the world depression made itself felt, it was
estimated that the average proportion of absentees was not
more than 15 to 20 per cent., and was in some districts as low
as 10 per cent. But by no means all of those who are still
absent are still at work. Some are being rationed as a reserve
force by the mines, others are simply living on their friends.[2]
Government provision for them is held to be unnecessary
seeing that all *could* obtain subsistence in the reserves. But
their forcible deportation has not been contemplated, and
some alternative policy will surely have to be found.

In the last year or two African administrations have been
brought face to face for the first time with the intimate connection between industrialization and periodic unemployment;
as a solution to the problems which result from this connection,
none seem to have looked beyond attempts, more or less
efficacious, to remove the unemployed natives from the
immediate vicinity of the urban areas. None is prepared to take
responsibility for the maintenance of a stable labour force by
means of a system of insurance. It is admitted that the financing
of such schemes is probably beyond most African revenues,
but this only means that once again the urban African population
is condemned to the worst of both worlds, and once again the
encouragement of European enterprise has gone on without
regard to the consequences for the native populations whose
labour is the condition of its success.

Northern Rhodesia is more liberal than its southern neighbour, both in the provisions of its labour legislation and in
their enforcement. The maximum period of an oral contract
is thirty days and of a written one two years, as against one
year and three years. Desertion is penal, but mere desertion is
distinguished from "desertion with intent not to return", and
classed as a minor offence. Arrest of deserters without a
warrant is allowed, but in practice the police do not make it
their duty to track them down except on a demand from the
employer. Natives are obliged to carry identity certificates,

[1] Native Affairs Report, 1930, p. 23.   [2] *Ibid.*, 1932, p. 27.

but since 1931 the provision that the certificate must be endorsed by the employer has been applicable only in the railway area. The Southern Rhodesian provision, by which the pass is exchanged for a certificate of contract and retained by the employer during the period of contract, does not apply in Northern Rhodesia.

Nyasaland.—A British Protectorate was declared in 1891 over those parts of Nyasaland adjoining Lake Nyasa and the Shiré River, but the rest of the territory was till 1896 administered along with Rhodesia, by the British South Africa Company. They acquired by means of agreements with native chiefs—whose validity and even existence was hotly contested by their successors before a Government Commission in 1929 [1]—free-hold rights over 2,700,000 acres at the northern end of the Lake, constituting practically the whole of the North Nyasa District; this is now in the hands of the African Lakes Corporation. At the other end of the territory the Livingstone-Bruce Estate Company own 320,000 acres in a single block, and the British Central Africa Company 170,000 in different parts of the Blantyre District, nearly half of which is in European hands.

These large-scale alienations of land, held under Certificate of Claim, which amount practically to freehold, were made during the first years of the Protectorate. The total area covered by them is 3,705,255 acres. Only a small portion of this is in actual occupation. In addition the Protectorate Government made further grants of 139,472 acres in freehold before the War, and in the post-war boom alienated 118,504 acres on short-term leases (seven years renewable up to 1921). The maximum area under cultivation by Europeans appears to have been 66,000 acres in 1922. [2]

Squatter Regulations.—While this does not represent a large percentage of the total land of the Territory, it accounts for a considerable proportion of what is cultivable, and in view of the continuous extent of the alienated areas there are inevitably large numbers of natives living on them. About 15,000 are resident on the Livingstone-Bruce estate; in the district

[1] North Nyasa Reserve Committee Report, p. 3 ; evidence, pp. 63–4.
[2] Annual Report, 1922, p. 7.

omba in 1921 about a quarter of the total native population
was living on alienated land; in that of Blantyre about half.[1]
Theoretically the grants were made subject to native rights—
a condition which, as we have seen, has been liberally respected
by Northern Rhodesia in the demarcation of Native Reserves
in the B.S.A. and North Charterland Concessions. In Nyasaland, however, the custom of shifting cultivation has provided
an excuse for refusing to regard as "original inhabitants" of
the land any natives not occupying the sites on which they
were at the time of alienation. Legislation passed with a view
to safeguarding the native's position was a dead letter,[2] and
all that the Land Commission appointed in 1921 could do was
to propose that labour tenancy, as the only basis on which
European landowners would permit natives to live in their
estate, should be officially recognized and strictly supervised.[3]
Where land was being developed it seems to have been found
impossible to protect against eviction natives who were not
willing to enter into such contracts. Discontent with the
existing system, in which the period of work demanded by the
landlord constantly increased, and the practice common further
south of refusing to allow squatters to seek work elsewhere
began to be followed, was found to be one of the causes of the
Chilembwe Rising of 1915.[4]

It was some time before effective legislation was enacted, but
eventually a measure was passed which safeguards the interests
of the squatters more effectively than is done anywhere else
where the system exists. This is the Natives on Private Estates
Ordinance of 1928, which, though it permits the conclusion
of a six months' labour contract, makes an agreement on a
cash basis the normal form of tenancy. The maximum rent is
fixed at the cash equivalent of three months' average pay for
agricultural labourers. The native is allowed, if he wishes, to
pay this by work for wages at current rates, on an agreement
whereby for each month worked between October and February
he is entitled to a rebate of one-third of the rent due, for every

[1] Commission on the Occupation of Land, 1921, p. 11.
[2] Land Ordinance (Native Locations) 1904; Native Rents (Private
Estates) Ordinance 1917. See Land Commission, 1921, p. 14.
[3] Ibid., loc. cit. [4] Ibid., p. 13.

other month one-sixth. Landlords who do not offer employ
ment to a tenant who elects to work must give facilities for th
cultivation of crops for sale, purchase by the landlord entitlin
the native to proportional rebates of rent. A good deal of nativ
tobacco is grown in this way.[1] The basis on which the rebate
are calculated is fixed from time to time by Government. N
rent may be charged unless the landlord offers employment c
gives facilities for cultivation.

Evictions for any other cause than misconduct or non
payment of rent can only be made at the end of a quinquenni:
period, and at any one time no landlord may evict more tha
10 per cent. of his total tenantry. At the end of the first suc
period only a few large estates evicted the full 10 per cent.
elsewhere the proportion varied from $1\frac{3}{4}$ per cent. to 5 pe
cent.[2] This measure also empowers Government to orde
landowners to set aside up to one-tenth of their estates fo
native occupation, but the use of this power has not bee
found necessary. These provisions, liberal as they are, hav
been considered to give the tenant insufficient security, an
further measures are under consideration.

The principle task of the Land Commission of 1921 was t
determine the areas required for native occupation, takin
into account the probable expansion of the native populatio
and the requirements of native production for export. The
rejected the demarcation of reserves as a method, holding tha
this would involve an undesirable concentration of native
normally living in small scattered groups, where they woul
be short of the water in search of which they scatter, an
would find themselves obliged to travel long distances to thei
gardens or to centres of employment. If these difficultie
were to be avoided, "Reserves would have to be of such :
size as practically to allow of the continuation of presen
conditions."[3] They proposed therefore the demarcation o
areas available for European settlement, all other land
being left for native occupation. Basing their calculations
on the estimated requirements of double the then existing

---

[1] Native Affairs Report, 1931, pp. 54–5. [2] Ibid., 1933, p. 9.
[3] Report, p. 5.

native population, they found that six million acres, or nearly twice the total already alienated, could be so thrown open.

The Present Land Regime.—Their recommendations were shelved, however, and when the East Africa Commission visited Nyasaland in 1924, they found the same feeling of insecurity among the native population as in Kenya, and recommended the same solution in the vesting of native lands in a Trust Board "so constituted as to command native confidence." [1] The Governor of the time, Sir Charles Bowring, who had recently been appointed, had already declared himself in favour of the development of the territory by native peasant production, and had expressed the opinion that "the blocks of Crown Land to be set aside for further European occupation should not be large or numerous, and that the amount of land which is suitable for that purpose, and which at the same time is not required for the present or future use of the natives, is not great ".[2] A Bill such as the Commission recommended was introduced into the Legislative Council in 1927, but did not become law.

In the meantime, however, areas closed to alienation have been proclaimed after survey and after consultation with the native authorities affected. These authorities have also been officially assured that no further land will be alienated without their full consent,[3] and the disposal of land to non-natives even of the areas which remain theoretically open for such disposal is subject to native requirements. In 1933 a new Lands Bill was introduced which follows the general phraseology of that in force in Northern Nigeria; the whole territory, that is to say, is native territory vested in the Governor as trustee. In settling the land question in this way the method of a final delimitation of native and non-native areas was definitely rejected in favour of the idea that future necessities might call either for the expansion of native populations into the territory now regarded as available for alienation, or for the "temporary alienation" of that which at present is not so

[1] Cmd. 2387 (1925), p. 109.   [3] *Ibid., loc. cit.*
[2] Native Affairs Report, 1932, p. 24.

available. The inclusion of the whole territory in a singl
system is defended on the grounds that it not only protect
the native population from alienations made against their ow
interests but prevents them from refusing to allow beneficia
alienation; the right to alienate vested in the Governor is
however, only to be exercised after consultation with th
native authorities concerned,[1] and it was expressly stated t
them that it would not be exercised without their consent.
Rents received will be credited to native revenue.

The significant new factor in the present situation is th
absence of any demand for alienation. The B.S.A. Compan
in 1927 asked for a Commission of Inquiry to delimit the lan
which under the terms of their title was subject to nativ
rights, and expressed considerable chagrin at finding that i
took into account not only legally valid claims but the require
ments of native commercial production and of the futur
expansion of population.[3] In 1933 they agreed to relinquisl
their surface rights in return for confirmation of their minin
rights.[4] Elsewhere estates are being surrendered in sufficien
numbers to justify a Government order empowering Nativ
Authorities to take measures to regulate the settlement o
natives upon them. The demand of Kenya for "mor
Europeans" as a means of remedying the bankruptcy o
those already there does not seem to have been heard i
Nyasaland.

Development by Native Production.—Of recent years th
Government has taken no active steps to direct labour int
European employment. Up till 1920 the native tax was 8s
with a rebate for 4s. for those who were a month in Europea
employment, but this was altered in 1921 to a flat rate of 6s
As early as 1920 demands for the institution of a pass systen
and the registration of natives were refused, and employer
urged to look rather to economy in the use of labour than t
regulations designed to produce "an increased supply ".[5] Th

[1] Speech by the Governor in Legislative Council, July 6th, 1933.
[2] Speech by the Governor to a meeting of natives at Zomba, 1933.
[3] North Nyasa Reserves Commission, evidence, p. 210.
[4] Native Affairs Report, 1933, p. 9.
[5] Governor's speech, Legislative Council, March 1921.

encouragement of native cotton and tobacco has been looked upon with suspicion by employers, but the majority of the 1921 Land Commission were of the opinion that "it would be unfair to the native to check it as a hindrance to European industry".[1] While administrative officials have been instructed not to divert labour from plantations to independent production, employers have been left to obtain it by offering satisfactory conditions, or to dispense with it by the use of machinery.[2] Government has used its influence in support of the view, said to be gaining favour among planters, that higher wages mean greater efficiency.[3]

The number of natives in European employment in the Protectorate reached 88,000 in 1929, before the world depression began to affect Nyasaland. In that year 35,000 natives were engaged in cotton and 48,000 in tobacco cultivation. There is also a constant emigration of labourers to the Rhodesian and South African mines, estimated at about 30,000 annually. From the North Nyasa District, which has remained undeveloped until the last few years, 50 per cent. of the natives are said to have emigrated annually to the mines.[4] One of the motives behind the encouragement of native production has been the hope that it would provide an alternative livelihood for some of this migrant population; but it has hardly affected the north.

A great stimulus was given to cotton-growing in 1922 by an agreement with the British Cotton-Growing Corporation to purchase the crop at a fixed price. The percentage of the total output of the Protectorate grown by natives steadily increased from that time on, and with the fall in prices, making the crop unprofitable for Europeans, it has passed almost entirely into their hands. Tobacco was first grown by natives for export in 1924, and by 1930 the native crop represented almost 60 per cent. of the total output of the territory. An

[1] Report, p. 7.
[2] Annual Reports, 1924, p. 9; 1926, p. 7. Instructions circulated January 15, 1927. These instructions closely resemble the Tanganyika circular of the preceding year discussed below, p. 144.
[3] Ibid., 1930, p. 45.
[4] Northern Nyasa Reserves Commission, Report, p. 88.

increasing quantity is grown by natives resident on privately owned land; they receive free seed and instruction from the landlord, who nominally buys the crop. There is no obligation on the tenant to sell to him.[1] A Native Tobacco Board was established in 1926 to give advice and supervision to native growers living on Crown lands; only seed approved by it may be planted, and it is responsible for the grading of the leaf.

The very serious falling off in revenue from native taxation during the economic depression has led to a new drive to increase native production. A Native Agriculture Committee was appointed in 1933 as part of this campaign. It has considered improvements in the native tobacco industry along with such matters as the destruction of forests and exhaustion of the soil by native methods of cultivation, fire protection, afforestation and irrigation.

Native Administration.—In Nyasaland the system of native administration has recently been remodelled. Since 1912 "Village" and "Principal" Headmen had been entrusted by Government with executive duties. In 1924 certain modifications were made in their position, but it was officially stated that "the new system is in no way intended to revivify or perpetuate governance by native chiefs". Under the 1924 system "Village" and "Principal" Headmen still had executive duties on behalf of Government, but no authority to administer their peoples in their own right. They had no revenues, and though they were still entitled to hold courts these received no legal recognition. Their principal new power was that of calling out compulsory labour for public purposes when required by Government. A series of village, section, and district councils were set up, consisting of headmen and other members nominated and removable by the Government. The village councils were to advise the headmen when called upon to do so. The function of the section and district councils was simply "to advise the District Resident in such matters as may come before them". They were to meet as and when required by him and follow his directions in the

[1] Agriculture Department Reports, 1929, p. 7; 1931, p. 8.

conduct of proceedings. The standing orders quoted above go on:

> "The position of Principal Headman [the head of a Section Council] is in no sense similar to the archaic one of chief. The Principal Headman and the Village Headman alike will look to their D.C. as the chief to whom each is responsible for the good order and supervision of his Administrative Section or Village Area."

Under this system it was usual to appoint hereditary chiefs as headmen, but there were cases where such a chief was passed over in favour of a subordinate, and expressed his resentment in an attitude of non-co-operation shared by his followers.[1]

The Northern Nyasa Reserves Commission, asked to recommend the measures best calculated to promote economic development within the reserves to be constituted, proposed that suitable powers should be given to these councils, along with the allocation of the necessary funds, but did not suggest any change in their constitution.

The creation of a more effective native administration was advocated at a conference of administrative officers in 1930, and after the Senior Provincial Commissioner had made a study of the Tanganyika system Native Authorities and Native Courts Ordinances on the lines·followed there [2] were introduced in 1933. This involved a few changes in personnel, but the recognition of several different types of Native Authority corresponding to the varying degrees of political integration in the different tribes, which characterizes Nigeria and Tanganyika, does not appear to have been found necessary. In only one case, that of the Atonga of West Nyasa, the four Principal Headmen who had held office under the Ordinance of 1924 were replaced, at the request of their tribe, by a Tribal Council of thirty-two chiefs.

The Nyasaland Native Authorities receive from the proceeds of the tax which they collect only 8 per cent., which goes towards their salaries. Their general revenue is derived from

[1] Cf. Northern Nyasa Reserves Commission, p. 32.
[2] See next chapter.

Court fines and fees, from "fees collected for certain services taking the place of customary tribute", and from half of the rents due from leases and the yearly tenancies of plots under ten acres, which are mainly taken up by natives for trading stores. The other half of these rents is paid into a Central Fund from which grants will be authorized to Native Authorities whose budgets have been approved. The object of this fund is to equalize the position of more and less wealthy native groups. Native Authorities may also raise local levies for special purposes.[1] At the time when the latest available Annual Report was made no grants or levies had yet been made.

It is too early yet to judge of the success of this, almost the newest adoption of the Indirect Rule system. The existence of a class of educated natives who have tended to regard themselves as wiser than the chiefs and set themselves up in opposition may hamper its working here as it has elsewhere—for in Nyasaland education, while more practical than in many other areas, has yet concentrated largely on fitting the native to earn a good salary in European employment. Both Tanganyika and Northern Rhodesia have drawn numbers of native clerks, foremen and skilled artisans from Nyasaland; and as the demand for their services has been shrinking both with the economic depression and the development of education in Tanganyika, the difficulty of finding the place for which their training has fitted them has become more and more acute.

The Educational System.—In 1932 inquiries were made into the conditions of village life with a view to modifying the training given so that the specialized skill acquired could be turned to account in the villages. The replies revealed the difficulty with which such proposals are everywhere confronted—that the general standard of village life is too low to enable the specialist to earn by his craft the income to which he considers his training should entitle him. Stress was laid on the improvement of agriculture with a view to raising the general standard; but for the present it was held that skilled artisans could only find employment with Europeans or in village improvement schemes undertaken by native administrations.

[1] Native Affairs Report, 1933, p. 7.

At the same time attention is beginning to be directed to the closer integration of the school with village life and to the organization on a sounder basis of the primary education which is all that the majority of the population receive. Provision for a thorough course of training for native teachers began to be made by the missions in 1929, and was given particular support by Government; by 1933 there were twelve Normal Schools in existence.

A Jeanes School was opened in 1928, and as a result of its influence it was reported in 1932 that "teachers and supervisors are being encouraged, as they have rarely been before, to study the relationship between the headmen and the people and the children".[1] It is true that the example of the result so enthusiastically referred to in a later report—the interest taken by the headmen in an inter-school competition in music and drill [2]—hardly represents that integration of the school with village life that a sociologist might look for. More important are the village meetings organized for the discussion of such subjects as hygienic housing, or the relation of education to native customs, the visits of the Principal Headmen to the Jeanes Centre and their requests for advice as to possible improvements to be made in their villages. One of them rebuilt his whole village on a new site under the supervision of the Jeanes staff and students.[3]

New syllabuses were drawn up in 1932 for girls' education, based on the general principle that training for the married life to which the great majority look forward should be its central feature.[4] Nyasaland has also produced a considerable number of vernacular text-books dealing not only with "school" subjects, but with such practical matters as child welfare, agriculture and cookery.[5]

[1] Annual Report, 1932, p. 29.
[2] *Ibid.*, 1933, p. 33.
[3] *Loc. cit.* and 1932, p. 30.
[4] Annual Report, 1932, p. 30.
[5] *Ibid.*, 1933, p. 25.

CHAPTER III

SYSTEMS OF NATIVE ADMINISTRATION

IN a number of British dependencies an economic development based primarily on native peasant production is combined with an administrative system allowing considerable powers of local self-government to native authorities. To this group belong Nigeria, the Gold Coast, Uganda, and the Mandated Area of Tanganyika.[1] Not all of these can be strictly said to follow the policy of Indirect Rule in the sense of government through indigenous institutions adapted to modern needs; for while in Nigeria and Tanganyika much patient research has been devoted to the study of native law and custom and the incorporation of recognized native authorities as part of the machinery of government, in Uganda native political institutions have been so radically modified from the very inception of Protectorate government that those now existing can hardly be said to rest on any traditional basis, and in the Gold Coast little has been done to develop the traditional system. In them all there is a certain amount of land alienated for agricultural purposes—in Tanganyika a considerable area—and in West Africa and Tanganyika there are mines. In none, however, is the native population primarily dependent upon wage-labour to meet its obligations and satisfy its material wants.

I. NIGERIA

The Birthplace of Indirect Rule.—For an understanding of the Indirect Rule policy in all its implications no area is more instructive than Nigeria, its original home. It is there possible

[1] The reasons for classing Northern Rhodesia and Nyasaland, despite their recent adoption of a system of administration through native authorities, with the White Man's Countries, are given in the previous chapter.

to trace its history from the empiric establishment of a system deemed particularly suitable to a group of Moslem Emirates, where an already literate hierarchy of officials administered a conquered population, to its acceptance as a principle of administration found to be equally applicable whatever the size and political configuration of the native unit concerned. We can follow its gradual extension from the Fulani Emirates of Northern Nigeria to the Yoruba kingdoms of the south, and finally—after the belief that other forms of government were more suitable for small groups of little political development had been somewhat rudely shaken by facts—to the tiny clans of the five south-eastern provinces. It is possible, too, to follow a development from a stage where the guiding principle was that of maintaining the prestige of traditional authority to one where its adaptation to modern needs becomes the predominant aim.

The extension of British authority over Nigeria was completed in 1900; the Colony and the two Protectorates of Northern and Southern Nigeria being amalgamated in 1914. The main aims in the establishment of British rule were to put down resistance to trading enterprises and to suppress various native customs involving bloodshed on a large scale.

There is little land in the colony high enough to be suitable for settlement, and its population of about 21,000,000 in an area of 365,000 square miles left none of those vast unoccupied areas, waiting to be developed, to which Europeans elsewhere have claimed a moral right. The Government was not faced at its inception with any pressing demand for alienation or any corresponding necessity for demarcation. The actual policy followed with regard to land is so closely bound up with the whole Indirect Rule system that it will be best described after that system has been explained, for it is a special feature of Indirect Rule that the recognition of native authorities, so far from being subsidiary to a programme of development imposed by alien agencies, is the foundation on which all development is based.

Its Introduction in the Moslem Emirates.—Indirect Rule was introduced by Lord Lugard in the Northern Protectorate as a form of administration for which the local native organization was peculiarly suited, and he himself would probably not at that time have regarded it as capable of general extension. He found in Northern Nigeria a series of Moslem Emirates formed through the conquest by invading Fulani of aboriginal Hausa. In some the entire population had adopted Islam; in others the subject tribes retained their pagan religion and customs. Economic development had reached a point of considerable specialization, and elaborate series of taxes on the produce of land, on cattle and on the practice of various trades, were collected by the nominees of the Emirs. Justice was administered by Alkalai learned in Koranic law. The Sultan of Sokoto, as Sarkin Musulmi, or head of the Mohammedans, received annual payments from the other States.

There was thus already in existence an organization which needed but little adaptation for the performance of the tasks required by a European government, and a personnel closely acquainted with the circumstances of the native population, and more numerous than any staff that a British administration could hope to provide. The Lugard policy was to utilize their services in the development of a native administration based on British principles of impartiality and financial efficiency.

The conquered Emirs who submitted to British authority were given Letters Patent confirming their position, subject to the right of the British Government to impose taxation and its ultimate control over the allocation of land; the latter being a power which by their own custom was held to pass to the conqueror.

Lugard then proceeded to the reorganization both of the system of taxation and the method of collection. The assertion of authority implied in the collection of revenue seemed to him to be essential to the maintenance of a prestige which would tend to be impaired by the loss of military power. The right of the native officials to a share in it he regarded as a necessary compensation for the loss of personal revenue which they were to suffer through the emancipation of their slaves and the suppression of such levies as were no longer countenanced. At the same time their emoluments were to depend strictly on services rendered; there was to be an end to the system whereby the recipients of the taxes lived at the Emir's court and periodically dispatched their agents for collection. The District Heads entrusted with tax collection were also to perform other administrative duties; and were obliged, therefore, to reside permanently in the areas for which they were to be responsible. Below them ranked the Village Heads, who were not emissaries of the Emir but the authorities recognized by the village groups. Allowance was made for immigrant groups who still owed allegiance to a distant chief to pay their taxes through their own recognized heads until such time as they should be willing to accept the territorial authority. Meantime, wrote Lugard in 1906,

"the application of British Crown Colony rules of accounting and audit to the native system will be difficult; but the whole object of this system of taxation in Northern Nigeria is that it shquld be based on native tradition and custom to an extent probably hitherto untried in any Colony or Protectorate." [1]

The Basis of Taxation.—The system of taxation was based on the amalgamation into a single General Tax of all previous dues except the Jangali or cattle tax, which had always been the only levy made on herdsmen. The elaborate assessment of the product of every kind of occupation, which had already been made by the Fulani, formed the basis of a system of taxation whose only counterpart in Africa is in the other predominantly Moslem area under British control—the Sudan. In Lugard's view the hut or poll-tax universally adopted elsewhere was suitable only to the lowest communities; for those which had attained any degree of economic development he advocated a graded tax based on the potentialities of the land. This is in his opinion preferable to a tax proportionate to the actual product, which may act as a deterrent to increased production; a tax based on estimated productivity, on the other hand, bears more heavily on the individual who fails to cultivate his land to the best advantage. [2]

[1] *Political Memoranda*, No. 5, in Cmd. 5103 (1912).
[2] *The Dual Mandate*, p. 239.

As soon as possible the Emirs' assessments were replaced by more accurate counts made by British officers together with the village heads. The object of the assessment is to estimate the total productivity of the village, including the wealth obtained by the collection of forest produce and by the practice of crafts, and taking into account such factors as the proximity of markets. The assessment, being based on potential productivity, is not subject to annual revision, but would be modified only in case of significant changes in the general economic situation of the village, such as a large accretion or loss of population, development of communications, or in more recent times violent fluctuations in prices. The total tax payable by each village is then assessed at $2\frac{1}{2}$ per cent. of this amount. Divided by the number of adult males, the lump sum assessment can be expressed as a flat-rate tax. Its actual collection is left to the heads of compounds, who apportion it as they think fit. This system is supported on the ground that the apportionment is graded according to individual capacity. The estimated individual rate is well known, so that each individual is in a position to express his opinion as to the contribution demanded of him.[1]

In some of the Southern Provinces an individual income tax has been instituted on incomes above a certain level. Both the rate and the minimum income appear to vary from one district to another. The minimum rate of taxation levied in Nigeria on the basis of these assessments is generally lower than the hut and poll-tax exacted in southern and eastern Africa. It varies at the present time from 6s. to 8s., where the poll-tax in many districts of Uganda and Tanganyika is 10s., in Kenya 12s., in South Africa £1. This statement, of course, provides no satisfactory basis of comparison with territories where the average native income is not known. From the administrative point of view the significant fact is that Nigeria is the only area where it has been calculated in any detail; elsewhere taxation tends to be considered in terms of the period of labour necessary to earn it.

[1] Report of Commission of Inquiry into the Recent Disturbances in Owerri and Calabar Provinces, 1930, pp. 460, 501.

The assessment system, in Nigeria as in India, has had the incidental advantage of necessitating that close study of native life which elsewhere tends to be reduced by pressure of other obligatory work to an occupation for leisure hours.

Native Treasuries.—Originally the revenue was divided equally between the British Government and the Emirs, with the exception of the Sultan of Sokoto, who, in recognition of his status as Sarkin Musulmi, was allowed 75 per cent. of the General Tax collected in his Emirate. While the Emirs' personal emoluments were not at first differentiated from the revenue available for public purposes, the subordinate officials were from the outset paid salaries in proportion to the amount of tax they collected. This proportion was estimated as the equivalent of the share to which they had previously been entitled, but the principle was insisted upon that they did not themselves appropriate it as the money passed through their hands, but received it in payment from their Emir. Later fixed salaries were assigned to the Emirs. Since 1928 Native Treasuries classified as "fully organized" receive 70 per cent. of the revenues collected by them, and meet from their own resources a correspondingly wider range of public services.

Characteristics of Indirect Rule.—This, then, was the Indirect Rule policy in its original form. Its essential characteristic in the eyes of its creator was that the government of the native peoples by their own rulers should continue to be a reality; that all orders should come from the native ruler, that the share of the European official in determining their nature should be genuinely limited to persuasion in all possible circumstances, and that where it did become necessary to put pressure on a native authority the appearance of his freedom of action *vis-à-vis* his subjects should still be preserved. This principle implies a difference, not of degree, but of kind, from that underlying system where native rulers are used as a mere mouthpiece for the issue of orders on behalf of European interests, and are rewarded in proportion to the efficacy of those orders. The lowest pygmy is not such a fool as to suppose that a chief in the free exercise of his own powers would accompany a recruiting agent on his rounds and require the appearance of the desired complement of labourers, or that a village authority would on his own initiative lead a contingent to a distant and unpopular employment centre; hence the utter hopelessness of any attempt to maintain traditional authority where such services are required of it. To Lugard Indirect Rule did not present itself as an effective means of coercion, because the policies which he favoured did not require coercion to make them effective.

To him the second essential was that from the outset the native administrations should collect and disburse their own revenues—again a principle in marked contrast with that of those governments which first constitute their native authorities, and then leave them to prove their efficiency before allowing them to deal with money matters. As a basis for the prestige of authority the financial power is perhaps more necessary in Moslem States, where the judicial function is already performed by a specialized personnel, than in those communities where the administration of justice is the essential attribute of political supremacy. But as the foundation for the development of a native administration adapted to modern conditions it is absolutely essential; for in the modern economy the apportionment of revenue takes the place of many of the basic functions of chieftainship in its traditional form.

This third aspect of Indirect Rule—the adaptation of native institutions to meet new needs—has been a later development, in which the moving spirit was Sir Donald Cameron. In the early days of Nigeria attention was concentrated rather on eradicating defects in the existing system, such as corruption in the collection of revenue, and on the suppression of slavery and of such practices as human sacrifice and the exposure of twins.

Finally, the whole system as inaugurated by Lugard presupposed an economic development through independent peasant production, which he held to provide a greater stimulus to industry than could ever be provided by plantation labour. Thus the problem of adaptation has not in West Africa been complicated by the immense social upheavals that attend an economic system based on migratory labour.

Legal Foundations of Indirect Rule.—The legal foundations of Indirect Rule as it at present exists in Nigeria are the Native Authorities and Native Courts Ordinances. The former empowers Native Authorities recognized by the Government to make and issue orders on specific matters of local government and also to make rules of general application; this provision is intended to allow for the registration of changes in native customs but not "to open the way to the substitution for native law of something which the British official thinks is better".[1] The Native Courts Ordinance provides for the constitution of courts of different grades according to their competence. These have been established throughout the Protectorate, and in the areas in the South where there was no organized Native State the Native Courts were at one time constituted Native Authorities.[2] In the Moslem States the courts of the Alkalai were constituted Native Courts and seem to have shown some skill in adapting Moslem law to Pagan customs. The latest development of the judicial system is one which it is not easy to harmonize with the principles enumerated above. It consists in the establishment of Protectorate Courts to hear appeals from Native Courts, which, as soon as the financial situation makes it possible, are to be presided over by professional judges. The role of the administrative official in the judicial sphere is to be reduced to the minimum, and with it the influence of a point of view that attaches more importance to native institutions than to legal principles evolved in an alien culture. Since the new system is not yet in full operation its results in practice cannot yet be discussed; one can merely express considerable doubt as to the prospects of an evolutionary development of native institutions in a system which gives so powerful a voice in that development to a body of persons trained to believe in the universal applicability of standards alien to those institutions.

The System as Interpreted by Sir Donald Cameron.—The relation aimed at between British and native authority is reasserted by Sir Donald Cameron in a memorandum issued

[1] Cameron, *Principles of Administration*, p. 24.
[2] See below, p. 128.

in 1934. The administrative powers assigned to Native Authorities are, he writes,

> "intended to restrict direct action by the British officer to cases of genuine necessity,"

and again,

> "It is believed to be the habit of some Native Authorities to cloak all orders in the form of a Government instruction. . . . It is apparent that this tendency will be accentuated if the Native Authorities are frequently induced to issue orders which they do not appreciate and to which they are possibly at heart opposed. Where it is unavoidable that the Administration should obtain the issue of particular orders Administrative Officers should seek to persuade the Native Authorities to take the necessary steps, refraining as long as possible from giving them direct instructions." [1]

Similar scrupulous insistence is laid on the strictly advisory relation to native administrations of the technical services, medical, education, agriculture or public works. Their members are reminded that

> "in its own area the Native Administration represents the executive Government so far as native affairs are concerned, and all executive action which may be required will be carried out through it. . . . All orders on matters other than of a purely technical nature . . . should in general appear to be those of the heads of the Native Administration. . . . Care must be taken to make the Native Authorities understand that orders issued by them within their unit must be issued by themselves and are to be considered as their own orders and not those of any other person who may instigate them to exercise their powers. It is for the Native Authorities to consider whether a particular order is called for and reasonable, and so long as they are not so satisfied they should refrain from issuing the order and seek the advice of the District Officer before so doing."

It is particularly emphasized that "progress" in technical matters such as sanitation is not to be sought by enforcing as

---

[1] *Principles of Administration*, p. 25.

orders of the British Government measures the grounds for which are not popularly appreciated;

"it should be impressed on Native Authorities that they are expected to exercise their influence in these matters rather than their powers of punishment. . . . These principles . . . are designed to ensure that by the use of proper channels the fabric of native political organization shall not be broken down under the pressure of modern demands, and that, whenever possible, for the sake of the future, development shall be carried out executively by the native organization." [1]

Much has been written about the difficulty of distinguishing persuasion from command in the relations between European and Native Authorities. From what has been quoted it will be seen that even in Nigeria the distinction has not always been made in individual cases. That it should be generally recognized involves a patience and understanding of the native attitude on the part of the British official, and a confidence on that of the native authority, that are not easy of achievement. It has been the strength of the Nigerian policy that a tradition regarding this as the first essential has been created and maintained.

Its Extension throughout Nigeria.—The most interesting aspects of the development of Indirect Rule in Nigeria are to be seen in connection with its extension from the Moslem Emirates first to the Southern Provinces, which were amalgamated with the Northern in 1914, and later to the Mandated Area of the Cameroons, which came under effective British control at an early period of the War. Here we can see how, on the one hand, the form of native authority which had been recognized in the Northern Provinces proved inapplicable in the South, and on the other the extension of the fundamental principles of Indirect Rule was found to provide the only effective system of administration to native groups who had at first been believed to be too lacking in organization to be brought within it.

It had at first been held that Indirect Rule involved the existence of relatively large areas subject to a single authority.

---

[1] Minute in *Nigeria Gazette*, December 22, 1932.

Accordingly small tribes were included in the jurisdiction of their more highly organized neighbours, pagan groups set under Moslem authorities, and district heads appointed to defined areas without much consideration of their relation to the populations under their jurisdiction. Not till later was full recognition given to Sir Donald Cameron's principle that "the allegiance of a people to a tribal head, freely given and without external cause, is the essence of true indirect rule ".

The widest divergence from this principle was made in the five provinces east of the Niger, which are inhabited by small groups of Ibo and Ibibio-speaking peoples, often owning no wider allegiance than respect for the head of a small kinship group. Here no attempt was made to set up native treasuries. No taxation was levied, and civic obligations were confined to the unpaid labour on the roads and rivers which up till 1928 could be called upon by native authorities on behalf of Government. Native Courts were constituted in which a group of villages recognizing no special relationships were represented each by a single member. These "warrant chiefs" were as far as could be ascertained persons entitled by tradition to exercise authority, but owing to insufficient knowledge of the native social organization many of them in fact held no such position even in the villages which they represented. In some districts the Native Court was constituted a Native Authority, in others not.

As early as 1922 it had begun to be realized that the mere fact that a constituted native authority was not British did not necessarily make him any the less alien to the population under his rule, and that where he was so alien, not all the determination of British officials to remain in the background could prevent his being regarded as their instrument, as indeed he was in those cases where his power had no other basis than their support. From that time onwards greater stress was laid on the selection as Warrant Chiefs of traditional authorities, and when, in 1927, it was decided to extend taxation and the native treasury system to these provinces, detailed inquiries were set on foot with a view to determining the most satisfactory basis for the new organization. The introduction of taxation, however, preceded these investigations in some districts; and its reception provided the most spectacular demonstration possible of the weaknesses of a native administration whose authority is not upheld by forces coming from within the group which it attempts to govern.

The Aba Riots.—In December 1929 an incident which occurred while a village assessment was being carried out led to violent demonstrations by great crowds of women, who destroyed native courthouses, looted property, and on more than one occasion had to be dispersed by firing with loss of life. Their main grievance—the rumour that women were to be taxed—was easily dispelled, but the hostility displayed towards the Warrant Chiefs, and the mere fact that the demonstrations could take place at all, made a significant commentary on the state of native administration. The Warrant Chiefs were widely accused of corruption, and even of having been bribed by Government to agree to the introduction of taxation. It was clear that they were not generally regarded with any particular respect; the women had been unanimous in their attack, and there was no movement among the men to support authority. The traditional village heads, asked why they had done nothing to restrain their women from such unprecedented behaviour, pointed out that their commands carried no weight when other individuals had an official recognition which was not accorded to them.

The comments of local officials on the working of the Native Courts illustrate the difficulties created by this attempt to disregard sociological fact in the interests of administrative convenience. The system whereby the members of the Court sat in rotation, a month at a time, meant that frequently a case would be judged by a body of men entirely strange to the village concerned;[1] so that neither the local knowledge which for a native court takes the place of general rules of evidence, nor the local ties which deter a native judge from giving a manifestly unjust decision, operated to secure that award to the satisfaction of general opinion which a "natural"

[1] Evidence before the Commission of Inquiry into the Recent Disturbances, 1930 p. 153.

native authority can generally be expected to give. A contributory cause of the inefficacy of the Courts was the arbitrary way in which officials insufficiently acquainted with native law had reversed decisions as being "contrary to natural justice",[1] while in the absence of the confidence in their own awards which would have come from a recognized position in native eyes, the Warrant Chiefs tended to become completely subservient to the literate clerks who kept their records and might be presumed to know what Government wanted.

Reorganization in the South-Eastern Provinces.—As a result of these disturbances, intensive investigations throughout the area were ordered, with a view to the reorganization of native authorities wherever necessary, and as a result it has been found possible to utilize the existing institutions even of these small units for administrative purposes. Each such unit retains its individual existence as a judicial and executive body, while federations are encouraged for the purpose of pooling financial resources. Thus the lowest unit is the village council consisting of the headman and elders. Villages are grouped, with their consent, into clan councils under the presidency of the clan head, at which all members of the village councils are entitled to be present; in practice the council consists of village heads or their representatives. If the villages cannot agree to unite, they are not forced to join a larger unit, but arrangements are made for meetings between heads of villages and the District Officer at which they can learn by experience the advantages of joint deliberation. In some cases a desire that the grouping should be of neighbouring villages united by economic ties rather than those of belonging to a single clan has been acceded to.[2] The clan or group council is a fiscal unit and constitutes a court of appeal. The executive action on behalf of the whole group which the administration of a common treasury implies is taken sometimes by the president, sometimes by an *ad hoc* committee. In some cases the heads of clan councils unite to form a wider deliberative body. The

[1] Memorandum on the Recent Disturbances, p. 46.
[2] See section, Onitsha Province, Southern Provinces Annual Report, 1932, p. 47.

Efik tribe of the Calabar Province have a council of 150 members, which meets once a month and receives reports from a committee holding weekly sessions.[1] Where even the clan is very small neighbouring villages may agree to share a treasury, but such unions are not made compulsory. This system is now in force in the Colony (with the exception of Lagos Township) and the Mandated Area of the Cameroons.[2]

Recent Modifications in the Northern Provinces.—Reorganization on these lines is also being carried out in other parts of Nigeria. It is now the policy to emancipate pagan groups from Moslem overlords when a break in continuity, such as the succession of a new Emir, provides a suitable occasion,[3] and in the last year or two steps have been taken to re-unite subject clans belonging to a single tribe under administrations of the same type as those of the South-Eastern Province.[4] It is interesting that one such group hesitated to accept the new system lest the common people should be denied access to their (Moslem) chiefs.

The age-grade system, so long frowned upon because of its connection with secret societies, has been made the basis of native authority in some cases, and where it has not been destroyed by the refusal of Christian missions to allow their adherents to enter the age-grades, it has been a means of incorporating the educated element into the native administration. In groups which are too backward to cope with accounting the native authorities nevertheless collect their own taxes, and are themselves responsible for the payment of salaries from a lump sum handed over to them by the European official.[5]

Development to meet Modern Needs.—Along with this stress on the native group as the basic unit of government and its traditional authority, however selected, as its only satisfactory

---

[1] Southern Provinces Annual Report, 1933, p. 21.
[2] Permanent Mandates Commission, Session 23, pp. 14–15. *Principles of Native Administration*, pp. 21, 32. Memorandum on the Recent Disturbances, 1930, pp. 6–7. Southern Provinces Annual Report, 1933, pp. 36, 47.
[3] *Principles of Native Administration*, p. 14. Cf. Southern Provinces Annual Report, 1933, p. 41.
[4] Northern Provinces Annual Report, 1933, pp. 15–16, 31, 45.
[5] *Ibid.*, 1933, pp. 24, 32.

representative, has gone an insistence on the need for a development corresponding to modern conditions. The creation where possible of wider groups for purposes of financial co-operation has been mentioned; it is a principle of this amalgamation that it does not involve any sacrifice of the executive independence of the individual members. Similarly federal courts of appeal are established, not as superior authorities but on a genuinely federal basis, the President being chosen in rotation and each chief undertaking to carry out decisions given on cases brought up from his area.[1] Smaller states, if their rulers agree, may be grouped with cognate neighbours.

In the Northern Provinces the development of a uniform policy on common problems has been sought through an annual conference of all the native authorities with the Residents and leading non-official Europeans, such as the representatives of banks or of the tin mines.[2] For the first of these, several Emirs left their own territories for the first time. The proceedings summarized in their records are genuine discussions of suggestions put forward by Government but not pressed in any way, and involving no undertaking to act upon them.

Increased administrative efficiency has been sought in the North by persuading the Emirs to consent to a devolution of authority in specific matters to their leading officials,[3] while in the South, where Indirect Rule is newer, several of the Yoruba chiefs have agreed to have the Resident take part in the discussions of their councils, to seek his advice in matters of daily administration and to consult him before issuing orders. This control is intended to be withdrawn as the native administrations become better accustomed to dealing with modern problems.[4] It is intended to provide for the representation of educated natives on the larger Southern Councils;[5] and it appears to be becoming more and more common for

---

[1] *Principles of Native Administration*, p. 19.   [2] See below, p. 134.
[3] *Principles of Native Administration*, p. 12.
[4] Speech by Sir Donald Cameron at the installation of the Awujale of Ijebu-Ode, November 11, 1932.
[5] *Principles of Native Administration*, p. 12.

Christian and literate natives to be members of the small clan and village councils.[1]

Finally, attention has been paid to the danger that Indirect Rule may mean the consolidation of a privileged oligarchy at the expense of the majority of the population. Alone among African authorities Sir Donald Cameron has drawn attention to the importance of finding what safeguards against oppression the native organization itself provides.[2] He has also suggested the possibility of arranging periodical meetings in the large native states, at which village heads and elders may meet representatives of the European administration and the native authority,[3] and this suggestion has been followed in the case of certain primitive tribes in the Bauchi Emirate.[4]

Land Tenure.—In such a system the legislation regarding land tenure could have no other basis than respect for native rights. In theory the system in the Northern Provinces, where British authority rests on the right of conquest, differs from that in the Southern, which were acquired by voluntary cession; in practice the difference merely means that rents received from leased land are paid into general revenue in the north, and into local native treasuries in the south, and that in the south even Government pays for land which it occupies. In neither Northern nor Southern Provinces is any distinction such as that between "native" and "Crown" land made; in the north the whole of the land is declared to be "native land", vested in the Governor "for the use and benefit of the natives", and in the south it is held to be directly vested in the native tribes. The Land and Native Rights Ordinance (1916) of Northern Nigeria further provides that no title shall be valid without the consent of the Governor. This provision has met with a good deal of criticism from legal authorities and others, on the ground that it deprives natives of all security and enables the Governor to alienate at pleasure.[5] Undoubtedly the words could be made to bear that interpretation in the event of a drastic reversal of policy such as it is difficult to regard as at all

[1] Cf. Southern Provinces Annual Report, 1933, pp. 21–2, 50.
[2] *Principles of Native Administration*, p. 16.   [3] *Ibid.*, p. 15.
[4] Northern Provinces Annual Report, 1933, p. 10.
[5] Geary, *Nigeria under British Rule*, p. 266.

probable. What is more relevant is their real purpose and the extent to which this has been achieved. The origin of the Ordinance was a recommendation that steps be taken to safeguard native rights "prior to the advent of Europeans in any considerable numbers".[1] Its intention was to maintain unaltered the existing system, the British administration holding the same position as ultimate authority as would have been taken up by any of the Moslem Emirs who might have made himself paramount over the rest, and leaving occupiers undisturbed as he would have done. It was not contemplated that native occupiers under this system would desire to take out titles, and reference to title, which could be revoked for non-fulfilment of obligations, was definitely intended to apply primarily to land granted to Europeans. There was also an idea that the assertion of the ultimate authority of Government would justify the charging of rent if, as land acquired a commercial value, a demand arose among the native community for individual titles; but no such development has taken place in the Northern Provinces.

Figures as to the area of land in European occupation are not available. In the Northern Provinces the only rights of any importance granted to Europeans are mining licences for tin on the Bauchi Plateau and coal at Udi. In the South rights to cut timber have been granted, and it is stated in the Annual Reports that large tracts of land are available for agricultural purposes, but there is no information as to the areas leased. In the Cameroons fifty estates, covering 258,000 acres, were leased by the German administration, and when auctioned for reparations were mainly repurchased by Germans. Only a few of these are under cultivation. In the Colony transactions in land take place freely according to European law.

An interesting development in the South has been the demand for a modification of the native land system in view of the enhanced commercial value of land. By native custom, here as elsewhere, the sale of land was not so much prohibited as inconceivable, and Government has refused to countenance such sales. But in the Yoruba country, as in other densely

[1] Memorandum by Sir Percy Girouard, Cmd. 5103 (1912), p. 4.

populated areas, native custom allowed for friendly arrangements whereby one individual could occupy land to which another claimed the prior right, the right being generally acknowledged by a present which was not thought of as bearing any relation to the economic value to either of the land. Recent developments have affected this custom in several ways. Sites in the towns which are part of the traditional Yoruba culture are so much in demand that people compete in offering money presents for them; the successful competitor invariably claims to have purchased the land outright, but the grantor, taking refuge behind native custom, continues to assert ownership over it.[1] In some cases the money received by chiefs in place of the old-fashioned gift on settling on their land has been used to build houses which are let to European banks or traders.[2] Again, when forest land, which used to be given outright, is used for the cultivation of a valuable crop like cocoa, the grantor sees no reason why he should not get a share of the return, and demands money payments which cannot be distinguished from rent.

It has not been felt that these changes should be met by the issue of a uniform system of rules applicable in all districts. What is proposed is that the native authorities should themselves make such rules as they may consider suitable, the general principle being that commercial transactions in land should be recognized as between natives, that provision should be made for the optional registration of sales subject to the right of persons holding a joint interest with the vendor to show cause against the sale; and as a further safeguard that no agricultural land be attachable for debt.[3]

Labour.—The main labour centres in the territory are the plantations in the Cameroons, which in 1928 employed 9000 labourers from within the territory,[4] and the tin mines, which in 1927—the last year for which figures are given—accounted for some 34,000.[5] The numbers employed on the coalfield are not stated in the official reports. No assistance of any kind

---

[1] Price, *Land Tenure in the Yoruba Provinces*, 1933, p. 43.
[2] *Ibid.*, p. 87.
[3] Cameron, *Note on Land Tenure in the Yoruba Provinces*, 1933, p. 7.
[4] Southern Provinces Annual Report, 1928, p. 126.
[5] Nigeria Annual Reports, 1926, p. 20; 1927, p. 15.

has been given by Government in the obtaining of labour.[1] It has been pointed out that the Nigerian taxation system is almost unique in being calculated independently of any estimate of the wages which the native can earn. It would be true to say of Nigeria perhaps alone that no consideration of its effect on the supply of wage-labour has ever influenced policy with regard to taxation. Indeed it has been made a criticism of the Nigerian Government that it carried the *laissez-faire* policy so far as to neglect provision for the treatment of wage-labour. The Labour Ordinance passed in 1929, however, makes the usual provisions for the supervision of contracts and the standard of conditions in labour camps.

Education.—Educational policy has been marked by the contrast between the very circumspect attitude towards the Moslem Emirates in the north and the rapid spread and great popularity of literary education in the south. The Moslem States had their own schools which concentrated on teaching passages from the Koran. The exclusion of missions from Moslem territory meant that so long as education was mainly in their hands the north must go unprovided for, and with the development of native administration it became necessary to recruit educated personnel from the south. Government established some elementary schools in 1910 through the Native Administrations, but it is only in the last few years that an attempt has been made to develop elementary education on a large scale by utilizing the Koran schools. Since 1930 special courses have been held at selected centres for the training of Koran teachers. There is also a training college at Katsina, opened in 1921, which supplies teachers for the Native Administration Schools. In 1928 a school was opened for the training of non-Moslem teachers for the Northern Provinces. Girls' education could not be begun till 1930 owing to the difficulty of overcoming Moslem prejudice.[2]

The Southern Provinces have been influenced from the coast, where a British Colony has existed since 1862. Here literary education based on examinations set in England has taken

[1] Cf. Temple, *Native Races and their Rulers*, p. 152.
[2] See Education Department, Annual Report, 1933.

a firm hold, and the demand for it further inland has grown far more rapidly than the supply. It was met by the opening of immense numbers of schools conducted by quite unqualified teachers, till the acceptance of full Government responsibility for the standard of education, on the lines of the principles adopted by the Colonial Office Advisory Committee on Education in Tropical Africa, led to the establishment of a system of inspection and the introduction of a uniform curriculum.

While in the Moslem areas the dominant consideration has been that education should not have a denationalizing effect, and above all that schools should not be suspected of attempting to seduce the pupils from their faith, the wider problem of the place of education in native development has received less consideration here than in East Africa. Meantime the European curriculum followed in the Colony has produced a generation entirely out of sympathy with everything that Indirect Rule implies, suspicious of a Government that denies to the Protectorates that civilization which they have been taught to regard as the highest good, and at any rate partially aware that if the territory were governed by a replica of the British Civil Service that bureaucracy would be recruited from their ranks. I do not believe with some of the critics of Indirect Rule that it is doomed to founder on their opposition, for they are now nearly as foreign to the up-country native as are Europeans; they will not persuade their compatriots to reject Indirect Rule, and there seems no immediate prospect of their being able to force the issue. There would be a greater danger from the educated natives of the Protectorate should they be allowed to feel that the system represented something they had left behind; but the Nigerian Government is alive to this danger, as has been pointed out, and is meeting it both by insistence on Indirect Rule as a means of development and by finding room in the native administration councils for educated young men. At the same time the coast natives have been encouraged, through their representatives on the Legislative Council, to take an interest in native administrations, and perhaps it may be hoped that one day they may come to base their criticisms on knowledge rather than on prejudice or hearsay.

II. TANGANYIKA

Principles of the Mandate.—Tanganyika is of peculiar interest because here a territory containing considerable areas of land suitable for European settlement is administered in accordance with principles established by international treaty, which differ widely from those of the White Man's Country policy, and because the system of Indirect Rule evolved in the different climatic and economic conditions of West Africa is here functioning alongside European enterprise on a relatively large scale. Tanganyika is administered under a Mandate from the League of Nations, whose terms are based upon the principle that "the well-being and development" of the native peoples form "a sacred trust of civilization", and which specifically lays down that land legislation must respect native rights and consider native needs, that all forms of forced or compulsory labour, except for public purposes, are prohibited and that the terms on which contract labour is permitted are to be severely scrutinized.

Sceptics as to the efficacy of international supervision may argue that the characteristic features of Tanganyika policy are the outcome, not of the provisions of the Mandate, but of the appointment as Governor in 1925 of Sir Donald Cameron with his Nigerian traditions. Only those in possession of inner knowledge can say whether the appointment was made because of the principles of administration required by the Mandate; what is certain is that Sir Donald Cameron publicly took his stand on that document [1] in defending a policy which contrasts strongly with that pursued in Kenya and is accordingly far from popular with the European unofficial community.

The point of view expressed by him before the Mandates Commission is that so far as agriculture is concerned "the non-native is an incidental and not the principal factor"; [2] that the basis of agricultural development should be native peasant production, and that the contribution of the European

[1] Or, in the opinion of Kenya settlers, " sheltered behind it ". See Huxley, *White Man's Country*, vol. II, p. 67.
[2] Permanent Mandates Commission, Session 11, p. 84.

should be made in those spheres where capital is essential—mining or the marketing of produce. European agriculture has, however, been allowed where it was held that land was not required by natives.

Allocation of Land.—Complete adherence to this programme has been prevented by the fact that when Great Britain took over the administration of the territory, 1,750,000 acres had already been alienated by the German Government. The greater part of the grants were made in the Moshi district, on the southern slopes of Mount Kilimanjaro, where the local native tribe, the Chagga, is in consequence seriously overcrowded. A reversal of this situation was precluded by the provisions of the Peace Treaty which required ex-enemy property to be auctioned for the benefits of the reparations account. Nevertheless the Government acquired some fifty square miles of this land in order to return it to the Chagga, and was only prevented by the depression in 1921 from making further such purchases.[1] Since that time further small areas have been acquired to be thrown open for grazing to the neighbouring Arusha and Pare tribes.[2] Elsewhere the natives themselves have combined to buy back land at considerable expense.[3]

In this area a good deal of alienated land is still unoccupied, and the effect upon native opinion is the same as has been created by a similar situation among many Kenya tribes. General resentment is felt against the Government, and any measure remotely associated with the tenure of land is viewed with suspicion. An inquiry into the tribal system, carried out in 1929 as part of a general survey of the Territory with a view to respecting native rights, was obstructed for some time by a boycott; and more recently, the offer by the Government of European seedling trees, to be planted along river banks as a protection against erosion, was refused on the ground that once planted they could be made a pretext for claiming the land on which they stood.[4]

---

[1] Annual Reports to the League of Nations, 1922, p. 20.
[2] Cf. Provincial Commissioners' Annual Reports, 1933, p. 56.
[3] *Ibid.*, p. 51. [4] *Ibid.*, p. 51.

Nevertheless, for reasons to be found in the general Tanganyika policy of native development, the lot of the Kilimanjaro tribes is in many ways more fortunate than that of their neighbours in Kenya, who have not only lost their land but have received little assistance towards the improvement of the resulting economic position.

The general land policy of Tanganyika is regulated by the Land Ordinance of 1923, which, while it respects the private rights acquired by Europeans before that date, applies to further grants the same strict control that is exercised under the legislation of Northern Nigeria. The Tanganyika Land Ordinance, indeed, exactly reproduces the wording of that in force in Northern Nigeria, which declares the whole land of the Territory to be vested in Government for the use and benefit of the natives, and makes the validity of titles dependent upon the approval of the Governor. The possibility that this provision could be interpreted so as to render native rights invalid in the absence of a title specifically granted, which has been mentioned in connection with Northern Nigeria, was considered by the Permanent Mandates Commission, who pressed for an amendment of the law to make this point clear. This criticism was met by Ordinance No. 7 of 1928, as the result of which native customary rights are recognized as equally valid with those held under certificates of occupancy. At a subsequent meeting of the Commission Lord Lugard suggested that even this was not sufficient, as rights of occupancy under the Land Ordinances are revocable at will; but it has since been officially stated that the provisions relating to revocation do not apply to native rights.[1]

Before 1923 no land was alienated, the attention of the administration being occupied in tracing and registering titles granted under the German regime.

Before proceeding to dispose of any land the Government declared closed to further alienation a large block of land in the north-east, including the area occupied by the Chagga, that of the cognate Arusha and Pare, the districts of Usambara, Tanga and Pangani, and the Masai Reserve. Within it five

---

[1] See P.M.C., Session 22, and Annual Report, 1932, p. 146.

mall areas are specified where applications for land will be
onsidered "for special purposes". The type of alienation
nat would be permitted here was defined later with regard to
Ioshi District as "the grant, in a few cases, of short-term
:ases of land which was not ·immediately required by the
Vachagga", the maximum term being thirty-three years, and
ne Government retaining the right to take possession at any
me after fifteen years without compensation if the land is
equired by natives.[1] Part of the Songea and Mahenge Districts
vere similarly closed later.[2]

The principles to be followed with regard to alienation were
ormulated by Sir Donald Cameron in his speech to the first
egislative Council in 1926: "Non-native settlement should
e encouraged wherever the climate is suitable and adequate
reas are available without depriving the native population of
ufficient land for its own use, provided that transport facilities
re available to evacuate the produce." He announced that
e would consider applications for land in specified areas in
he Southern Highlands.

Before this date certain alienations had in fact been made.
Sut in 1927 the whole system was reorganized with a view to
ubstituting for the previous haphazard picking up by private
ndividuals of the best pieces of land all over the territory a
ystematic development under the control of Government.
Government itself assumed responsibility for selecting suitable
reas and throwing them open for settlement. A Land Develop-
nent Survey was set up to investigate the possibilities of the
egions selected, and alienation was suspended pending their
eport.[3]

The areas so far dealt with in this way have been the high-
ands of the Iringa, Mahenge and Mbulu Districts and the
Eastern Province. The Survey covered an investigation both
f native requirements and of the possibilities of European
nterprise with given soil and climatic conditions, and facilities
or the evacuation of produce.

[1] Legislative Council, December 3, 1929.
[2] Land Department, First Annual Report, pp. 4–5.
[3] See First Annual Report of the Land Department, 1929.

The Commission based its decisions on the view of th
Hilton Young Commission "that the creation and preservatio
of a field for the full development of native life is a duty accepte
by Government and that it must precede any alienation o
tribal land to non-natives".[1] As an example of a conscientiou
inquiry taking into account the necessities of the actual nativ
way of life rather than the common arbitrary estimate of th
area that *ought* to be required, its reports are worthy of stud
Basing its calculations of the needs of the native populatio
on the estimate of half a square mile per family among pastor
tribes, the Commission recommended the closing to furthe
alienation of a considerable part of the areas surveyed. N
all its reports give detailed figures of the relative areas close
and open for settlement. In the Iringa Province the are
thrown open in the Uhehe and Ubena country is 637 squar
miles out of a total of 15,526; in Morogoro and Kilosa in th
Eastern Province 7705 out of 12,776.[2] The Government ha
announced that no land will be alienated contrary to thes
recommendations without the express sanction of the Secretar
of State.[3]

In view of the decrease in applications for land and th
surrender of numbers of farms owing to the economic depressio
it has been announced that for the present new alienations wi
not be made even in the areas recommended by the Surve
with the exception of that part of the Mbulu District in th
Northern Province where land was declared to be available
Similar surveys are to be made in the extreme south of th
territory in the Western Highlands bordering Lake Tanganyik
But since 1933 policy has been to sell abandoned farms rathe
than open up new areas.[5]

In 1931, on the recommendation of a conference of admini
trative officials which met at Dar-es-Salaam in 1929, the are
now forming the Lake, Central and Lindi Provinces we
closed, not on economic grounds but with a view to "preservin
the existing racial homogeneity". Here applications a

[1] Land Development Survey, Third Report, p. 7.
[2] Land Development Survey, Reports I, p. 12; V, p. 11.
[3] Land Department Annual Report, 1931, p. 2.
[4] *Ibid.*, 1932, p. 3; 1933, p. 3.   [5] *Ibid.*, 1933, *cit.*

considered from Europeans only if they are prepared to invest capital on a large scale in such works as irrigation.

Only 250,000 acres all told have been alienated in Tanganyika by the Mandatory Government. The area in European hands reached its maximum of 2,000,000 acres in 1930 (3125 square miles in a total area of 340,500 as against 10,375 in Kenya out of a total of 225,000). Since that date new alienations have been roughly balanced by the surrender of leases whose holders have succumbed to the economic depression. It would fairly sum up the position to say that in Tanganyika under Mandate, alone of territories where white settlement is possible, native interests have in every case of conflict been given the benefit of the doubt.

The Scientific Treatment of the Labour Question.—Although the native population of Tanganyika is twice that of Kenya and the European population half, the difficulty of obtaining labour is complained of just as bitterly here as in Kenya. The official remedy, however, is very different. The land policy has just been described. It has in no case had the effect of reducing native tribes to dependence on wage-labour. The one congested area, on Kilimanjaro, is conspicuously not a labour reservoir; its inhabitants grow at considerable profit the Arabica coffee which Kenya natives are not allowed to cultivate. The preference of the average native for village cultivation, even when European employment is offered close to his home, is noted without regret in official publications. The Land Development Commission report, for example, that in several of the areas surveyed the number of young men seeking employment is decreasing with the development of cotton cultivation. Of one tribe they write that "although the bulk of the Kisaki Vakutu live cheek by jowl with non-native plantation owners, not one of them works on the plantations". In connection with the possibilities for increased European production should a new railway be built they point out that this would also increase native production and *pro tanto* reduce the labour supply.[1]

The sources of labour for the plantations have in the main

[1] Land Development Survey Reports, I, pp. 1, 3, 15; III, p. 9.

been those tribes where lack of transport facilities at first mad
village production unprofitable and agricultural instructio
took some time to penetrate. A general policy of encouragin
all natives to "develop some form of active work",[1] necessaril
means in their case persuasion to undertake wage-labou
chiefs were encouraged to use their influence in this directio
At the same time there is no question of making Governme
approval of the chiefs dependent on the success of their pe
suasion, and the offer of money by recruiting agents to chie
is heavily penalized.[2]   More important still, every effort h
been made by the development of agricultural propaganda t
ensure that in all parts of the territory the natives shall be ab
to choose between the alternatives of village production an
wage-labour. The cultivation of coffee, cotton, rice, groun
nuts, maize, onions, wheat, garlic, tobacco and coconuts has bee
actively encouraged, the trade in cattle and cattle produc
and in bees-wax fostered, and instruction given in the makir
of ghee and the preparation of hides for marketing. It is tr
that the circular already quoted forbids officials actively
divert from wage-labour individuals accustomed to it: but t
reports cited above[3] indicate that such active intervention
not necessary. On the other hand, in cases where "the peop
have generally been shown to be unfitted for labour on t
farms or are unwilling to undertake it", the area in questic
may be declared to be one where the development of nativ
production should not be left to the propaganda of agricultur
demonstrators but actively encouraged by administrativ
officials.

The Tanganyika administration has held to the princip
that employers must obtain their labour by offering con
ditions that will attract it—and it has been further laid dov
in connection with the recruiting of labour for public wor
that if the private employer can obtain his labour witho
compulsion Government should be able to do the same.[4] T

---

[1] Agriculture and Labour Circular, 1926.
[2] Masters and Servants Ordinance, as amended in 1927.
[3] See above, p. 143.
[4] Recruitment, Employment and Care of Government Labour, circul
1933.

emand that Government should make itself responsible for
recruiting for private employers was categorically refused.[1]   In
his opening speech to the Legislative Council in January 1928
the Governor referred to a popular demand for "a policy of
employing force in order to 'make the natives work'" and
repudiated "repressive measures, such as any form of forced
labour or any measures designed to keep the natives in a
servile state" as incompatible with the terms of the Mandate.
With regard to the effect of taxation as an incentive to seek
employment the Governor wrote in 1926:

"I have steadfastly refused to increase the tax in the districts
in which the natives cannot augment their earnings by
working for themselves. . . . Coercion of labour by pressure
of direct taxation is little, if anything, removed from coercion
of labour by force; the latter is the more honest course."

Commenting on the point of view expressed by the sisal
growers that it is essential, in order to reduce absenteeism, to
develop "a labour force wholly dependent on wages", the
special report on labour presented to the League of Nations
in 1933 stresses the advantages of the present system in the
maintenance of native home life, the prevention of detribaliza-
tion and the absence of any liability for the maintenance of the
unemployed.   This, it is held, may "come to be regarded in
time as definitely preferable to a process of industrialization".[2]
In any case it indicates the Government's attitude towards
industrialization.

Policy with regard to labour, however, has had in it more
elements of "planning" than of *laissez-faire*.   While it is left
for employers to obtain their own labour by offering conditions
which will compete with the attraction of alternative occupations,
Government has been concerned with measures designed as
far as possible to counteract the evil effects which labour
migration may have both on the physique of the individual
worker and on the maintenance of a healthy tribal life.

To this end a Labour Department was established in 1926,
which undertook not only the supervision of contracts and of

[1] Legislative Council Debates, 1928, p. 113.
[2] Annual Report to League of Nations, 1933, pp. 11-12.

the activities of recruiting agents, and the investigation
complaints by labourers or employers, but the study of tl
prevailing flow of labour migration with a view to directing
to the best possible advantage, of the aptitudes and inclinatic
of certain tribes for particular types of work, the effects up
them of changes of diet and climate, and so forth.

This department made it its aim as far as possible to dire
natives seeking employment to areas not far from their home
Where, as was often the case with the remoter tribes, this w:
impossible, they concentrated their efforts on the provisic
of railways along the principal routes followed, which w:
carried out on their recommendations. A feature taken ov
from Uganda, but considerably developed, was the establisl
ment of labour camps at strategic points, with a view to inducin
natives travelling on foot to pass that way: when once such
camp became known others were opened along the same rout
Here any native traveller, not necessarily going to or from worl
can obtain free accommodation for three nights. Kitchen
with ·cooking arrangements of native type are provided, th
travellers making their own arrangements for food, firewoo
and water. Rations are sometimes provided in case of need
and the cost recouped from recruiters or employers. Insigh
into native ways is shown by the provision at the original cam
of four separate buildings, "allowing various parties to remai
apart, thus eliminating a possible source of quarrelling betwee
tribes of different habits in eating". To each camp is attache
a dispensary. There are now eleven such camps in existence.[1]

Through their influence, along with the efforts of Labou
Officers to induce employers to look to the nearest sources fo
their labour and recruiters not unnecessarily to engage me
for work at long distances from their homes, much needles
travelling has been eliminated. The sisal plantations on th
coast no longer obtain their labour from the extreme south-west
but either from regions closer at hand or from those wester
areas which are served by the railway, while the Songe
labourers who formerly travelled to them on foot now fin
employment close at hand on the Iringa farms.

[1] Labour Report, 1927, p. 14.

Conditions on plantations have been considered not only from the point of view of the obvious sanitary precautions but also from that of the provision of suitable diet. Instructions on the subject have been issued to employers, which invite special attention to the case of men who have left home owing to a local shortage of food and arrive in a half-starved condition. The employment of tribes whose normal diet—bananas and milk—cannot even be approximated to on plantations is discouraged, and in some cases efforts have been made to prevent natives whose homes are at high altitudes from going to the coast to work.[1]

The recruiting of labour and engagement on contract have been studied more exhaustively here than in any other colony. The position originally taken up by the authorities was that employers offering reasonable conditions should be able to obtain labour without the assistance of recruiting agents. The Labour Department, however, took the view that the contract system, if controlled, can be of considerable value to natives going long distances to work. The expense of providing transport and provisions for such natives will not be undertaken without some guarantee that they will remain long enough with the employer who pays the cost to make it worth his while. Recruiters can provide information as to the sources of employment for natives who have not left home before, and can advance the tax which many are anxious to pay before leaving.[2] Moreover, if Government provides special transport facilities for natives travelling to work, someone must be responsible for their *bona fides*.

It is the opinion of the Labour Department that the contract itself can be made a safeguard to the native if it is understood, and if it is as specific in the obligations which it lays upon the employer as in those to which the native is subject. The legal provisions to this end do not differ from those in force in Kenya, but the existence of a staff of officers whose sole concern was the welfare of native labour made much closer and more sympathetic supervision possible.

[1] Provincial Commissioners' Annual Reports, 1933, p. 58.
[2] Labour Reports, 1927, pp. 7, 20.

The legal maximum contract is for two years, which has been reduced by proclamation to twelve months; the usual period in practice is for nine months or 180 working days, whichever finishes sooner.[1] Since the desire to return to the villages at the planting season has been a common cause of breaches of contract, the Labour Department has urged officials to make it clear to natives entering upon such engagements if the term is to extend over this period, even though this might deter them from making the contract.[2]

Since 1928 desertion by contract labourers has not been an offence cognizable by the police; the apprehension of a deserter requires that his employer should first lay a charge against him. The prevention of desertion has in the main been sought in other directions than by penalizing it. Sometimes it was found to be due to a panic caused by epidemics, to unpopular innovations in food or living conditions, to mere misunderstanding or to the desire of the native to return home during the planting season or for family reasons. Explanations of misunderstanding by Labour Officers have done a good deal to remove causes of friction on plantations where employers have had difficulty with unfamiliar tribes. Native authorities have been encouraged to use their influence in explaining that the proper remedy for a grievance lies in an appeal to the Labour Officers rather than in desertion, while they exert their authority in sending back deserters to finish their contract.[3] The number of desertions due to unsatisfactory conditions on estates has been reduced, through the closer supervision exercised by Labour Officers.

The demand for a pass law to be operated in the interests of employers has been rejected.[4] But the advantages to natives at work far from their homes of a system of registration have been recognized. A means of identification enables communication to be made with the relatives of men who die at work and compensation to be paid to them; it obviates the hardship of a double demand for payment of tax, which it is reported that many of the natives are afraid to refuse. It also

[1] Labour Report, 1927, p. 27. [2] Ibid. pp. 24–5. [3] Ibid., p. 26.
[4] Legislative Council, January 16, 1928.

148

eliminates the possibility of substituting children or unfit persons after the medical inspection of contract labourers. In order to avoid incurring the suspicion that it was felt would inevitably attach to any provision for compulsory registration, the system was followed up till 1929 of entering on each labourer's contract the number of his tax receipt ticket and asking him to carry the ticket with him.

In 1930 the new Governor, Sir Stewart Symes, abolished the Labour Department in the interests of economy and made administrative officers responsible for the duties which up till then had devolved upon its members. The Permanent Mandates Commission expressed misgivings at this step in a report endorsed by the Council of the League of Nations, and with a view to testing the contention that it would not involve any decrease in the attention devoted to the welfare of the native labourer, invited a special report on labour conditions to be presented for consideration at their next session. The result, though necessarily a much shorter document than those submitted in previous years, does indicate that the standards developed by the Labour Department are as far as possible kept up by its successors.[1] Yet one must regret that Tanganyika is now deprived of the synoptic view of the labour problem in its sociological setting which that Department's work provided, and that the future treatment of labour questions is to be left to the unco-ordinated efforts of individual goodwill.

The number of native wage-labourers in Tanganyika was estimated in 1927 at 139,000–140,000, of whom 18,000 were engaged under contract. This is the only year in which an estimate of the total has been made.[2] With the economic depression Tanganyika, like other territories, has had to cope with a surplus of natives seeking employment. Steps have been taken to "ensure as far as possible that natives did not leave their homes in search of work unless there was a reasonable prospect of such work being found for them". For the benefit of the literate natives monthly bulletins stating where employment is offered are published in the Government Swahili

[1] Appendix IX to Annual Report to League of Nations, 1932, pp. 139 ff.
[2] Labour Report, 1927, p. 59.

newspaper.[1] At the moment, the most prosperous European enterprise in Tanganyika is gold-mining. The Lupa goldfields in Mbeya District, where important reefs have been found, are expected to absorb up to 20,000 natives.[2] This does not of course by any means account for the total thrown out of employment by the slump. Every possible effort has been made to keep up the native standard of living by increasing propaganda for the extension of native-grown crops; and it seems that the native with his low overhead costs is still able to sell his product at the low prices of the present day. Relief has also been given to areas hard hit by the slump by the reduction of taxation and by provision for the payment of tax in instalments.

Indirect Rule and the Mandate System.—The system of Indirect Rule in its final form, with its various types of native authority, as it has already been described in connection with Nigeria, was first worked out in Tanganyika. Here the first experiment was made, not without some misgiving, in that utilization for purposes of native administration, even of the smallest village authorities, which forms such a striking feature of recent Nigerian developments.

In Tanganyika the utilization of native political institutions has been justified by Sir Donald Cameron not only for its administrative convenience, but as the inevitable outcome of a strict adherence to the conception of the Mandate as a *temporary* tutelage.[3] The duty of the Mandatory, as interpreted by him in a Memorandum published in 1930, is "to train the people so that they may stand by themselves *at least* as part of the whole community of the territory, however long that training may take", so that "when the time comes a full place in the political structure shall be found for the native population". During the period of training, he holds, the Government "must make no disposition in the political field which would impair its power to give effect to any decision it might have to make in order to comply with the spirit and the letter of the Mandate", and he bluntly ascribes to the European population

---

[1] Annual Report, 1932, p. 62.   [2] *Ibid.*, 1933, pp. 145–6.
[3] Introduction to *Native Administration Memoranda*, pp. 1–3.

the aim of attaining a position "so securely entrenched that there will be no place for the natives in the political structure *unless you please to give it to them*".

After thus rejecting by implication any proposal for the grant of responsible government in the European population until such time as the natives can share in it, he goes on to adumbrate a future constitution involving a Central Native and a Central Non-Native Council, with delegates sitting jointly for most of the business now conducted in the Legislative Council. To that end the native authorities must be entrusted with responsibility and trained to take that independent interest in the conduct of their own affairs which alone can fit them for participation in such a political organization.

The German administration had been organized through Arab officials—*akidas* and *jumbes*—who, as foreigners to the tribe over whom they were set, were frankly the emissaries of the European Government. The British authorities at first were content to restore to power the chiefs of large and politically well-organized tribes, but to leave the *akidas* and *jumbes* in control of groups which were at first believed to be too small to be recognized as administrative units. Up till 1925, therefore, half the territory was administered under Indirect Rule, the rest under alien authorities on lines which have nowhere else been adopted by British Administrations; while Native Authorities were given "only so much of the business of Government as the Administrative Officer is himself unable to undertake".[1] In that year Sir Donald Cameron took office as Governor and set about the recognition of all indigenous authorities as part of an administrative system in which they should exercise real responsibility. An important amendment made in the Native Authorities Ordinance is that which empowers European officials to issue orders in matters for which the chief is normally responsible only if the latter has neglected or refused to do so.[2]

Immediately upon Sir Donald Cameron's arrival five Native Authorities were gazetted, in Tabora, Mwanza, Bukoba,

[1] *Native Administration Memoranda*, No. I, p. 14.
[2] *Ibid.*, No. I, p. 18.

Dodoma and Moshi, and throughout the next years there went on a process of patient inquiry, redrawing of boundaries, and the restoration of power to the individuals of each community in whose hands it traditionally lay. Stress is laid upon the point that it is the *office* and not the incumbent which receives recognition from Government; while the authorities of course must retain an ultimate right of interference, in normal circumstances succession to office is determined entirely by native custom. It is also made clear that the recognition by Government of the status of Subordinate Native Authorities does not affect the right of their native superiors to appoint or dismiss them.[1] In point of fact it is interesting to note that where chiefs have been removed it has nearly always been at the request of their own elders. In one case two elders were made responsible for the conduct of native administration on behalf of a chief who proved completely incapable.[2] In another a chief was sent, on a petition from the elders, to the court of a more efficient neighbour to learn his business.[3]

The greatest difficulties arose in the coastal areas. Here it was for a long time held that groups recognizing no authority over a wider area than the village were too small to constitute units of native administration. The first step taken here towards administrative reorganization was to establish in the Rufiji District a number of "chiefs", apparently acceptable to the people concerned, but appointed to exercise authority over groups of villages inhabited by different tribes. In 1931, it was reported that "for some time past there have been signs that the chiefs in some cases have not maintained, if indeed they ever possessed, the goodwill of all sections of the people living within their jurisdiction".[4] In the meantime village headmen had been constituted Native Authorities in neighbouring areas of the same region, and although these number as many as 131 in Dar-es-Salaam District and 30 in Morogoro, and have not been found to be remarkable for personality or initiative, it is nevertheless recognized that their status as part

---

[1] *Native Administration Memoranda*, No. I, p. 12.
[2] Provincial Commissioners' Reports, 1931, p. 17.
[3] *Ibid.*, 1930, pp. 52–3.   [4] *Ibid.*, 1931, p. 13.

of the tribal system gives them a qualification for their part which no alternative candidates would have. Accordingly it is proposed to remodel the Rufiji District on the same lines.[1]

Another tribe who have presented particular problems are the Masai, organized as they are without central political authority, and recognizing no individuals as entitled to exercise the powers conferred by Government upon a Native Administration. After some difficulty had been experienced in finding any person who would regard himself as qualified to issue orders, the matter was discussed in a council of the whole tribe. Here it was agreed that "the headmen were not expected to act as individuals but as a council, the Laibon (religious head) being expected to delegate any duties that were not his of heredity to chosen members of the council". A system of administration, arbitration and debate by local councils was accordingly recognized and approved.[2]

The Grouping of Native Administration Units.—The gradual building up of larger and larger units for purposes of financial co-operation has been a feature of Tanganyika as of Nigeria. At first a "Paramount Chief" was appointed to preside over some of these, but this practice has now been abandoned in favour of a system whereby the presidency is held in rotation, so that no one chief is obliged to reside permanently at the headquarters of the group, where he cannot supervise the affairs of his own tribe. Here, as in Nigeria, no attempt is made to form of such a group a centralized political unit. Its members may exercise joint executive authority in matters of enterprises undertaken jointly, and act jointly as a Court of Appeal from decisions of any one of them, but each retains full powers over its own area in every other respect. At the same time meetings for the joint discussion of problems within the sphere of individual members are encouraged, and it is becoming the practice to hold them at regular intervals. The most spectacular gathering of this type was inaugurated in 1932, when fifty-two chiefs of the four Sukuma Districts of the Lake Province met on the initiative of two of them to discuss an agenda entirely

[1] Provincial Commissioners' Reports, 1932, p. 10; 1933, p. 16.
[2] *Ibid.*, 1933, pp. 61-2.

drawn up by the chiefs themselves. This included among its items the marketing of native produce, the improvement of agriculture, the issue of game licences to natives, the proportion of taxes to be assigned to Native Treasuries, and the unification of tribal law throughout the four districts, especially with regard to marriage.[1] This Conference is now an annual event.

Equally interesting in its way is the incident recorded in 1932 of the Pare Council, which two years earlier had been rent by dissension and intrigue. In this year they on their own initiative dispatched one of their members to investigate a district represented in the Council where administration was considered to be "a disgrace and a drawback to the whole of Upare".[2]

The initiative shown by these native authorities is as striking as is the freedom of action left them by Government. They deliberate intelligently on such matters as re-afforestation, irrigation and the dipping of cattle.[3] They have made rules of various kinds dealing with the cultivation of modern crops and with excessive consumption of beer; in one case a Native Treasury has arranged to make advances to individuals for ghee production and maize-growing on a large scale.[4] Foresight and decision have been shown in taking precautions against locust invasion, and the orders given have been obeyed with a readiness which only traditional authority could command.[5] Such is the general interest in the public works which are undertaken that these are frequently carried out by voluntary communal labour.

As cases where decisions of some importance have been left to the responsibility of native authorities one might quote the appointment of a commission of Native Elders to delimit the boundary between Ukuguru and North Usagara;[6] or the comment on the situation among the Sambaa, where "stranger" natives who have come to the district to work are beginning to settle on the land in some numbers and demanding to be administered by their own headman: "It will be interesting to watch how the Native Administration deals with the matter finally."[7]

[1] Provincial Commissioners' Reports, 1932, p. 21.
[2] *Ibid.*, 1932, p. 52.   [3] *Ibid.*, 1933, p. 64.
[4] *Ibid.*, 1933, p. 60.   [5] *Ibid.*, 1932, pp. 5 ff.
[6] *Ibid.*, 1933, p. 18.   [7] *Ibid.*, 1933, p. 64.

New Native Organizations.—The development of new native groupings is an interesting feature of Tanganyika. Such groupings do not constitute a form of opposition to constituted authority, and are sometimes even utilized for administrative purposes. The most conspicuous is the Kilimanjaro Native Planters' Association, formed for the co-operative marketing of coffee and purchase of spraying materials, etc., by means of a levy on produce sold. This Association was somewhat shaken by the malversations of its native treasurer, but now pays for the services of a European manager.[1] Corresponding societies were formed in 1933 by the Arusha and Meru; here the accounting and the annual sales are dealt with by the native president and vice-president, the only European assistance being the advice of the local District Officer.[2]

Less reputable are the *ngoma* or dance societies which have grown up among the town natives. Their main function is to compete with one another in singing or dancing performances, and the competition has been known to lead to bloodshed. An affray of this sort, which occurred in Ujiji in 1932, drew attention to the place of these societies in urban life. The method of avoiding their recurrence was to entrust the leaders of the tribal groups with responsibility for order among the members, and in particular for seeing that those who had no fixed employment were occupied in the rice cultivation [3] which was provided by Government as a means of unemployment relief. The incident has also, however, given rise to a proposal that they should be utilized as recognized organs of native administration. The Provincial Commissioner, Western Province, writes: "We should endeavour to mould them whilst young in order to use them eventually just as we use the organizations of the tribes outside the towns." [4] Since some such groupings are found among all urban native communities, this experiment in Indirect Rule for the detribalized may have a relevance to the problems of many other administrations.

Native Courts and Native Law.—The development of Native

[1] Provincial Commissioners' Reports, 1931, pp. 61–2.
[2] *Ibid.*, 1933, p. 56.
[3] Annual Report to the League, 1933, p. 13.
[4] Provincial Commissioners' Annual Report, 1932, p. 66.

Courts has shown a flexibility and an understanding of native custom greater than is found in most other African territories. They are of two grades, the lower having competence in civil cases up to 200s. or one month's imprisonment, in criminal up to 50s. or one month's imprisonment, the higher being competent to deal with civil cases up to 600s. and criminal up to six months or 200s. Tribal Councils or Federations can be constituted appeal courts at discretion: the intention is that in time they should all exercise this power.

It is recognized that many cases are settled by family councils or groups of village elders, and while such bodies have no legal authority to enforce their decisions, no attempt is made to interfere with a practice which saves the time of the Courts and gives satisfaction to all concerned.[1] Officials are instructed to take a liberal view of those aspects of native law which are not compatible with European principles. They are warned that "that which is different is not necessarily repugnant", and advised in particular not to lay too much stress on a distinction between civil and criminal law which "often depends simply on the nature of the judgement", and not to insist on the imposition of fines where this would be in accordance with the principles of European courts, if native law in those cases awards compensation.[2] An interesting case of an adaptation of the Courts Ordinance to local circumstance is that of the Mbeya district, where five chiefs have been given extended jurisdiction to deal with marriage cases in which the money value of the cattle at stake exceeded the limit of their competence.[3]

Education.—Before the onset of the financial depression Tanganyika possessed a somewhat ambitious educational system, including eight Central Schools, six of which had departments giving industrial training in carpentry, shoe-making, tailoring, motor mechanics, metal working (leading up to employment in railway workshops), and printing. A clerical course with instruction in typewriting and accountancy was also given at Tabora. Loss of revenue on the one hand and the

[1] Provincial Commissioners' Annual Reports, 1930, p. 37; 1933, p. 60.
[2] *Native Administration Memoranda*, No. II, pp. 9, 11, 12.
[3] Provincial Commissioners' Annual Reports, 1930, p. 33.

curtailment of opportunities of employment on the other led to a reorganization of the system in 1931, and as at present constituted it lays much more emphasis upon the requirements of village life. One of the Central Schools (Bukoba) was converted into an agricultural school paying special attention to coffee. Three of the others were devoted to training for village life with a syllabus designed to produce "practical handymen", and English taught as a subject only. Their new syllabus is recommended for adoption in Native Administration Schools. The industrial schools have been cut down to two, the standard of qualifications for entry increased and the training extended from two to three years in order to reduce the number of pupils seeking employment. The principal attention of Government has been directed to the village vernacular schools, which have received a larger share of total education revenue than ever before. This reorganization may lay the foundations of an educational system more closely in accord with the needs of native society as a whole than that of many other territories.

III. The Gold Coast

Indirect Rule as "Laissez-faire".—In point of actual chronology the recognition of native authorities by the British Government is older in the Gold Coast than in Nigeria. But the policy which until very recently has been pursued there has resembled rather the *laissez-faire* of Basutoland than the constructive adaptation which in Nigeria and Tanganyika have been regarded as the essence of Indirect Rule; and the result has been to develop that opposition between an educated generation and its traditional rulers which is sometimes held to be the inevitable consequence of Indirect Rule as such, and necessarily fatal to its prospects of success. I have already suggested that this is not an inherent characteristic of the policy which I believe to hold out better hopes than any other for the assimilation by African societies of those new cultural elements which the modern world has thrust upon them; and I hope that the comparisons made in this chapter will bear out my view.

The Akan peoples of the Gold Coast Colony and Ashanti are divided into States in each of which a group of chiefs recognize one paramount authority which has attained this position by conquest; the Ashanti Confederacy, with its capital at Kumasi, was the largest such group. The chief was chosen by tribal councillors from a number of eligible candidates. He ruled with his council of elders and other officials, and in many of the groups custom provided that in case he abused his authority he might be deposed or "destooled"—the stool being the concrete symbol of his office.

The Gold Coast Native Jurisdiction Orders of 1883 confirmed the authority of Paramount and Divisional Chiefs (as they came later to be called) though without recognizing the right to be consulted which the councils possessed by native custom. Paramount chiefs were empowered to make bye-laws covering a wide range of subjects, including the administration of unoccupied lands and forests, subject to the approval of the Governor. Native tribunals were recognized in about half the States, but up till 1910 they had only concurrent jurisdiction with the British Courts and no power to enforce decisions. There is still no direct taxation in the Gold Coast, though chiefs have the right by tribal custom to make levies for specified purposes, and no provision was made for the administration of any tribal revenues. Nor did Government assume any rights over land even for the purpose of controlling alienation to Europeans. Thus, in sum, the chiefs were given very wide freedom to meet new situations in their own way—or disregard them—while they lost not only their former power of life and death but their position as the one source of justice, and the cessation of warfare removed a situation which had made tribal cohesion a necessity of survival.

The British administration was regarded from the outset with hostility and suspicion by the Gold Coast chiefs. Instead of the sympathetic co-operation which characterizes Nigeria, its influence seems to have taken the form of spasmodic pressure to obtain the enactment of urgent measures which, being passed unwillingly and without any appreciation of their necessity, were not then enforced. This in itself would tend to reduce the respect shown to native authority. Its efficacy has been further weakened by a state of chronic political uncertainty directly traceable to ill-considered actions over which British authority exercised no control. Here, as elsewhere, the conception of land as a saleable commodity, suddenly introduced into a society previously innocent of it, has had unexpected repercussions throughout the social organization; though the type of transaction in land which characterized the Gold Coast has not resulted in the loss by any tribe of its subsistence.

Native Rulers and Land Alienation.—There has never been much demand by Europeans for land for cultivation in the Gold Coast. The problem of alienation first became acute with a gold rush in 1896, when Europeans vied with one another in seeking, and chiefs in granting, mining concessions. Government sought powers to regulate such transactions in a Bill which would have given it the same right of ultimate disposal which it holds in Northern Nigeria. This measure evoked violent protests against "attempts to deprive the natives of their land", and was withdrawn after a native deputation had visited London and put their case before Mr. Joseph Chamberlain. The organization of this deputation was the origin of a permanent body, the Gold Coast Aborigines Rights Protection Society, which is managed by educated natives and supported by contributions from the chiefs, and which until very recently regarded itself as the most authoritative channel for the expression of opinion on measures affecting native interests.

Accordingly the land tenure of the Colony is regulated only by the Concessions Ordinance of 1900, which controls alienation by the provision that concessions do not become definite until a certificate of validity has been granted by the Courts. This must be refused in the case of concessions which cover an area of more than five square miles or do not give reasonable protection for native rights of hunting, shifting cultivation and collecting firewood. Later amendments safeguard rights to the collection of forest produce and access to "fetish Lands".

The original Concessions Ordinance did not cover agricultural concessions. In their case concessions of more than one square mile required the approval of the Governor, but concessions for smaller areas, and leases, however great the area, were made subject to no control.[1] In 1917, however, these concessions were brought within the scope of the original Ordinance. By 1931, only one European agricultural enterprise had failed to succumb to the prolonged economic depression.

In Ashanti there is the further safeguard that the concessionaire first approaches the District Commissioner, and negotiations are carried on under his auspices. In the Gold Coast Colony, however, he has no *locus standi* whatever, and unless his advice is voluntarily asked, the first intervention by a European authority occurs when the negotiations are completed and the concession presented for validation.

That this system has not deprived the native population of a large proportion of their territories can be mainly ascribed to the fact that the mineral wealth of the Gold Coast proved to be much less than had been supposed. The motive which weighed most strongly with the chiefs was the "consideration money" paid down at the time when the concession was granted. Its terms, drawn up in English legal language, read out and explained by a native lawyer, had the minimum of meaning for them. Most of them had no idea what a square mile meant; and many alienated the same area twice over or made grants which in the aggregate covered more than the total extent of their territories. By 1913, indeed, the alienations made by chiefs in the Colony amounted to 25,108 square miles, or more than its total area.[2] The concessions validated by the Courts covered only 1084 square miles, and alienations covering 10,279 square miles had been disallowed; the rest remained in suspense till such time as the concessionaires should take up the question with a view to working them. By this time, however, palm nuts had come to bulk larger than gold mines among the natural resources of the Gold Coast, and there was a fresh rush for concessions which should give a monopoly of the right to set up machinery for the extraction

[1] Order in Council of April 11, 1916.
[2] Report of West African Lands Committee, 1917, p. 53.

of oil. The worst danger of these concessions was obviated by legislation bringing agricultural concessions within the scope of the Concessions Ordinance, and amending it so as to render invalid any agreement which gave rights to collect any produce to the exclusion of the native population, or to move them from their homes.

A Royal Commission appointed in 1912 expressed concern at the extent of alienation and recommended legislation to check it, but this was still felt to represent too great an encroachment on native rights. Only in the Northern Territories has legislation been recently passed providing for Government control on exactly the same terms as in Northern Nigeria.[1] The demand for concessions has decreased, however, partly perhaps because the terms of agreement which Government is prepared to sanction are so much less favourable than those granted by the French and Belgian Governments.[2]

The area of valid concessions in the Colony in 1925 amounted to 2361 square miles, or one per cent. of its whole area. Of these 607 square miles were not being worked. Of the remainder 870 square miles were represented by agricultural concessions, all of which appear to have been abandoned as the result of the present economic depression. Comparable figures for Ashanti are not available.

Thus modern development on the Gold Coast has not been affected by land shortage. Nor has the demand for labour affected more than a small percentage of the population. Complaints of shortage from the mining companies met with no response in the shape of official assistance beyond instructions to officials to let the native population know that work was available and encourage them to undertake work of some kind. No more sympathy was offered to the rubber plantation in Ashanti which was unable to obtain labour owing to the demand

---

[1] Northern Territories Land and Native Rights Ordinance, 1931.

[2] The Apol Palm Concession of 72 square miles, granted in 1912, in its original form provided for the renunciation by natives of their customary rights over the oil or fruit of palm-trees within the area, and the renunciation by chiefs of their jurisdiction over the Company's employees, and gave the Company the right to dam any watercourse within their concession. All these provisions were excised by Government. Terms in Africa 1048 (1917), p. 106.

for "prohibitive wages". By 1927 the mines were able to obtain locally their total labour force of 10,000, and in 1929 it was reported that with the development of transport facilities for the cocoa crop and consequent decrease in head porterage, there had been no difficulty in finding the requisite 12,000. From that time the number in employment remained fairly stationary till 1933, when it rose to 16,000, but continued apparently to be found easily obtainable.[1]

The repercussions of land alienation in the Gold Coast have accordingly been of a different nature from those which attend a policy of development primarily by European enterprise. It has affected principally the internal political structure of the native States, in creating a cause of serious friction between chiefs and subjects. The results illustrate not only the fact that tribal obligations are not strong enough to outweigh the attractions of pecuniary gain when this can be obtained in circumstances for which tribal customs do not provide, but the impossibility of arriving at a just distribution of the cash proceeds of land in a community in whose whole system of land tenure the idea of the transfer of rights over land for pecuniary consideration plays little or no part.

The chiefs who so readily signed concessions were certainly unaware of their exact terms, and content to believe that their people's rights were not being prejudiced. But when they realized the new value which land had acquired, they began to press claims over disputed areas, in litigation which involved them in debts often far greater than the value of the land in dispute. The only way to meet their debts was by granting further concessions, for they were far too heavy to be met in the traditional manner by levies on the tribe.

In a system where it is impossible to say with regard to any area of land that a given individual has a right to dispose of it for cash, it is impossible to settle the question of the distribution of the proceeds by trying to find individuals entitled to a share. Where, as one finds in all native societies, a number of different individuals have rights of a different nature over

[1] Annual Reports, 1933–4, p. 35.

the same piece of land, it is impossible to arrive at a numerical proportion between them, and equally unsatisfactory to suggest a distribution of the proceeds in equal shares. No theoretical principle as to the type of right which carries with it a claim to share in the proceeds has ever been laid down. Is the prior claim that of the individuals dispossessed? In this case there were very few, and their case was met by compensation. Is it that of the chief as ultimate authority? Yet he in fact gives up nothing in the transaction. If all land is held in trust by the chief for the tribe, are not all members entitled to a share in the proceeds of any land? The point was mentioned with judicious levity by some members of the West African Land Commission who suggested the possibility of paying the rent to the whole tribe at the rate of, say, 6d. a head. Or should the individuals actually in occupation of the land, with or without persons having contingent claims, such as relatives who might wish to join them, receive special consideration? The problem is not an imaginary one, for the legislation of New Guinea specifically provides that the proceeds of land alienation shall be paid to all those who by native law can claim a share.

When such an innovation as the receipt of revenue for land is made, it is really impossible to square the old with the new by attempting to find individuals entitled by native law to the proceeds. The solution which in fact corresponds to the native conception of the land as the land of the tribe, and involves neither undue profit to the chief, injustice to the commoner, nor the dislocation of native economic relations that must result from the creation of a *rentier* class, or the confusion of economic values produced by money payments not made in exchange for any visible commodity or reward,[1] is to have such revenues paid into a tribal treasury and expended on public works. But in the Gold Coast the resentment by the chiefs of all control seems to have made this impracticable.

[1] This too is not a figment of the imagination, but can be observed among the North American Indians. See Mead, *The Changing Culture of an Indian Tribe*.

Consideration money and rents were accordingly divided by the chiefs into three parts. Each chief took one part as his personal share, another as "stool" or tribal revenue, which was devoted largely to meeting debts already incurred, but in part also to paying the expense of tribal ceremonies, and distributed the third among the elders who formed his council, who appropriated it to their personal uses.

Discontent with Tribal Rule.—The disposal of these funds, along with the levying of taxes held to be oppressive, and the arbitrary action of chiefs whose councillors Government had not recognized, appears to be mainly responsible for the ill-feeling between the tribal authorities and the educated natives —a group which has long ceased to include only the younger generation. The gulf between these groups has grown ever wider as education entirely along European lines has been developed, the more so as in Ashanti native opinion has been consistently opposed to the appointment of an educated man as chief.[1] There is now not only a large section of opinion which resents the very existence of the native form of government as obsolete and oppressive, but endless cliques who in one State after another demand and obtain the destoolment of the chief in order to substitute their own nominees. The custom of destoolment has spread to tribes which formerly did not recognize it, and in many States constructive administration has been paralysed by irreconcilable feuds.

Such intervention as has been made by the British authorities has aimed at strengthening traditional authority and respect for custom. Since the Chiefs Ordinance of 1904 there has been an appeal to Government in case of a dispute regarding the validity of an election or destoolment, its object being solely to determine whether native custom has been followed; and since 1925 Government has taken power to order the removal of a destooled chief from his residence. But all such measures have been received by the Aborigines Protection Society as attempts to transform the chiefs from representatives of their own people into servants of Government: while such innocent provisions as that the Government shall determine

[1] Ashanti Annual Report, 1923, p. 22.

tribal boundaries are hailed as the first step towards "land control".[1]

Reorganization through the Legislative Council.—Finally the rehabilitation of the chiefs' authority, as far as the Colony was concerned, was sought indirectly through a reconstitution of the Legislative Council which paradoxically gave to native authorities, who had so far done little or nothing to develop administration within their own territories, a more direct voice in the government of the Colony as a whole than have native rulers anywhere else in Africa. The new Legislative Council comprised nine African members, three elected by the towns, and the other six chiefs, elected by Provincial Councils of Paramount Chiefs constituted at the same time for the discussion of all matters of native interest.

At these Councils each Paramount is accompanied by eight of his subordinate chiefs whom he must consult before expressing his opinion. For purposes of election to the Legislative Council the voting strength of each is calculated in proportion to the number of his subjects.

Although at first some chiefs boycotted these Councils, and the representative of the Western Province had at first to be nominated by the Government, by 1927 all the elections had been regularly held and by 1928 the system could be said to be in full operation.[2] It is now regarded by Government as the correct channel for the expression of native opinion, in contradistinction to the Aborigines Protection Society.[3]

The Legislative Council in its new form passed in 1927 a Native Administration Ordinance on lines largely suggested by the chiefs, which aims at the establishment of native authorities on a more stable basis and in some aspects extends their powers. This Ordinance recognizes as part of the hierarchy of administration not only the chiefs but the State Councils with their traditional personnel, and makes them responsible, subject to appeal to the Provincial Council, for the decision in disputed questions of election and destoolment.

[1] Mr. Casely Hayford in debate on Native Jurisdiction Bill, Legislative Council, 1922–3, p. 513 ; the Bill was withdrawn.
[2] Governor's speech to Legislative Council, 1929.
[3] Annual Report, Central Province, 1931–2.

The Provincial Councils are given authority to decide such questions, along with the demands of subordinate chiefs for independence, the final decision resting with the Government, to be exercised in accordance with native custom. Land disputes are also referred to the Provincial Councils, with an appeal to the Supreme Court. The Ordinance empowers the Governor to refer any matter to the Councils for hearing and determination. The jurisdiction of Paramount Chiefs' Tribunals is extended in civil cases to matters involving up to £100 where it previously only covered cases up to £25, and decisions are made enforceable by execution against property.

These measures seem to have produced a somewhat greater degree of continuity in personnel but hardly any improvement in the direction of administration. It remains necessary for the Government, when action becomes urgent—as in the case of forest conservation—to take powers by Ordinance for the enforcement of measures which constitutionally fall within the sphere of native administration.

Native Treasuries.—Not until 1931 was legislation passed providing for the establishment of Stool Treasuries. Although the measure allows very great freedom of chiefs in the disposal of their revenues, leaving them free to specify which Stool revenues are to be paid into the treasury, not more than two or three have actually been constituted. Elsewhere it has not been possible to overcome the chiefs' refusal to submit the disposal of their revenues to any form of inspection or control, or even to divulge their sources, and their suspicions that any Government supervision means the appropriation by Government of their revenues.

The official attitude towards the native authorities seems to be one of disillusionment. The Governor in 1933 foreshadowed the enactment of measures increasing the supervision to be exercised over native tribunals and the administration of Stool funds,[1] and in 1934 referred to "the deplorable waste of time and money involved in the political disputes and litigations unfortunately so common in many parts of the Colony".[2]

[1] Address to Legislative Council, 1933, p. 10.
[2] *Ibid.*, 1934, p. 12.

The educated native remains as hostile as ever, and the Gold Coast is appealed to as proof that Indirect Rule is incompatible with the necessary and desirable spread of European education.

Ashanti and the Northern Territories.—At first sight the argument might seem to be supported by the relatively greater success of the system in Ashanti and the Northern Territories where education is less widespread. Stool Treasuries were introduced into Ashanti in 1928. By the end of that year twenty-nine Head Chiefs were keeping Stool accounts in accordance with the provisions of the Ordinance, and in 1929 it was applied to eleven Stools. By 1930 one chief had voluntarily decided to pay himself a fixed salary, another had divulged "secrets" referring to the property and lands of his Stool and their sources of income, and the publication of statements of expenditure had done a good deal to allay political discontent.[1]

In the Northern Territories it was not till 1933 that Indirect Rule generally took the place of direct administration by European officials. After investigation into the nature of the various tribal groupings and a good deal of readjustment of administrative boundaries, Native Authorities were recognized and Tribunals were set up by Ordinances of 1932. Stool Treasuries had already been constituted in one or two areas, and by 1931 there were twelve in existence, and it could be reported that fuller statements of revenue were made as the chiefs realized that disclosure did not mean loss of control, and that in one division the elders were considering the payment of fixed salaries to chiefs.[2]

Education and Indirect Rule.—It is arguable that the opposition of the educated natives in the Colony has developed so far that it is no longer possible to reconcile them to the continuance of their traditional institutions. But this is not equivalent to saying that in no case is the maintenance of traditional institutions consistent with the spread of education. Had the guidance which is now being given to Ashanti and the Northern Territories been given at an earlier stage in the Colony; had the educated natives not at that stage been

[1] Cf. Annual Report, Ashanti, 1929–30, p. 11; 1930–31, pp. 8, 12.
[2] Northern Territories Annual Report, 1931–2, pp. 18, 28.

encouraged to regard themselves as alien to their own institutions; the chiefs could have become rulers whom even a modern African could accept, and the literate class might have found a place in the government of their own people such as they are finding in Nigeria. No more here than in Basutoland can a policy almost innocent of any constructive plan be used as an argument against the constructive adaptation of native institutions.

Prince of Wales College, Achimota, the great pride of the Gold Coast, has set before it the aim of providing an African education on African soil. To this end it encourages research by its students into native customs and folklore. It provides also for the practical application of education in agriculture and hygiene in visits to neighbouring villages. But the aim set before its best students is education up to a university standard, and therefore the acquisition of the knowledge which is necessary in order to pass examinations such as are set by English universities. This education it offers in order that the African may not have to procure knowledge at the cost of detachment from his native environment. But the benefits of a university on African soil will be illusory if the mental environment is such as to range the Achimota graduate with his brother student from Edinburgh or London in opposition to the majority of his compatriots, if the type of interest in native tradition that is encouraged is the sentimental and antiquarian. Perhaps the influence of Achimota has not yet had time to effect any reintegration of the new generation; perhaps it cannot be such as to produce that result.

IV. Uganda

Imitation rather than Adaptation.—The system of native administration in force in Uganda differs so much from those of Nigeria and Tanganyika on the one hand, and that of the Gold Coast on the other, that it is doubtful whether the name of Indirect Rule is really applicable to it at all. In the kingdom of Buganda the present system represents an imitation rather than an adaptation of the traditional institutions, while outside it the Buganda system is imitated rather than that of the various other tribes. The authority of the hereditary kings in Buganda, Toro, Ankole and Bunyoro is the only feature of the existing native administration which can really be said to derive from the indigenous system.

The development that has produced this result has been determined partly by the provision of the Agreement made with the native kingdoms soon after British authority was established in Uganda, partly by the desire to secure an administrative personnel better trained for the necessities of modern times. It resembles the Indirect Rule system principally in that there has been no attempt, at least in the political sphere, to substitute European for native institutions as superior on their merits. The adequacy of the system that has evolved in this way has varied with the degree of artificiality in its application to different tribes. At its best it is a demonstration of the vitality of African society, and its ability to make its own response to changed conditions, provided it is not deprived of the economic basis of a stable existence; at its worst it can become a tyranny of despots for whom authority has no traditional meaning and no sense of responsibility checks its abuse.

The Character of Indigenous Institutions.—The political organization that prevailed before the British occupation among the people bordering Lake Victoria was the typical Bantu hierarchy of chiefs owing allegiance to a superior who appointed and could depose them. On his behalf they administered justice, allotted land, collected taxes and organized their subjects for war and for such "public works" as the clearing of roads and the upkeep of houses in the royal enclosure. They were rewarded with a share of taxes collected and of booty captured in war, and had the right to services from the peasants under their authority. They could evict a peasant from his holding for any misconduct, and peasants who were dissatisfied with one chief could leave him for another. The chieftainships were not hereditary, individuals holding office at the pleasure of the king.

In the smaller kingdoms of Toro, Bunyoro and Ankole there

was a more or less rigid division between an upper class of cattle-owners, from whom the chiefs were selected, and a lower class of cultivators, but in Buganda there was no such distinction, and any peasant might rise to be a chief. In Busoga, east of the Nile, a similar but less highly centralized system seems to have prevailed. Among the Nilotic peoples in the northern part of the Protectorate nothing resembling it existed; for them the effective political unit was the village group.

Their Modern Counterpart in Buganda.—The system of native administration which is followed throughout the Protectorate is that which was first devised in Buganda. Buganda was divided under its own kings into a number of "counties" or *sazas*, in each of which one chief held a position of seniority, rather than authority, over the others; he decided cases which they failed to settle, but issued no orders to them. On this organization is based the present grading of native courts. All the chiefs spent a considerable part of their time at the capital, and when there attended daily upon the king and gave their opinion upon cases which came before him. On this custom is based the present Lukiko, which combines the functions of a court of appeal and a native Parliament.

But these institutions function in a social structure radically different from that to which their prototypes belonged. The change has been effected by means of the system of land tenure introduced by the Uganda Agreement. This Agreement, dominated by the European conception of the exercise of rights over land as a purely economic matter, envisaged the administration of land as a perquisite rather than as one of the duties of office. Accordingly it allotted a definite area as an "official estate" to each *saza* chief (eight square miles each), and to the three native ministers appointed under the Agreement (sixteen square miles each), and from the rest allotted in individual tenure 350 square miles to the king, 148 square miles to his relatives, and an average of eight square miles each to "one thousand chiefs and private landowners" as "the estates of which they are already in possession". Some of these chiefs continued for a time to exercise political powers, though as it was from the start the policy of the Government to encourage the appointment of administrative chiefs with the necessary educational qualifications, they soon came to be superseded. Many had never any recognized place in the scheme of government, while continuing to hold the position which in native eyes qualified them to exercise authority. Freed from any responsibility towards the peasants living on their land—whose legal status was now that of tenants at will—they were simply presented with a lucrative source of revenue. Fortunately many of them found the revenue by selling portions of the land to peasants rather than by extorting rent from them, or a very serious situation might have arisen. For the peasants another result of this divorce is that they are now liable to two sets of obligations—the payment of rent and other dues to their landlord and of taxation or services to political authority.

Meantime the chiefs of the native administration had lost, except as regards the population of their official estates—a very small proportion of the total under their authority—what was formerly the central bond between them and their subjects. To this day, where large estates have not been broken up for sale, it is the landowner who is the real centre of importance not only to his tenants but to those who, having bought land from him, are legally independent of him; and this is true even if his only interest in them is the collection of rent. The good old days, it is true, are over; the peasants no longer look to the landlord for help in need. But they do not turn instead to the chief who represents Government. "The chiefs are Europeans now", people say; although, as the Uganda Agreement provides, they take their orders from their own king, they are the emissaries of the alien rule of "these new times" in all matters but the collection of taxes.

The Judicial System.—Yet in fact they are not mere mouthpieces; they do administer native law in a manner which commands confidence and respect, and by a procedure which commends itself to native opinion as a fairly close approximation to what it has always been accustomed to. There are two classes of court, the *gombolola* or district, and the *saza*, with an appeal from *gombolola* to *saza* and thence to the central

Lukiko (this is the native word for any chief's court). The Lukiko has full jurisdiction in all cases arising under native law except homicide or murder. Matters concerning clan status and inheritance go straight to the Lukiko without passing through the lower courts. A District Commissioner may direct the re-hearing of a case or its revision by the next highest court, but he can only transfer to his own court cases in which both parties are not natives of Buganda; and while the proceedings of the Lukiko are subject to revision it is not open to the parties to appeal against its decisions except where they are not natives of Buganda.

The *gombolola* chief has a small area of official land in addition to his salary. His court consists of *miruka* chiefs, whose status roughly corresponds to that of a village headman elsewhere. The *muruka* is generally a small landowner; though this position carries of course no legal right, the extent of a man's land is popularly held to determine his claim both to office and precedence. Three constitute a quorum, and certain individuals are called upon in rotation to attend for this purpose; but the average number present is usually from twelve to twenty. The *saza* court consists of the *gombolola* chiefs or their representatives; the Lukiko of the "three native ministers" —Prime Minister, Chief Justice and Treasurer, the Chief Justice being a creation of the Uganda Agreement—the *saza* chiefs or their delegates and "three notables" from each *saza*, selected by the Kabaka.

The development of a superior native court with permanent personnel was initiated in 1929, when the provision that any seven members of the Lukiko constituted a quorum for judicial purposes was amended so as to set up the king, three ministers and three other members as the court of the Lukiko. The king is empowered to set up special courts from among the members of the Lukiko for the hearing of appeals if the number of cases pending becomes unduly great, and to provide for the trial by a specially constituted court of *saza* chiefs of any case unsuitable for trial by the regular Lukiko court. It is not clear whether these powers have been used.

The Lukiko as a Legislative Body.—The legislative powers

of the Lukiko are exercised at an annual session, whose agenda, drawn up by the Provincial Commissioner of Buganda, includes items submitted by him and by the chiefs. The laws which it has passed relate to such matters as the making of wills, cotton cultivation, the imposition of special taxation, the relations of landlord and tenant, sometimes to the suppression of native customs now held to be objectionable. In this connection its constitution, though unexceptionable by native standards and similar in many ways to that of the Tribal Councils of Nigeria or Tanganyika, has disadvantages in view of the economic situation created by the Uganda Agreement; it represents, no longer a group of persons responsible for the welfare of the inhabitants of their estates, and liable to suffer if they take their responsibility too lightly, but a class with a common interest in exploiting a privileged position. Thanks to timely pressure from Government the Lukiko has in fact passed legislation for the protection of the tenant and the taxation of the landlord. But as a basis for that native self-government which is generally accepted as the ultimate goal of Indirect Rule, it is open to criticisms on the ground of its undemocratic constitution which do not apply to native authorities within the native system.

The Division of Administrative Responsibility.—Though as a legislative body the Buganda Lukiko is older than any other native authority under British rule, its administrative functions are extremely limited. In Uganda there are no Native Administration schools, dispensaries, seed farms, though the Lukiko may vote taxes to contribute to the cost of such services, as it did with the Development Fund of 1922, part of whose proceeds were devoted to education and the treatment of venereal diseases. Though it makes grants towards public services from its general revenues their organization is in the hands of missions or Government. The native government is responsible for the organization of markets and the survey and registration of native lands, for the construction of local public works and for the policing of the kingdom. It administers sanitary and agricultural regulations, some made by itself, others by the British Government.

It does not handle the poll-tax rebate allotted to the native administration; this is paid directly by Government in salaries to chiefs. The revenue which actually passes through the hands of the Lukiko is derived from court fees and fines, market dues, licences and land registration fees, and from the annual payment of 10s. made by those who wish to commute the obligation to give thirty days' *luwalo* or unpaid labour on public works. The works in question consist in road maintenance and in the building of courthouses, rest - houses, prisons and dispensaries. Theoretically the unskilled work is done by those who do not commute, while the contributions of the rest pay the wages of the skilled workmen. Actually the *luwalo* budget brings in far more than is necessary for this purpose, and it is expended partly on the salaries of the *luwalo* inspectors, native sanitary inspectors and the Lukiko police, partly in grants to the missions and hospitals.

Till 1926 the Lukiko accounts were subject to no external control. In that year the king offered to submit them to audit, so that there is now a safeguard against wild extravagance or actual malversation. But the essential disadvantage of the system, in comparison with Indirect Rule proper, as a form of native local government remains: that in so many spheres the Lukiko is concerned only with the allocation of the sums collected to other bodies, government or missions, with whom the entire executive responsibility rests. To a large extent Buganda does not manage its own affairs but pays Europeans to manage them. The experiment which was tried at Budo School, of appointing a preponderantly native governing body, met with difficulties, perhaps inevitable in an institution whose driving force is European, that do not arise in the case of the Native Administration Schools of Kenya and Tanganyika.

Under this system a native government containing men of such outstanding ability as Serwano Nkulubya, the Treasurer, who made such a profound impression on British opinion when he gave evidence before the Select Committee on Closer Union, is in a position which calls for no initiative and gives no practical training. It is true that Uganda has gone further than many colonies in the appointment of native representatives to such special bodies as the Advisory Council on Native Education, the District and Provincial Education Boards, the Coffee Board, and so on; [1] but participation of this kind in the affairs of government has a serious disadvantage in that it is purely advisory.

The stimulus and encouragement to undertake new tasks which is the essential vitalizing principle of the Nigeria and Tanganyika systems is at present lacking, and there is real danger that the ability which ought to be directed to this end may spend itself instead on the type of obstructive criticism that comes so readily to those who cannot be called upon to put their theories into practice.

The Extension of the Buganda System.—The Agreements made with the kingdoms of Toro and Ankole only provided for the grant of freehold land to the kings and a few leading chiefs, so that the territorial basis of native political organization have not there been undermined in the same way. Bunyoro, as a conquered territory, was denied the privilege of an Agreement till 1933. In all these areas, and recently in Busoga, there has been a demand for the Buganda system from the class which expected to profit by it, but the demand has been successfully resisted. Hence there has been no difficulty in commuting to a money contribution to native administration revenue the dues and services traditionally owed to chiefs.

Organizations corresponding to that established in Buganda, with *saza* and *gombolola* chiefs and courts, with or without central councils, have been progressively extended to the other tribes of the Protectorate. In all districts outside Buganda there is an appeal in all cases from the highest native to a European court. The extent of jurisdiction varies in different districts. The councils do not have legislative powers until they are expressly conferred, and then their powers are limited to the amendment of native law; they have been conferred in the case of Busoga, Toro, Ankole, Kigezi and the Nilotic tribes of Teso, Acholi and Lugwari. While the system in Busoga represents no greater innovation than the federation of a number of closely allied groups, and in Toro and Ankole

[1] Annual Report, 1930, p. 47.

175

a modification in the functions of already existing institutions, in the Nilotic kingdoms it is something as alien as a purely European organization could be. When it was first extended to other tribes Buganda "agents" were appointed to advise and train the authorities in their new duties. Most of these have now been withdrawn. Whether or not their presence constituted a check on arbitrary government, it seems to be widely true at the present time that chiefs entrusted with the operation of a foreign system which has no place in the society to which they belong use their new powers largely for their personal advantage.

Land Policy.—The policy of Uganda towards land alienation has been to respect native rights to a degree which is remarkable in a territory that in its early stages looked to the plantation system as the most hopeful form of economic development. Whatever the disadvantages of the Uganda Agreement from the point of view of the internal structure of Buganda, it did preserve in the hands of the tribe as a whole ample land for their needs. In Buganda land not included in the Agreement, and elsewhere "waste and uncultivated" land, is held to be Crown land and available for alienation. The area so available was stated in 1920 to be 2745 square miles out of a total land area of 94,131 square miles.[1] Natives living on this land pay rent to the Crown. Before 1920 native landowners were allowed to sell up to half their land to Europeans, and some 55,000 acres were so sold, but sale to Europeans is now prohibited. Land was at first in demand for cotton and rubber cultivation, but little interest has been taken in either by Europeans since the depression of 1921. In 1927 a certain number of coffee estates were taken up in the high country of Toro. But the total area of alienated land in the Protectorate by 1930 was only 300 square miles, and many estates have been abandoned since that date.[2]

Nevertheless there has been a demand, in the kingdoms of Toro, Ankole and Bunyoro, and in Busoga for some legal recognition of individual native rights comparable to that which exists

[1] Annual Report, 1920, p. 4. *The Statesman's Year Book* for 1935 gives the total land area as 80,588 square miles.

[2] Annual Reports, 1930, pp. 36–8; 1931, p. 24; 1932, p. 24; 1933, p. 25.

in Buganda, as a measure of protection against possible alienations and in order to give security for economic development.
While the demand has come mainly from those who under the
Buganda system would be landlords, it has been met in a
manner· expressly designed to prevent any individual from
acquiring rights over land which he cannot himself cultivate.
The form of title which has been granted in Toro and Ankole
is a Certificate of Occupancy which confirms the right of a
given individual or his heirs to occupy, cultivate and dispose
of the produce of a given area of land. The holder of such
a certificate is stated to be the owner of the produce of the
land, of trees planted and buildings erected on it, but not of
the land itself, and he is expressly debarred from collecting
rent from any resident on the land. The introduction of a
similar system in Bunyoro was recommended in 1931.

The Buganda system has necessitated a series of measures
designed to counteract the economic inequality it has created.
A law was passed by the Lukiko in 1927 limiting the obligations
of the tenant to a rent of 10s., a gourd of beer in every brew,
one barkcloth yearly for every five barkcloth trees on his
holding (few holdings contain as many) and a payment of 4s.
for a plantation of cotton or coffee trees in bearing, plus an
additional 4s. if the area exceeds one acre. The growing
practice of commuting the tribute of beer for a money payment
was legally recognized in 1934.

In 1922 a tax of 20s. was imposed on every owner of more
than five acres, while a levy of 1s. was made on each payment
of rent, the proceeds being devoted partly to meet the expenses
of the native administration and partly to meet educational and
anti-venereal services provided by the British Government.
This tax was imposed for a limited period, and was replaced
in 1928 by a tax on owners of more than ten acres of 25s. in
the richer and 15s. in the poorer districts, while a landlord
with only five tenants or less was only obliged to pay 5s., the
levy on rent being retained as before. In 1929 the latter was
raised to shs. 1/50. In 1932 the amount of the tax was made
variable from time to time according to the directions of the
Lukiko with the approval of the Governor.

Labour Shortage and the Government Attitude.—The complaint of shortage of labour, in a territory with a maximum of
230 estates and a native population of 3,500,000, throws into
relief a characteristic attitude of the average European employer throughout Africa that does not appear so clearly in
territories where the native population is actually insufficient
to meet the demands upon it—the conviction that he has a
right to expect such labour as he requires on whatever terms
he is prepared to offer, born often of an economic situation in
which a precarious margin of profit depends upon the reduction
of labour costs to a minimum. A Development Commission
in 1920 recommended the demarcation of reserves sufficiently
restricted to force the native population to "come out to work".
More recent complaints have been directed against the rate of
wages offered by the Public Works Department. There is in
fact a constant flow of labour from the outlying districts where
native production has not yet been developed; though it is not
of course the policy of Government to leave these areas indefinitely without some source of revenue from village production. They have held to the position that the employer
must offer inducements sufficient to compete with alternative
occupations, and the question asked in the Legislative Council
in 1924, whether the newly constituted Labour Department
was "averting an increase in the wages of unskilled labour",
was answered by the statement that its object was "to create
an efficient and adequate labour supply and not to depress
wages".

The Labour Department.—Government works were up till
1922 carried out entirely by compulsory labour, in the belief
that this represented a legitimate adaptation of the services
rendered to the native chiefs. After this system was abolished
difficulty was experienced in getting labour for work which
had been deservedly unpopular, and eventually a Labour
Department was established in 1926 whose main business was
the recruiting of volunteers for Government works by the
offer of suitable wages and conditions, but which has devoted
such time as could be spared to the inspection of conditions on
plantations. A few camps for migrant labourers have been

built; at first these were only available for natives recruited for public works, but later they were thrown open for general use. No such systematic survey of the labour situation as was made in Tanganyika from the point of view of the special needs of different tribes has been attempted here, but the Labour Department has had considerable influence on the standard of conditions, both through its example and through direct advice to employers on such matters as diet. The monthly average of natives working for wages in 1933 was 49,685.[1] Reports for previous years give the total of "all natives in employment", including independent cultivators, as over 400,000.[2]

Education.—Uganda is one of the territories in which up till very recently education has been almost exclusively literary. It has aimed, and aimed successfully, at giving a training which will enable intelligent natives to qualify for any profession. But it has envisaged the creation of a far larger professional class than the territory, even in prosperous times, could be expected to absorb. Its culminating point is Makerere College, destined by its founders as the future University of East Africa, where boys who have completed four years in primary and six in secondary schools can be trained in medicine, veterinary work, surveying or agriculture, or as schoolmasters, or can take matriculation through the Cambridge certificate. Makerere was planned in 1926 to accommodate 340 students; its numbers had reached 117 by 1933, but only seven of these were taking the matriculation course.[3]

In the last few years there has been a reaction, first against the purely literary curriculum followed in many schools, and later against the emphasis on a training suitable only for those boys who would be able to leave their villages and enter some profession. In 1930 a new Central School syllabus was drawn up for Buganda, which substituted the vernacular for English as the language of instruction, and included such subjects as agriculture, carpentry, clerical work, an elementary business course and instruction in the keeping of Native Court records

[1] Annual Reports, 1933, p. 33.   [2] *Ibid.*, 1931, p. 31 ; 1932, p. 33.
[3] Education Department, Annual Report, 1933, pp. 15, 43.

and the collection of poll-tax. In this year also provision was made for all teachers to attend courses at the Government agricultural school at Bukalasa. A more important move has been the opening of two farm schools at which up-to-date agricultural and stock-rearing methods will be taught on model small holdings. Here farm work is not a subject among many but the sole object of the course; the pupils work on the farms in the morning, and in the afternoons write up records and attend lectures on subjects closely connected with their practical work. Similar courses have been started at the Government experimental stations for adult natives, who require no qualification for acceptance beyond a knowledge of the three R's.

There has also been a shift of emphasis from concentration on the minority who can attain to higher education, can afford to pay for it, and may hope to gain some advantage from it, to consideration of the needs of the majority who will never complete the full course. Definite steps have been taken only in the discontinuance of grants to the two "women's colleges", neither of which had been in existence very long. In 1933 the Education Department expressed the view that two secondary schools preparing pupils for entrance to Makerere, one for Protestants and one for Catholics, would be sufficient, and that the rest of the seven now in existence "should be utilized for secondary education of a type more suited to the needs of African rural communities". The recent appointment of Mr. Harold Jowitt as Director of Education will doubtless lead to a reorganization on these lines comparable to that already carried out in Southern Rhodesia.

V. THE SUDAN

The Sudan, in view of its peculiar international status as an Anglo-Egyptian Condominium, is controlled not through the Colonial Office but through the Foreign Office, and in its case the detailed information which the Colonial Office places at the disposal of the public is not available. Nevertheless a study of the systems of native administration which have been evolved under British rule cannot omit all mention of this area. An outline of the policy pursued there is given by a former Governor, Sir Harold MacMichael, in a recently published book.[1]

From the establishment of the Condominium in 1898 till 1920 the administration was carried on by a Civil Service organized on British lines, in which the responsible officials were British and their subordinates Egyptians and Sudanese. At first only the lower posts could be filled by Sudanese, but one of the aims of the Gordon College, founded by Lord Kitchener in 1902, was to train Sudanese for employment in the higher ranks.

The Milner Mission and Decentralization.—A departure from this policy in the direction of increased utilization of native institutions was recommended by the Milner Mission in 1920. With regard to the Sudan they wrote: "Having regard to its vast extent and the varied character of its inhabitants, the administration of its different parts should be left as far as possible in the hands of the native authorities, wherever they exist, under British supervision. . . . Decentralization and the employment, wherever possible, of native agencies for the simple administrative needs of the country in its present stage of development, would make both for economy and efficiency." In education the Sudan is advised "not to repeat the mistake which has been made in Egypt, of introducing a system which fits pupils for little else than employment in clerical and minor administrative posts, and creates an overgrown body of aspirants to Government employment. . . . Education should be directed to giving the Sudanese a capacity and a taste for employment in other directions, such as agriculture, industry, commerce and engineering."

The devolution of administrative powers to native authorities has been carried out progressively. A recent article by E. N. Corbyn describes the process as follows:

"Some ten years ago, when the foundations of the present development were laid, the decision was very wisely taken, on the recommendation of an annual conference of Governors

[1] *The Anglo-Egyptian Sudan*, 1934.

of Provinces, to commence by devolving magisterial and judicial functions, and, by their handling of these, to judge the capacity of the bodies entrusted with them to go on to the charge of other administrative duties. The Native authorities to whom functions are devolved are thus continuously by methods of trial and error passing judgement upon their own capacity, and the stage of advance is not at any time universal, nor constant even throughout a Province." [1]

Devolution in Practice.—These principles appear to have been followed in a spirit of extreme caution. At first judicial powers were- conferred only on nomad sheikhs, since it was held that nothing short of an entirely different mode of life could justify a preference for native rather than British legal procedure.[2] In 1926 Sir John Maffey extended the recognition of Sheikhs' Courts over a much wider area, and they now function throughout the Sudan. Those sheikhs who demonstrated their efficiency in this field were next entrusted with responsibility for the maintenance of order through their own police, and the assessment and collection of taxes. What further powers are exercised it is not very easy to discern from published reports. Some native authorities employ medical dressers trained at the Gordon College, and are responsible for their own veterinary and agricultural inspectors. "Wherever possible" they take responsibility for the maintenance of roads, wells, and water storage.[3] The prevention of sleeping sickness and the supervision of village schools, the enforcement of forestry regulations, and the registration of transactions in land and date trees are also mentioned.[4] The entire administration of a gum forest in the Kassala Province is stated to be in native hands,[5] and native authorities co-operate in the allotment of land for cultivation in the Gash Delta.[6] The Native Court at Tokar in the Red Sea Province is responsible for the management of a co-operative society.[7]

The Sultanate of Dar Masalit, in the extreme west, was

---

[1] *Journal of the African Society*, April 1935, p. 182.
[2] MacMichael, *op. cit.*, p. 248.
[3] Annual Report, 1929, p. 12.   [4] *Ibid.*, pp. 104, 123 ; 1930, p. 127.
[5] *Ibid.*, 1926, p. 90.   [6] *Ibid.*, 1929, p. 117
[7] *Ibid.*, 1928, p. 10.

recognized as a Native Authority soon after, in 1919, it was included within the territory of the Sudan.[1] The Sultan retained full powers of internal administration subject to the advice of a Resident; but he had no budget till 1925, and by 1928 the stage reached was only that "proposals [had] been approved for the eventual delegation to [him] of real responsibility".[2] In the same Province (Darfur) the Emirs of Rizeigat and Zalingei were later given similar recognition. By 1929 a few tribal treasuries were in existence,[3] and they were extended in 1930. A "tendency to coalition" among the smaller units has been encouraged for the sake of its administrative advantages.[4]

Side by side with the increased utilization of native authorities has gone a shifting of the emphasis in educational policy. Since 1922 its aim has been, while maintaining the high standard of advanced education given at the Gordon College, to concentrate on the provision of facilities for the great majority who will never go beyond an elementary education. An interesting step in this direction was the payment of subsidies to those village Koran schools (Khalwa) which attained a certain standard of efficiency in teaching the three R's, and the institution of training courses for the teachers. In the present economic depression the Sudan Government, like many others, has turned its attention to the development of a curriculum directly related to that village life from which the school in existing circumstances can no longer be a way of escape.

Criticisms of the New Regime.—Much stress is laid in the Annual Reports of the Sudan on the economies of "devolution", and the whole system, administrative and educational, has been criticized by Sir James Currie, the first Principal of Gordon College, as no more than a device for saving money. In his view the future of the Sudan lies in the speediest possible development of a highly educated native Civil Service. It is the converse of the same theory that those Sudanese who have attained education deserve to take their share in the advance-

---

[1] MacMichael, *op. cit.*, p. 249.
[2] Annual Report, 1928, p. 111
[3] *Ibid.*, 1929, p. 12.
[4] MacMichael, *op. cit.*, p. 253.

ment of their own country. The present policy saves money on the salaries both of teachers and of administrative staff, denies to the Sudan that technical equipment which is the condition of a successful existence in the modern world, and panders to the vanity of officials who like to play the part of "county squire".

In essence this is the same argument which is brought against Indirect Rule wherever it has been established. Put in its crudest form, it would not be unfair to say that it makes the final criterion of a system which affects the welfare of some six million villagers the prospects of Government employment which it offers to a certain number from a group estimated at about 12,000.[1] Sir Harold MacMichael has characterized the attitude of the younger urban population as "a form of patriotism generally indistinguishable from a desire for office";[2] it is easy to imagine the indignation with which the patriots would reject the description—but is not the element of truth which it contains found too in the case which their British friends put for them? They are anxious to "do their share in uplifting their country", certainly, but would they be as anxious if it was a share not involving power, prestige and a salary much higher than the income of a villager? And, unless we are convinced on other grounds that a transformation from top to bottom is the best way of achieving that adaptation to modern needs that all African peoples are now forced to make, is this a sufficient reason for making it?

Some of these educated young men are in fact finding employment under the native administrations of their own tribes; some have left Government service for the purpose. With the extension of the executive functions of the native administrations there should be scope for many more in the future; and this is perhaps an argument for a more confident advance in that direction.

---

[1] MacMichael, *op. cit.*, p. 268.   [2] *Ibid.*

CHAPTER IV

FRENCH POLICY

THE French possessions in Tropical Africa cover an area of 2,000,000 square miles, nearly ten times that of France itself; though this area, it is true, comprises the greater part of the desert of the Sahara, for which no use has as yet been devised other than as a potential route for the transport of West African troops required for service in a European war. In the West there are two federal groups, French West Africa and French Equatorial Africa, better known as the French Congo. These are approximately equal in area, French West Africa being slightly larger; but the difference between them in population is enormous, that of A.O.F.,[1] as it is officially designated, being 14,000,000, while that of A.E.F.[2] is only 3,000,000. To these must be added the two Mandated areas of French Togoland, an area of 21,000 square miles with a population of 750,000, and the French section of the Cameroons, which, with a population of 2,000,000 in an area of 166,000 square miles, is easily the most densely populated region under French control. In the east, France possesses the island of Madagascar, an area of 241,000 square miles with a population of 3,500,000.

The French Theory of Colonization.—French colonial policy is unique among those represented in Africa in being governed, in theory at least, by a clearly formulated body of principles, which are supposed to be equally applicable to all French colonies. Local differences, historical events prior to the formulation of this policy, and the initiative of individual

---

[1] Afrique Occidentale Française : this comprises the formerly separate colonies of Senegal, French Guinea, the Ivory Coast, Dahomey, Sudan, Mauretania, the Niger, the Upper Volta, each of which remains a Colony with its own Lieutenant-Governor.

[2] Afrique Equatoriale Française.

administrators, have resulted in certain variations in practice; but the theory adopted by all exponents of French coloniza- tion is the same. It is most adequately expressed in the writings of M. Albert Sarraut and Marshal Lyautey; though the actual method so successfully followed by the latter in Morocco remains without its counterpart in any other French possession.

The guiding principle in this theory is the unity of France with her possessions overseas, from which it follows that all the subjects of France are alike her children and have the same patriotic duties to the mother country. The exact nature of these duties is laid down by M. Albert Sarraut in his book *La Mise en Valeur de nos Colonies*, in which he presses for a policy of intensive economic development in the colonies as an essential element in the post-war reconstruction of France. The first question which he asks is in what way France's children from overseas can come to her aid. What can they give her?

He finds three answers.

"Des hommes, d'abord."

The population of the colonies, added to that of France, brings up the total from 40,000,000 to 100,000,000 and thus gives her a numerical preponderance over the 65,000,000 of Germany. The ability to mobilize her colonial troops rapidly in time of war is regarded as an indispensable element in French security. Upon the necessity of maintaining her sea communications for this purpose rested her insistence on naval parity with Italy at the London Conference of 1930, and for this purpose it has been proposed to build a railway across the Sahara which would have almost no economic value. The maintenance of her colonial army for use in Europe has been one of the fatal obstacles to any agreement between France and Germany on the question of disarmament, and so much importance does she attach to it that she insisted upon the right, denied to other Mandatories, to use troops recruited in her mandated areas outside those areas "in case of a general war". Colonial troops are frequently employed outside their native areas—Senegalese in the Ruhr occupation, for example, and Malagasy troops during the Druse revolt in Syria—while the West African troops regularly serve their term of conscription in France.

The second form of assistance which the colonies should give to the mother country consists in financial contributions. These are made, above all, for military expenses. Sarraut envisages a time when the whole upkeep of colonial troops shall be borne locally. The sum to be provided is determined by the Minister for the Colonies. Colonial budgets contribute also towards the maintenance of various institutions which are considered to advertise the colonies and thus assist their development, such as the Institut Colonial Français. A voluntary contribution was also invited in 1926 to assist in maintaining the franc, and brought in nearly 7,000,000 francs from West Africa. The degree to which this contribution was really voluntary was questioned with some acerbity in a Parliamentary debate, but only with reference to Indo-China.

The third form of assistance which France should be able to call upon is the provision of raw materials for her industry. English readers, accustomed to being invited to buy colonial products as a patriotic duty, will be surprised at the insistence of continental writers on this point. It is not until the appearance of Lyautey's *Empire Colonial Français* in 1930 that one finds any reference to that economic function of colonial possessions which to us appears to be of preponderant importance—as markets for our manufactured goods.[1] For France, however, especially in the years immediately after the War, the essential seemed to be an assured source of raw

---

[1] The English reader will be surprised also to find British policy characterized in such terms as these: "The world is, in the eyes of the British, a vast garden destined to furnish to the United Kingdom all that an ignorant nature has refused to the factories of Liverpool and Manchester." Or again: "The dominant motive in British colonization has been the most complete and conscious egoism, national and imperial. Colonial expansion has but one end: to supply British manufacturers with raw materials and with an assured market for their products." Guernier, *L'Afrique Champ d'Expansion de L'Europe*, p. 165. Without attempting to deny the interested element in British, as in all other, colonization, one is impelled to ask in what respect these statements describe a difference between British policy and that outlined by Sarraut and Lyautey.

materials which would make her independent of foreign countries. This demand had a rational basis in the depreciation of the franc, which raised the cost of foreign goods to her manufacturers; but it is upheld to a surprising extent by mere expressions of indignation that France should buy from abroad goods which her colonies could produce—an indignation not founded on sympathy with the French colonial producer, since at that stage production of many of the commodities discussed was non-existent—and by rumours that other nations contemplated refusing to sell their goods to France.[1]

To meet this last and all-important requirement Sarraut devised a twofold plan. The products particularly suited to each colonial area were to be determined and their intensive cultivation begun, while this increase in production was to be accompanied by a rapid simultaneous development of communications in all the colonies, in order to transport the goods produced. The scheme, which is published in his book, was worked out in detail as regards both its aspects and laid before the French Parliament. Its application as a whole would have cost four milliards of francs, and this the French budget has never been able to undertake, perhaps fortunately in view of some results of the method which has been adopted of carrying out his suggestions piecemeal. It was to be accompanied by a policy of the "conservation, amelioration, increase and education of the labour supply".[2]

Civilization as a By-product.—The role of the native seems to be clear. He is to fight and produce for the mother-country like a good Frenchman. There is an additional element in the theory, however—the belief that the native will be necessarily and inevitably civilized by this process so that in helping France he also helps himself. The increased productivity of which the native is going to be the source will inevitably redound to the advantage of the native population, while the members of it who show themselves worthy will be associated with the Government in its civilizing mission. The Sarraut theory is "a doctrine of colonization starting from a conception

---

[1] Cf. M. Georges-Barthélémy in the Chambre, December 21, 1922.
[2] Sarraut, *Mise en Valeur*, p. 344.

of power or profit for the metropolis, but instinctively impregnated with altruism".[1]

The assumption which governs the whole attitude of France towards native development is that French civilization is necessarily the best and need only be presented to the intelligent African for him to adopt it. Once he has done so, no avenue of advancement is to be closed to him. If he proves himself capable of assimilating French education, he may enter any profession, may rise to the dignity of Under-Secretary for the Colonies, and will be received as an equal by French society. This attitude towards the educated native arouses the bitter envy of his counterpart in neighbouring British colonies.

In the fate of the majority who do not attain to "civilization", however, French policy has in the main taken little interest. The principle which is held to characterize British administration, that indigenous institutions should be preserved and developed, appears to the French to be nothing but a disguised form of colour bar—a means of perpetuating the gulf between the dominant European and the subject native. Convinced as they are that native institutions are doomed to perish, and that soon, the emphasis of their policy has always lain on the encouragement of the privileged *élite*, while the conception of the *system* as the subject of development rather than the few selected individuals appears to have presented itself to no one.[2]

For the purposes of this study, the question is what this conception means in terms of the evolution of native society and of the actual administrative system under which that society now lives. The belief in the superiority of French

---

[1] *Mise en Valeur*, p. 81. The phrase irresistibly recalls the dictum of Sir Harry Johnston to the effect that the Slave Trade, like most other instinctive human procedure, contained in it elements which were necessary for the progress of humanity, including that of its victims. *The Colonization of Africa*, p. 101.

[2] Cf. M. Sarraut at the African Society in June, 1933. " You err, perhaps, by excess of scepticism about the feasibility of transforming souls long steeped in heredity. We may err in our turn by excess of faith in the virtue of doctrines and the logic of principles. You build day by day on what already exists. We dream of new and rectilinear architectures. You listen especially to the prudent but rather cold counsel of experience. We warm our action in the flame of apostleship. You, in sum, wish the native races to place themselves in a condition to make their own happiness. We wish ourselves to make their happiness, urgently and with authority."

civilization is reflected in the judicial system, in the attitude towards native law in general, to native authorities and native rights in land, in the educational programme, in the convenient belief—not confined to the French colonies—that the first duty of civilization to the savage is to give him "a taste for work", even in the justification for the colonial contributions to the metropolitan budget on the ground that the beneficiaries of civilization should contribute to the expenses of the country which brings them its benefits,[1] and, above all, in the privileged status conferred on those Africans who are deemed to be civilized.

Since the attainment of this status by all is the theoretical goal of French policy, it will be interesting to see how it is attained and in what its privileges consist. It will be seen that they cover an extensive field.

The Privileges of Citizenship.—In theory the educated natives become naturalized *citizens* of France and are then not legally differentiated in any way from her European citizens, whether in France or overseas, while the mass of the population are classed as subjects. In practice, the distinction is not based solely on educational qualifications, partly because in the greater part of the French colonies the process of attaining recognition as a citizen is complicated and does not seem to be very widely taken advantage of, partly because in Senegal, the oldest possession of France in Africa, citizenship is the right by birth of every native of the territory in virtue of a law of 1833.

The general legislation applicable to the acquisition of citizenship in the French colonies lays down the following criteria of eligibility: ten years' service in French employment, the ability to read and write French, and evidence of good character and the possession of means of support. Exemption from the requirement of a knowledge of French can be granted in the case of persons deemed to have rendered conspicuous services to France, and is automatic for anyone who has received the Legion of Honour or Médaille Militaire. Any application for naturalization is sent by the local official to the Lieutenant

---

[1] Cf. Homberg, *La France des cinq Parties du Monde*, p. 19, where this principle is described as theoretically valid though unsound in practice.

Governor of the Colony, by him to the Governor General of the Federation; thence, with the approval of the Governor General in Council, to the Ministers of Colonies and Justice in Paris. If all these authorities approve the application, naturalization is granted by a decree of the President of the Republic.[1]

The attractions of French citizenship do not seem to have been sufficient to lead many natives to embark upon this tedious process. In all West Africa, excluding Senegal, there were by 1922—ten years after this legislation came into force—only a little over 2000 French citizens; and since the number of naturalizations in A.O.F. between 1914 and 1922 was only ninety-four, it seems that the majority of those who availed themselves of the right must have been natives already established in town conditions who had something immediate and definite to gain from the change of status. Its advantages would appear to have been recognized by the highly sophisticated, but it cannot be said to have provided any effective stimulus to the adoption of European ways by the natives at large—even, apparently, those who have had considerable education. As the culminating point of the "new and rectilinear architecture", the entry of the civilized native into the ranks of the citizens of France seems, therefore, to have rather failed of its purpose, and so long as this is the case the "association of the *élite*" in the great task of France has very little meaning. Association on terms of equality does not seem to be ardently desired, and its alternative, association in a position of subordination, while it may provide the administration with useful instruments for effecting the changes which it desires to make, contradicts the avowed purpose of the "*mission civilisatrice*"—the free access to civilization and all its benefits for all those who show themselves worthy. In the last resort, it appears that France offers to her subjects only something which they do not want; but the bases of her policy are such that she is precluded from seeking measures which would lead to the development of their own culture in a way that they would accept.

The existence of this very small citizen class would be of

[1] Buell, *The Native Problem in Africa*, vol. I, pp. 946 ff.

slight significance were it not for the fact that its privileges are shared by all inhabitants of that part of West Africa which was already French in 1833. The inhabitants of the four communes of Senegal acquire by birth the full status of French citizenship, including the right to elect a deputy to the Paris Chambre, to vote for the mayors and town councils of the communes, and to elect their representatives to a Colonial Council for the whole Colony of Senegal (including the hinterland), which has considerable control over the budget. Thus we have the paradoxical situation that, out of a total of 25,000 French citizens in A.O.F., over 22,000 have acquired their status in a purely fortuitous manner, and that in Senegal European representative institutions are being managed by natives whose sole qualification is their place of birth.

The privileges of the citizen are of value first and foremost in connection with his obligations towards the State. His name is entered on a register of taxpayers and he receives a receipt for his tax, while in the case of subjects a lump sum is calculated as due from each administrative division and the chief is left to raise it as he thinks fit. As regards the annual *prestation* of a given number of days' unpaid labour on public works, citizens are entitled to commute the service for a money payment, a privilege which is shared by the natives of Togo and the Cameroons, owing to the requirements of the Mandate. Most significant of all is the privileged position of citizens as regards conscription: while subjects are called up for three years' service, which is spent in France, citizens are enrolled in a special formation, whose period of service is the same as that for European French citizens and which does not leave the colony.

In the eyes of justice, citizens are subject to French law and have access to French courts presided over by a professional judge, while subjects come before administrative officers' courts as elsewhere in Africa. Citizens are exempt, moreover, from the *indigénat*—a summary penalty of imprisonment for two weeks which may be imposed by administrative officers at their discretion for a number of offences, including "any act of a nature to weaken respect for French authority". Though two weeks' imprisonment is the theoretical maximum, there is nothing to prevent the imposition of a second sentence as soon as the first is served, and there is no appeal against the sentence. By a decree of 1924, exemption from the *indigénat* is granted to natives who, without having attained citizenship, have risen to positions implying a certain standard of Europeanization— chiefs recognized by the Government, Government employees, members of the various native councils and tribunals, merchants, persons who have passed certain school examinations, as well as those who have received a decoration or served in the War; while a special exemption may be given to "natives who have particularly distinguished themselves either by participating in the commercial or agricultural development of the country and generally in works of public interest, or by services rendered to the French cause".[1]

Land Tenure.—While no specific privilege with regard to the ownership of property is possessed by the French citizen, the legal system in force up till 1925 had the effect of recognizing only individual claims to land formally registered in accordance with European law. Any claim brought before the notice of the authorities was announced in the *Official Journal*, published in French, and if no counter-claim was brought in three months, the claimant received a title to the land in question. Since 1925 the law has been modified to the extent that the onus of proof rests on the person claiming title, but since French law refuses to recognize the ownership of a group, and no native African system recognizes individual tenure in the European sense, it is clear that the titles which are granted must still be granted in disregard to native law. This method of dealing with land is consistent with the theory, expressed by more than one French writer, that the individual ownership of property is the basis of civilization and the essential prerequisite of all progress.[2] It has the advantage over general individualization that it does not modify the native system in the advance of demands from the native producer such as would

---

[1] Buell, *op. cit.*, vol. I, p. 1017.
[2] Cf. Olivier, *Dix Ans de Politique Sociale au Madagascar*, pp. 25–6, and Sarraut in the introduction to the same book.

indicate a need for change, and it does not seem to have been appealed to much in practice. On the other hand, no attempt has been made to envisage or allow for the conflicts between the new and old regime which must arise in areas where a part only of the land has become individual property, or for the confusion which equally ensues when the holder of an individual title continues to follow native custom with regard to the utilization and disposal of land.

These then are the privileges open to the Europeanized *élite*. The rest who have not attained their degree of civilization have, nevertheless, all the patriotic duties of "children of France"—to fight, pay taxes, cultivate the soil or work on transport developments, according as the exigencies of France require. Since the administration does not envisage any other future for them than their ultimate Europeanization, and regards this as inevitable, it is in the main concerned with the fulfilment of their duties—the organization of conscription, taxation and public works—while its provision for their advancement takes the form of a considerable interest in public health and the establishment of an educational system in which the *élite* can go as far as they like in the acquisition of European knowledge, while the remainder are trained first and foremost to be good workers and loyal citizens.

Native Production.—The economic development of the West African Federation is based in theory on native peasant production, though in A.E.F. the legacy of the large concessions granted in 1899 presents an obstacle to the realization of this policy. Moreover, peasant production has a sense here considerably different from that which it bears in other African territories. It has been mentioned that the respect for native lands which is a fundamental principle of the Indirect Rule policy is not marked in the French territories in West Africa. While the Government of the Belgian Congo attempts, by a system of compulsion, to further cultivation of crops for sale by natives in their own villages, the French method in many districts—not in all—is to select a large continuous area near a road or railway and organize its cultivation by labour brought, if necessary, from a distance. Ground-nut cultivation has been developed in this way along the Thies-Kayès railway in Senegal, where a French writer refers to the "hundreds of thousands" of labourers.[1] An article in *L'Afrique Française*,[2] anticipating the construction of the Congo-Ocean railway, forecast the immediate introduction along the route, and particularly near the stations, of food crops of all kinds, as well as coffee, cocoa, and the development of stockbreeding. Cocoa, cotton and kapok cultivation have been pushed in other regions. A considerable area in the Niger Valley has been irrigated for cotton-growing, and in 1927 employed over 12,000 natives. All of these had to leave their homes for the work; very few undertook it voluntarily, and, while it was hoped that they would see the attraction of productive employment and would settle permanently in the areas of cultivation, not many in fact did so, and Abadie describes the natives engaged in this work as " prestataires payés ".[3]

It has been officially stated, however, that in connection with the agricultural stations of Niénèbalé and Baguinéda in the irrigated part of the Niger Valley, there were over 4000 natives settled in 1931.[4] In 1932 an organization was formed, under Government control, which is to complete the irrigation works and supply seed to natives, who will own the land and the produce while paying interest to the Company. Two native notables are to be members of its local committee.[5]

Elsewhere governmental encouragement of commercial culti-vation does not involve the migration of labourers to places far from their homes. Exactly how it is organized it is difficult to discover, and the nature of the obligation resting on the native does not seem to have been clearly defined. A circular

[1] M. Abadie, *Nos Richesses Soudanaises*, p. 33 ; and M. J. Raffin, quoted in *Renseignements Coloniaux*, 1921, p. 228.

[2] June 1924, p. 369.

[3] Abadie, *Renseignements Coloniaux*, 1921, p. 229. Work of this kind is sometimes undertaken voluntarily by natives in order to earn the amount of their taxes. Raffin, *loc. cit.*

[4] M. Brévié in address to Conseil de Gouvernement, J. O., 1931, p. 964:

[5] *Afrique Française*, August 1932, p. 479. An agricultural training station opened in 1926 adopted the method of settling families in the neighbourhood in native conditions with possession of their land and crops. Though the scheme seems to have been very successful, it cannot have affected a very large number of persons. See J. Renkenbach in *Renseigne-ments Coloniaux*, 1928, pp. 626 ff.

of A.O.F. of April 21, 1912, asserted "Il y a pour l'indigène l'obligation stricte de cultiver le coton", while another, as late as March 21, 1928, issued by the Lieutenant Governor of the Upper Volta, states that only constant action by administrative officials can induce the natives to undertake the regular and efficient cultivation of kapok.

Cocoa cultivation was introduced into the Ivory Coast by Angoulvant when Governor-General. In a recent article he explains that his method was to induce native chiefs, "par une propagande inlassable et aussi par des récompenses ou par des refus de faveurs", to give the necessary orders to their subjects.[1]

The possibility of resorting to any other stimulus than compulsion, or of leaving the natives to make their own response to their new economic circumstances, does not appear to be envisaged. As late as 1929, M. Carde, Governor General of A.E.F., spoke thus to his Council:

> "Take a native who has paid his tax, performed his *prestations*, done his military service and fulfilled all the requirements of the written law. A new burden is imposed on him, which certainly is soon going to bring him appreciable benefits, but whose advantages do not appeal to him at the outset. Granted that the moral right to impose it is inherent in the meaning of colonization, the text which would legalize it does not exist. We must establish it, and in the present state of political development of A.O.F., the most rational method consists in an annual programme approved by the Conseil de Gouvernement. . . . Plans of production will be drawn up by the Lieutenant Governor of each Colony, modified, if necessary, by the Governor General, and approved by the Council. For the execution of this programme the Lieutenant Governors are responsible, but they have no authority to modify it."[2]

The Lieutenant Governor of the Moyen Congo issued a circular in 1931 instructing his subordinates to require each

---

[1] " La culture du cacaoyer ", *Revue Internationale des Produits Coloniaux*, November 1932.

[2] Journal Officiel de l'A.O.F., 1929, pp. 1025–6. In an earlier circular (see J. O., 1924, p. 173) M. Carde described the recourse to compulsion as futile, but there is so little information on the actual administrative methods employed that one can only guess how these two statements can be reconciled.

adult male to plant ten palm-trees a year and keep them in good condition.[1]

The same process as applied to cotton is described in greater detail in a report quoted by Bloud in *Le Problème Cotonnière et l'A.O.F.*, which calls it the method of the "champ du Commandant":

> "The administrator orders the chief of a tribe to have an additional area of cotton planted and cultivated by the natives of that tribe. This is the 'Champ du Commandant'. At harvest time the administrator auctions the cotton and turns over the proceeds to the chief, who distributes it among his subjects. All are agreeably surprised at not having been compelled to give unpaid labour to the administration and next year there is no need of constraint—a striking example of pressure combined with persuasion."

The system of the "plantation communale" was instituted in the Mandated Area of Togoland in 1925, and in 1926 462 such plantations were in existence.[2]

This system is regarded with less favour by two other French writers, who criticize it from different points of view. Abadie asserts[3] that the maximum development from the *prestation* system will soon be reached, and stresses the necessity of giving the native cultivator some interest in his work—a result which, in his opinion, the present system does not produce.[4] He proposes as an alternative the commercialization of millet, the traditional food crop of the Sudanese villages. R. Delavignette, an administrative officer, writing of the Upper Volta, also advocates a return to millet, though his argument for it is that the existing system not only diverts labour from the fertile soil round the villages to inferior areas along the roads but has

[1] Journal Officiel de l'A.E.F., 1931, p. 654.
[2] Annual Reports to the Permanent Mandate Commission, *passim*. It is stated in the Report for 1925 that there has been no question of imposing this system against the will of the natives.
[3] *Nos Richesses Soudanaises, loc. cit.*
[4] The obligation imposed on the native by the *prestation* system is legally limited to a maximum of ten to fifteen days' unpaid labour in a year on public works of local interest; but it seems to be taken for granted that any recruiting can be done in the name of *prestations*. The natives are unlikely to be aware of the exact legal position.

decreased the native food supply.[1] According to him, the division of the proceeds among the natives is purely theoretical.[2]

At present there appears to be a certain reaction towards methods which would involve less dislocation of native life and would commend themselves by their results sufficiently to make compulsion unnecessary.[3] Delavignette in *Les Paysans Noirs* describes his own success in substituting for the "collective" cultivation of ground-nuts under the direction of the chief individual production in the villages alongside the normal native crops. It is perhaps due to his efforts that there has been a reversal of policy in the Upper Volta, where the cultivation of food crops is now encouraged and the demands for labour and for cotton controlled,[4] while the attempt to substitute cotton suitable for the European market for the native-grown variety which provides the local population with clothes is not being pressed. In his interesting article *Sénégal et Niger* [5] already quoted, he advocates an economic policy adapted to the existing circumstances of the different tribes, in which some regions would not be expected to produce goods for the European market but might be encouraged to trade with their neighbours, while modern methods and new crops should be kept for peoples who were so situated as to be able to take advantage of them. He also suggests the development of native industries. It appears that this is the policy of the present Governor of A.O.F.[6]

Labour for Public Works.—The development of communica-

---

[1] This has been the case also in those parts of Senegal where the cultivation of ground-nuts has been pushed. M. J. Raffin, *loc. cit.*

[2] R. Delavignette, "Une Nouvelle Colonie", *L'Afrique Française*, September 1932, pp. 530. This writer characterizes the existing system as "une copie mégalomane des vieilles formes de l'exploitation mercantile". M. Henri Labouret is quoted by him as referring to "La tyrannie stérile des champs collectifs".

[3] Cf. Delavignette, *loc. cit.*, p. 532. "De même que la production exportable de la Haute-Volta n'eut jamais du être que le surplus de la production familiale consommée sur place, de même la migration de la main-d'œuvre doit représenter un surplus de population paysanne et s'écouler en courants organizés à l'indigène, protégés a l'européen."

[4] Delavignette, *loc. cit.*, p. 531.

[5] *Afrique Française*, August 1932, p. 481. See above, p. 195 *n*.

[6] "Le Gouverneur-général cherche à ajuster la production, non seulement aux besoins de la Métropole . . . mais encore à un meilleur 'standard' de vie locale." Delavignette, *loc. cit.*

tions is an indispensable complement to the development of production, and this too creates a great demand for labour. This is met in three ways. In the first place, under the *prestation* system, every adult native is liable to give ten to fifteen days' unpaid labour, according to the district, on work of public interest in the neighbourhood of his home.[1] This obligation strictly interpreted would not go far to satisfy the requirements of railway construction carried out often in very sparsely populated country, but it appears that it is not infrequent for a contingent of *prestataires* to be called up and then simply transported to the point where labour is required, however far distant this may be. Needless to say, labourers recruited in this way are not sent home at the end of ten days.

The second system is that of the "deuxième contingent", a system devised by M. Olivier in 1925 when Governor of Madagascar. This consists in utilizing for work of public importance those men found fit for military service who are not actually required for service with the troops. These M. Olivier organized into the Smotig or Service de Main-d'œuvre Obligatoire des Travaux d'Interêt Général. The members of this body are organized under military officers in exactly the same way as their comrades who are chosen by lot to serve under arms, and they are then drafted wherever their labour may be needed. The purposes for which it may be utilized include the requirements of private employers, since it is admitted that without government assistance in obtaining labour, nine-tenths of the European enterprises in Madagascar could not continue.[2]

The Smotig battalions live under the same conditions as military camps, recruits being allowed to bring their families with them, and it is claimed, doubtless with justice, that this represents a higher standard than is provided for the ordinary labourer. They are enrolled for two years' continuous service,

---

[1] Certain classes of natives are entitled to commute this obligation for a money payment. In A.E.F. women also were subject to it up till 1925.

[2] Olivier, *Six Ans de Politique Sociale au Madagascar*, p. 91. " In such circumstances ", M. Olivier asks, describing an urgent demand for extra labour in the almond-picking season, " A-t-on le droit de se refugier à l'abri d'un principe ? "

without leave, since the effect of a period of leave in the middle of a longer term of service was found to be demoralizing. The long period of continuous service is said to give them, "avec le gout du travail, la possibilité de vivre desormais une existence nouvelle", while at the same time they can enjoy "family life in an environment identical with that of the village ".[1] The number of recruits enrolled in the Smotig was 10,000 in 1929; in 1930 the organization of voluntary labour for public works along the same lines was begun.[2]

The same system was adopted in A.O.F. in 1926, but not used extensively, only 1500 labourers having been recruited in that way in 1928.[3] It could not be introduced in A.E.F., where the labour problem is most acute, because conscription itself has not been applied in that colony. It was the subject of acrimonious debate in the course of the discussions at Geneva of the International Convention on Forced Labour, when it was defended by M. Blaise Diagne, the native deputy from Senegal, on the grounds not only of the sovereign right of France to impose conscription in whatever form she pleased, but of the educational value of conscription itself to native peoples. The inclusion in the Convention of a clause limiting the employment of conscripts to purely military purposes caused France to refuse to ratify it and produced a small crop of publications by French writers in defence of the system of "obligatory"—as distinguished from "forced"—labour.

The Concession System.—The drain on native labour has been particularly heavy in A.E.F. owing to the very small population, to the programme of railway construction pursued by the Government, and to the demands of the Concession Companies which have been mentioned above. These Concessions in their original form represented a successful attempt to evade the Open Door clauses of the Berlin Act of 1885. The provision for equal treatment for the commerce of all nations does not specifically limit the disposal of property rights, and, although a corresponding regime in the Belgian

[1] Olivier, *op. cit.*, pp. 129, 131.
[2] See *Industrial and Labour Information*, January–March, 1931, pp. 370 ff.
[3] Mercier, *Le Travail Obligatoire dans les Colonies*, p. 65. For text of legislation see Journal Officiel de l'A.O.F., 1927. p. 431.

Congo evoked protests from Britain and America, France successfully took up the position that the grant to forty French companies of absolute rights to the wild products of one-third of the territory of A.E.F. was not contrary to her international obligations.

The original concessions were modified in 1910 with a view to reducing the areas covered by monopoly rights in the interests both of the native population and of European trade. Eleven original concessionaires merged in the Compagnie Forestière Sangha-Oubanghi, which accepted a new agreement giving it a monopoly for rubber only, with the right to acquire land which it had brought under cultivation. At the end of ten years the Company was to obtain freehold rights over all such land, and for the next ten years its rubber monopoly was to extend over ten times the area so acquired. At the end of that period, any further land brought under cultivation was to become the property of the Company, but the rubber monopoly was to expire. In 1920, however, a new agreement was concluded which prolonged the monopoly for fifteen years.

By this agreement the C.F.S.O. received, in addition to 10,000 hectares for the collection of wild palm fruit and 40,000 hectares for agriculture, the exclusive right to exploit rubber over an area extending right across the colony from the Cameroons to the Belgian frontier, with the possibility of a renewal of the concession in 1936 if, by that time, the annual export of rubber had reached 500 tons of plantation rubber, and the absolute right to receive in full possession four times the area cultivated during the preceding six years.[1] The area covered by the rubber monopoly was slightly increased by the incorporation of another company in 1925, though the maximum to be acquired in freehold was reduced in the 1920 agreement from 110,000 to 50,000 hectares.[2] Wild rubber is in fact the Company's main source of revenue, and while the natives are under no legal obligation to work for it, they have no other means of earning their tax money. The "agreed salary", even with the bonus, represents much less than the market price

[1] Text of Convention in Journal Officiel de l'A.E.F., 1921, pp. 166–9.
[2] J. O., 1925, p. 596.

of rubber, though estimates of the difference vary.[1] The Company is authorized to enter into contracts with the local natives—*les collectivités indigènes* is the phrase used—for the recruiting of labour for the collection of wild rubber or for the creation of "new agricultural enterprises". These contracts require administrative sanction. Only natives who pass a medical examination are to be employed in the forests: they are to be guaranteed suitable food and "a hygienic dwelling where they can live with their families". The Company is to maintain a hospital at its expense. The wages paid for the collection of rubber are to be supplemented by a bonus, whose amount will vary with the market price of rubber. According to M. André Gide, these provisions have remained a dead letter, and it is not difficult to estimate the value of a habitation suitable for family life in a fly-infested forest.[2]

In 1929 the contract of this Company was revised in such a way as slightly to increase the guarantees given to natives employed in its service.[3] A clause was inserted to the effect that natives who engage individually must receive the same treatment as those recruited by collective agreements, on pain of the same penalties for infraction. The minimum payment to natives is fixed at three francs the kilogram of dry rubber, while in the case of rubber which is not held to be dry the payment is not to be less than two-thirds of the rate paid for dry rubber. Instead of the former bonus in proportion to the price of rubber, the Company undertakes to pay a regular "abonnement" of 75 centimes per kilogram of dry rubber, from the funds of a "caisse de compensation" financed by contributions deducted from the proceeds of its sales of rubber and varying in amount proportionately with variations in the price. It may be noticed that the minimum price envisaged in the contract

---

[1] Gide quotes an official report stating that the price paid was two fr. the kilogram and adds that the market price in the neighbouring district was ten to twelve fr. These figures are disputed by M. Weber, the Director of the C.F.S.O., in a letter which he reproduces. See Appendix to *Le Retour du Tchad*. In a debate in the Chambre, the Company's price was given as 1200 fr. a ton as against a market price of 10,000 fr.

[2] See a medical report quoted in *Le Retour du Tchad*, p. 242. For the bonus, see *Voyage au Congo*, p. 103.

[3] See Journal Officiel de l'A.E.F., 1929, p. 914.

is eight francs.   If the funds of the "caisse de compensation" show a surplus, this is to be handed over to the administration to be utilized for the benefit of the Company's native labour. Restrictions are also imposed on the right of the Company to deduct from wages the value of the food ration allowed to its employees.   In 1927 the Company appeared to be counting on the renewal of its concession in 1936,[1] though the present state of the rubber market may have caused it to alter its views.

An agreement similar to that made with the C.F.S.O. was concluded in 1912 with the Société agricole forestière et industrielle pour l'Afrique, in which four of the original concessionaires were merged.   Those who insisted upon retaining their rights until the original grants expired were to receive at that date only land actually brought under cultivation.   At various times from 1918 onwards others of them agreed to an earlier termination of their monopoly in exchange for freehold rights over fixed areas, or to the restriction of their monopoly to specified products (usually timber and rubber).[2]   The remainder made new agreements by which they were entitled to erect oil mills at points selected by themselves within the limits of their old concessions, and were guaranteed against the establishment of other mills within a radius of thirty km. of each.

Smaller concessions continue to be accorded in large numbers and, though the agreements now made contain more effective guarantees of native rights than their predecessors, this does not alter the inevitable effect of the constantly increasing demand for labour.   The grant of two timber concessions in the Gabon in 1920 was followed a few months later by an Order fixing, for the Colony of Gabon, the proportion of the population which might be employed at one-third of the able-bodied males.   Despite this provision, the numbers in employment had by 1929 reached a point at which the Governor could write that "if the withdrawal of men from certain districts continued, there would be a risk of famine in the near future"

[1] Statement in *l'Information* of November 29, 1927, quoted by Gide, *Le Retour du Tchad*, p. 240.
[2] Girault, *Colonization et Législation Coloniale*, vol. III, pp. 153 ff.

From that date the numbers whose recruiting is authorized—which do not account of course for all the natives employed—have been considerably reduced.[1] In 1930 the Governor General, M. Antonetti, in his opening speech to the Conseil de Gouvernement, suggested the transformation of the Congo "in a future nearer than is often supposed" into a colony of settlement. In the same speech he repudiated the idea of recourse to compulsion in order to provide labour for private purposes, only to add that compulsory labour on plantations must be exempt from this condemnation since a plantation is "a school where the well-fed labour can learn profitable forms of cultivation at his employer's expense".[2] Since 1923 the total number of natives who may be recruited throughout the Congo, with the areas open to recruiting, have been prescribed at the beginning of each year by the Lieutenant Governors of the four colonies. The percentage estimated as available, and the definition of the term "recruit", vary in the different Colonies.[3]

The other serious drain on the labour resources of the Federation was caused by the construction of the Congo-Ocean Railway, an enterprise whose history, as revealed in the debate on an interpellation in the Chambre, seems almost too fantastic to be credible. Yet the facts alleged were not denied by the Minister for the Colonies. The object of this railway, which was completed in 1934, was to link up the port of Pointe-Noire with Brazzaville on the Congo and free French exports from dependence on the overcrowded Belgian line from Kinshasa to Matadi. It runs through the mountainous and unhealthy region of Mayumbe, where construction is particularly difficult and population particularly sparse. A contract was made in 1921 for its construction with a company known as the Société des Batignolles, in which the Government undertook to provide a permanent labour force of 8000 and to pay an indemnity proportionate to the number by which those

[1] *Report on the Recruiting of Labour*, International Labour Office, 1935, p. 72. See Appendix to this chapter for statistics of authorized recruiting in A.E.F.

[2] Journal Officiel de l'A.E.F., pp. 972–3.

[3] See Appendix for details.

actually in employment fell short of this total.[1] It is asserted that this indemnity has been up till now the only source of revenue for the company. No stipulations of any kind were made with regard to the use of machinery in the construction work. Very little progress was, in fact, made till 1925, when credits for the purpose were voted by the Chamber and an accelerated programme was begun, with a view to the completion of the line in 1930.[2] Work was begun at various points, a method which necessitated the construction of a road parallel with the railway. Labour had to be recruited from the far north of the territory, where climatic conditions were entirely different. No provision whatever was made for the transport of the labourers, who made the journey on foot, sometimes taking as much as a year on the way. The mortality among them was appalling, reaching in one contingent the figure of 94 per cent.

The difficulty of obtaining labour soon became extreme and any pretence that volunteers could be expected to offer their services was abandoned. The administration continued, however, to regard the needs of the railway as of paramount importance, and instructions to subordinate officials, quoted in the Chambre,[3] contain orders to conscript the necessary numbers despite "les conséquences regrettables qui doivent fatalement en resulter". One of these consequences was a widespread revolt in 1928 in the Ubangi-Chari region in the north, which cannot really be explained away as the work of the subversive "féticheurs" who are such convenient scapegoats.

Successive discussions in the Chambre elicited statements that the agreement with the Batignolles Company has been revised so as to reduce the guaranteed contingent of labour first in 1927 to 4000 and then in 1930 to 2000, while a series of decrees were passed in 1928 and 1929 regulating conditions on the journey and in labour camps, which have led to a

[1] See Débats Parlementaires, Chambre, June 14, 1929. The number estimated as necessary by the Governor-General of A.E.F. in 1925 was 10,000–15,000. Journal Officiel de la République Française, 1927, p. 8177.
[2] L'Afrique Française, June 1925, p. 290 ; Mercier, Travail Obligatoire, p. 53.
[3] Débats Parlementaires, Chambre, November 23, 1927.

decrease in the death-rate, and the company was given a bonus in proportion to the quantity of machinery used.[1] In 1929 a contingent of Chinese coolies was introduced, who were at first said to be more satisfactory than local labour,[2] but by the following year it was admitted that they "had not given the desired results".

This is an extreme case which has obtained a certain notoriety. Its real significance lies much less in those aspects of it which aroused public sentiment by their enormity than in those which are typical of the whole system. The drain on the energies of the people for work which brings them no apparent advantage, on their health in long migrations to unaccustomed climates and new types of heavy physical effort in strange conditions, leads everywhere to constant emigration to neighbouring territories, to rapid depopulation and sporadic revolt. Delavignette writes of the combined effect of plantations and railway development on the Upper Volta: "Ce fameux réservoir de la main-d'œuvre—avec quelle hâte s'est-on empressé de le vider." According to his estimates 93,000 men were removed from their homes in this region during the ten years preceding 1932, while every year 80,000 went to the Gold Coast to earn better wages than they could obtain in French territory.[3] The mortality among labourers employed on the Central Cameroons railway was commented upon by the Permanent Mandates Commission, who secured an improvement in health conditions.[4] This railway employed an average of 6000 workers during the period 1922–27. It was then announced that a period of rest was necessary, and that recruiting would be discontinued till 1939.[5] But by 1931 the continuation of the

[1] Cf. Mercier, *Le Travail Obligatoire dans les Colonies*, pp. 53–7. It was asserted in the Chambre (June 14, 1929) that these machines are simply allowed to rust.

[2] Débats Parlementaires, Chambre, December 5, 1928. It was stated in November 1930 that 75 per cent. of the labour employed on the railway was voluntary. Antonetti in Conseil de Gouvernement, J. O., 1930, p. 968; 1932, p. 10.

[3] *Une Nouvelle Colonie, loc. cit.*, p. 530.

[4] This railway was built by compulsory labour imposed in accordance with a decree of 1924 as a penalty for "l'insoumission aux réquisitions de l'administration pour travaux publics essentiels". Mercier, *Le Travail Obligatoire dans les Colonies*, p. 43.

[5] International Labour Office Report, *The Recruiting of Labour*, p. 70.

railway was under discussion, the view being held that in the meantime a new generation of labourers had grown up; however, financial considerations have made it impossible to begin this new work yet.[1] M. André Gide, whose book bears all the appearance of a sober record of things seen, describes his meeting in the Cameroons with natives who had fled from their villages to avoid conscription for road work, and in the Ubangi region seeing large areas of native crops unharvested owing to the absence of the men from their villages.[2] R. Mercier, one of the advocates of the compulsory system, states that the public works carried out in A.O.F.—railway construction, the development of harbours and irrigation—require a growing number of labourers who must be brought from great distances.[3]

Regulations on the Recruiting of Labour.—The compulsory recruiting of labour, other than that authorized by the *prestation* and Smotig systems, is regulated by legislation applicable to all Colonies, which makes the highest authority in the Colony responsible for the annual programme of public works and for the allocation to different areas of their quotas of labour. The decree of 1930, which constitutes the existing law, states that recourse to compulsion is a temporary measure, but lays down no time-limit.[4] It prohibits recourse to compulsion for the benefit of private enterprise. The only condition laid down as necessary to justify the recourse to compulsion is the absence of voluntary labour. The imposition of compulsory cultivation for educational purposes is expressly authorized; the method by which it is carried out is still left to the individual initiative of administrative officers.

The principles to be followed in the recruiting of labour were laid down in a circular of general application issued in 1931, after discussions in the Chambre in connection with a large loan which was raised in 1930 for colonial development.

---

[1] Permanent Mandates Commission, Session 21, p. 135.
[2] *Le Retour du Tchad*, p. 65 ; *Voyage au Congo*, p. 104.
[3] Mercier, *Le Travail Obligatoire dans les Colonies*, p. 44.
[4] The Geneva Convention of the same year provided for a further discussion five years from its entry into force with a view to the complete abolition of compulsion. For a comparison of the terms of the Decree with those of the Convention, see *Industrial and Labour Information*, October–December 1930, p. 241.

Their tenor is inspired in part by the conclusions of the Commission on Labour in the Belgian Congo which reported in 1925 on the dangers of removing from their homes a large proportion of the able-bodied males, though the proportion which they estimate as available is much larger than that recommended by the Belgian Commission.[1] The circular instructs local authorities to refuse authorization for any new works unless the programme includes "a plan (to·be approved by them) for the demographic protection of the communities from which the workers were to be drawn". This plan must take into consideration the requirements of native food-crops and native production for sale. The limitation of recruiting to 50 per cent. of the males between 20 and 45 is held to be in principle sufficient to achieve this end. In addition regard is to be had to the labour requirements of local employers. Sleeping sickness areas are to be closed to recruiting. In the selection of individuals the maintenance of family life is to be sought by the exemption of fathers whose children are dependent upon their work at home for subsistence. Despite the success claimed for the "natural" living conditions of the Smotig system, these instructions recommend the granting of fairly frequent leave to married workers rather than measures to enable wives to accompany their husbands.[2]

As far as A.O.F. is concerned the most recent legislation on recruiting suggests that the Smotig system has not been found satisfactory there, since it provides a different basis for the systematic organization of the labour supply for public works. An Order of February 18, 1933, lays down that the programme for each year is to be submitted in advance to the Governor General by the various Lieutenant Governors, with a statement of the labour required, the amount of compulsory labour available, and the estimated voluntary supply. On this basis the Governor General fixes the quota of compulsory labour to be contributed for each colony. The maximum period for which a man can be requisitioned in a single year is six months,

---

[1] See below, p. 233.
[2] Summary from *Report on the Recruiting of Labour*, International Labour Office, 1935, p. 66.

including the time spent on the journey, and proof of having completed six months' employment exempts him for the next five years. This exemption does not appear to apply to time spent in compulsory cultivation.

Native Administration.—The French administration, like all others, has been driven by necessity to utilize the services of subordinate native officials. These officials are called chiefs; but until quite recently there has been little attempt to select for the position persons whose authority is traditionally recognized, and none at all to develop the exercise of their authority along traditional lines. A deliberate policy of suppressing those native authorities who were powerful enough to constitute a potential danger to French authority, combined with a failure to recognize the existence of any authority in tribes which were not highly centralized, and with the general indifference to the fate of the indigenous civilization, have made any idea of Indirect Rule in the Nigerian sense inconceivable. The tendency of the French administration to think in terms of grand general schemes, applicable to a whole federation of colonies simultaneously, militates equally against any recognition of local differences of culture.

While there were advocates of the recognition of native authorities as long ago as 1909, their views have so far prevailed only to the extent that a traditional chief possessing the qualifications regarded as essential would be appointed to authority in preference to another candidate. Moreover, once appointed, he would be as much liable as any other official to be moved from place to place and even set in authority over an alien people.[1] The qualifications desired are literacy, ability in accounting, loyalty, assiduity in carrying out official orders. M. Angoulvant's method of encouraging cocoa cultivation by rewarding those chiefs who organized it among their subjects has been mentioned; more recently the Decree of December 1931 regulating recruiting for the Congo-Ocean

[1] A " School for the Sons of Chiefs " is not, as the British reader might suppose, an institution for educating future chiefs to govern their own people but a training ground for civil servants, who concentrate on the study of French law. When their training is over, they become clerks in Government offices, and are appointed to chieftainships as vacancies occur.

Railway expressly states that chiefs are to be rewarded for their success in furnishing labour.[1]

It is obvious that the new orientation of native life which European government produces calls for different qualities in the native chief than were expected of him in the days of inter-tribal warfare. It is obvious too that no administration would or could maintain in office a chief who persistently obstructed its policy, and that all colonial governments have introduced into native life changes which were unwelcome at the outset. This is true irrespective of the value to native society of these changes. That in the case of some of the measures introduced into French colonies this value may appear doubtful, is irrelevant to the essential weakness of their system of administration—that it makes no attempt to make the novelties palatable by enlisting on their side the persons whose authority carries weight among the natives concerned. It is true that to utilize traditional native authorities as the instruments of a policy which must be detrimental to native society would be in the long run equally fatal to native respect for such authority. Such measures as the large-scale recruiting of labour can in any case only be achieved by force and·will be welcomed no more readily if it is the traditional chief who carries out the coercion. But the appointment of aliens or persons with no recognized claim to command as " intermédiaires " — the customary French word — of the European government can only arouse unnecessary resentment and mistrust of the most salutary measures. Moreover, the " chiefs " have no judicial powers, so that their function is reduced to that of a mouthpiece for orders emanating from outside; and they receive a rebate on taxes collected, which, in some cases, constitutes their sole income.[2]

Such a case as has been made for the recognition of native authorities has rested entirely on the argument that the orders of the Government will be more readily obeyed if given through the mouth of one with a right to command. The idea of a native ruler exercising any kind of independent initiative seems

[1] *Industrial and Labour Information*, April–June 1932, p. 22.
[2] See Buell, *op. cit.*, vol. I, p. 991.

to be alien to the conception of most French colonial authorities. An official circular of A.O.F. in 1917, advocating the reinstatement with due ceremony of traditional chiefs wheresoever they could be discovered, continues: "They have no power of their own of any kind. There are not two authorities, French and native; there is only one".[1] On the other hand, M. Carde, Governor General of A.O.F., in addressing the Conseil du Gouvernement in 1929, said: "Les conseillers . . . prennent même l'initiative de suggestions, parfois très heureuses, que l'administrateur retient avec le plus grand interêt". But even this is a long way from any idea of local autonomy. In the same speech, M. Carde alluded to the mistakes which had often been made through the substitution of educated natives for traditional chiefs who were believed to be inefficient, but what he advocates is to only select the most suitable person among "those who can claim to rule with the consent of the population ".[2]

M. Antonetti in his first speech as Governor General of A.E.F. announced as part of his policy "the reconstruction of traditional groups".[3] More recently, M. Brévié, the present governor of A.O.F., in a circular to administrators, has called for more patience in finding out the native authority and retaining him in power. He writes in terms which presuppose the permanent residence of the native chief among his own tribe, and deprecates the hasty deposition of a recognized authority for offences against the ·Government, recommending instead temporary suppression. But he stresses the need for "rigorous supervision", and regards the knowledge that his every action is being followed by the Government as the main motive for satisfactory conduct by the chief.[4]

Where this is the basic theory of the relation between native and European authority, one cannot expect to find native councils developed as organs of local government. Such councils have been part of the administrative structure of

---

[1] Quoted in Buell, *op. cit.* Vol. I, p. 997.
[2] Journal Officiel, A.O.F., 1929, p. 1019.
[3] J. O. de l'A.E.F., 1929, p. 820.
[4] " Le sentiment d'être étroitement surveillés sera le plus efficace sauvegarde contre les mauvaises tentatives." Circulaires sur la Politique et l'Administration indigènes. Gorée, 1932.

A.O.F. since 1919. Their functions, however, are strictly parallel with those of the native chiefs. The aim of their establishment is stated to be the "formation of an *élite* which will later be able to co-operate more closely and in a more personal manner in the economic and financial life of the Colony".[1] They are a means of bringing a slightly larger number of people into personal touch with the French official —of enabling a larger audience to hear his views from his own lips. They are to consist of from eight to sixteen members, chosen by the chiefs and notables of the district for a period of three years, and to meet at least once annually under the presidency of the administrator of the district. They must be consulted in all matters relating to taxation, *prestations* and programmes of local public works.[2] But given the general attitude of the administration towards native authorities, it is difficult to see how this consultation can be more than a formality. There is no question of proposals emanating from the native members of the council, of any power of local legislation, still less the administration of a local budget. Native society is always to be refashioned from without, not from within; and the establishment of local councils does not affect this principle. Similarly, the constitution, announced in 1931, of a central native council for each colony, consisting of delegates from the local councils with consultative powers, is recommended not only as a means of "éclairer notre action" but because "Là encore, les Chefs des Colonies auront une excellente occasion de former des chefs".[3]

The circular in which M. Brévié elaborates this policy is interesting as showing a real attempt to make of the native administration an instrument for the representation of the native point of view. He proposes to establish native councils in each administrative area—"important villages, cantons, provinces"—consisting of a chief and a body of notables who will "each bring to the superior organ the support of their knowledge, their advice and their authority when decisions have to

[1] Statement by Minister for the Colonies, quoted in Buell, *op. cit.*, vol. I, p. 999.
[2] Decree of June 16, 1919, J. O., p. 410.
[3] Brévié, address to Conseil de Gouvernement, J. O., 1931, p. 968.

be taken or carried out". The village council is to consist of heads of families, the council of the canton of village chiefs, and so on. But these councils are to have no executive authority; they may merely present resolutions (*avis et vœux*) to the European administration. The experiment is an interesting one, but it could hardly be described as a great step in the direction either of local autonomy or of the re-establishment of native authority. Nor can the establishment in 1925 of elected native Councils in Togoland be said to serve the latter purpose, though reports to the Mandates Commission stress the active part taken by their members in the discussion of legislation.[1]

Education.—The system of education is characterized by a sharp distinction between the provision meted out to the *élite* and that reserved for the masses—a distinction which will commend itself to many educationists familiar with tropical countries where the training given by the European school equips the pupils only for professions in urban centres which many of them have no hope of entering. The aim of the system, however, is not so much to improve native life as to inculcate an appreciation of "civilization" and the qualities required of loyal French subjects. Thus a knowledge of French is the first essential, "pour assurer la cohésion de notre empire". M. Georges Hardy, the Director of the Ecole Coloniale, in a very complete exposition of the French theory of native education,[2] defines the aim of the higher schools as "amener [l'indigène] à l'intelligence de notre œuvre", and writes of the instruction of future native officials: "Il faut qu'ils soient parfaitement au courant de nos intentions civilisatrices". Of the rest he says, "Nos autres écoles ont pour objet d'attacher les elèves au sol et de les accoutumer au travail manuel ou de preparer les agents pour certains services techniques", and again, "Préparer à la France des sujets loyaux et reconnaissants". Every subject is presented in the light of its relation to the aims of French policy. History is taught so as to justify the French occupation of the territory. Geography, while it serves to widen the mental horizon and

[1] Cf. Report to P.M.C., 1924. [2] *Une Conquête Morale.*

thus destroy ignorance and superstition, is also of value because the French policy of economic development will become more acceptable when its geographical basis is understood. This recognition of the necessity of relating the subjects taught to the native environment is very valuable. More work has been done in providing suitable textbooks, in which school subjects are presented through the medium of familiar experiences, than in most other African territories.

In its fundamental principle of directing village education exclusively to subjects which will be of use in village life, French policy has shown an admirable independence of thought, but the practical application of the theory is impaired by the necessity of creating loyal citizens and of teaching the French language to this end. M. Hardy argues that this is necessary in view of the impossibility of establishing a *lingua franca*; and his point of view has its advantages for the teacher and the official, who are exempt from the necessity of learning any native language. French is taught by the direct method, and other subjects begin to be added when the pupil has a sufficient vocabulary. M. Brévié's circulars, pointing out the time that has to be wasted under this system before any information of practical value is imparted, represent the first reaction against it.

The underlying principle of the system is that the largest possible number of people should be brought into contact with the essential aims of French civilization, though only a minority are expected to be sufficiently intelligent to assimilate much learning. The instruction given to the minority comprises simple French, the three R's (arithmetic being made the basis for the inculcation of thrift), hygiene and morality. "Il faut réformer les mœurs", says M. Hardy, "de fond en comble". The system established in 1926 in A.E.F. contemplates only a year's schooling for those pupils who have no hope of being able to proceed to higher education. In this year they are taught spoken French, mental arithmetic and hygiene. Those who are found worthy to proceed further spend two or three years on the three R's, after which they are ready to go on to a "regional school", and thence to the Ecole Primaire

Supérieure at Brazzaville, where they can be trained for crafts or professions.[1]

In A.O.F. the village schools give a course of three or four years, but the general principles governing the curriculum are the same. Where it is necessary to restrict the numbers from lack of personnel, much emphasis is laid on the importance of educating the children of chiefs, whose prestige will help to advertise the advantages of civilization.[2] There should be one regional school for each "cercle"; there are 115 such divisions. In 1927 there were seventy-eight regional schools and eight "écoles supérieures."

The aim of the system can be summed up in the phrase of M. Carde: "Instruire la masse et dégager l'élite".[3] But here, as in every other aspect of French policy, it is only the *élite* who are really considered, and they are only considered from the point of view of detaching them from their own culture and incorporating them into another. That they will be incorporated and not find themselves barred from entry into European society seems certain; but what effect can that have upon the mass who will always remain the vast majority? Their leaders are not allowed to lead them but removed to another world, and the creation of that gulf between the educated and uneducated native which other colonial administrations are now deploring and seeking to bridge remains to French policy a desirable end. Certainly the education given to the masses is hardly of a type to make them discontented with their lot as agriculturists, but it is difficult to see how it is likely to do much to improve that lot.

A different attitude towards native education began to be apparent with the appointment of M. Brévié as Governor General of A.O.F. In his address to the Conseil du Gouvernement in 1931 he said: "Il s'agit de faire évoluer la société indigène dans son cadre . . . en se dégageant, sans bruit et sans trouble, de ses seules traditions trop tyranniques". The

---

[1] Gamache, *Renseignements Coloniaux*, 1928, pp. 756 ff.; and O. Nilambé, " L'Enseignement en A.E.F.", *Revue d'Afrique*, November–December 1928, pp. 32 ff.
[2] Cf. Circulaire sur l'enseignement, J. O., 1929, p. 69.
[3] Quoted in Guy, *Afrique Occidentale Française*, p. 109

programme of village education which he outlined resembles that indicated by Georges Hardy in *Une Conquête Morale*, but goes far beyond the meagre curriculum at present considered sufficient for the requirements of the mass, and aims at a real evolution of native life. While remaining faithful to the teaching of French, he urged the necessity of using the native language to convey that elementary practical instruction which is in his view important.[1]

In accordance with these principles the whole educational system of the Federation is being reorganized. Vernacular textbooks are being prepared for elementary village education. A new orientation is being given also to the schools of the next grade ("préparatoires") which previously had served simply as feeders for the Regional Schools with their literary programme.[2] They are now to concentrate on hygiene, agriculture,

[1] J. O. de l'A.O.F., 1931, p. 972. "Attendrons-nous qu'ils connaissent suffisamment le Français pour leur divulguer que l'anophile véhicule le paludisme ? "

[2] H. Labouret, " L'Education des Masses en A.O.F.", *Africa*, January 1935.

FIGURES OF NATIVES WHOSE RECRUITMENT IS AUTHORIZED IN THE FOUR COLONIES OF A.E.F. FOR THE YEARS 1924–1933

Year	Gabun	Moyen-Congo	Ubangi-Chari [1]	Tchad
1924	8,000	32,871	4,333	9,575
1925	7,200 [2]	29,165	8,118	9,575
1926	7,750	figures not given	8,318	9,575
1927	{ 8,300 away from home [3] { 2,800 for work in locality	22,450	5 per cent of adult males	5,100
1928	{ 5,000 away from home { 200 for work in locality	9,300	5 per cent of adult males	5,100
1929	{ 4,500 { 3,300	5,750	4,650	5,450
1930	{ 3,800 { 33,000	figures not given	15,200	4,950
1931	{ 2,800 { 3,700	3,510 [4]	9,700	4,950 [5]
1932	{ 2,800 { 3,700	2,450	6,500	4,950
1933	{ 2,500 { 3,700	2,530	5,150	5,000

For footnotes to Table see facing page.

with the senior administrative official as chairman; this Committee is to make periodic inspections.

The centres are being established for purposes of supervision near administrative headquarters — a policy criticized by M. Marzorati, a former Governor of the Eastern Province, who would have preferred to see them placed near important lines of communication where they could profitably grow export crops.[1]

The decree itself does not indicate what is expected to be the basis of economic life in these centres. The provision regarding passes makes it clear that some of their members will be expected to earn their living as wage-labourers, and since they are *ex hypothesi* men who have engaged in this work and become unwilling to return to tribal life, there is no hardship in this assumption.

The centres are to be established within reasonable distance of industrial neighbourhoods with a view to obviating the disadvantages of the long journey to and from work. To a certain degree they represent an extension of the policy pursued by the Union Minière of establishing labour villages in the immediate vicinity of the mines, and the date of the decree may indicate that they have been devised as a means of providing for the large numbers of natives accustomed to wage-earning who have been thrown out of employment by the slump. If these colonies are given constructive guidance in the utilization of such education and technical skill as their members may have learnt at the mines, and if they are enabled to become economically self-supporting, their creation may prove the best solution yet devised for the problem which industrial Africa is now everywhere having to face—but when a new demand for labour arises they may not prove such rich sources as might have been expected. If the "extra-customary centres" are simply left to work out their own salvation in complete dependence upon the European demand for labour, they will be merely one more way of dealing with a difficulty by putting it out of sight. The experiment is still too new for estimates of its effects to be profitably made.

[1] Article in *Revue de l'Institut de Sociologie*, quoted *Congo*, December 1931, pp. 710–11.

CHAPTER VI

OUTLINE OF PORTUGUESE POLICY

DESPITE the extreme scarcity of documentation on the subject it seems impossible to leave out of account altogether, in a study of this kind, a Power which controls so large an area of African territory as Portugal. I propose therefore to give a summary of legislation relevant to native policy, with the reminder that legislative texts without any evidence as to administrative practice can only present a very incomplete picture.

The principal African possessions of Portugal are Angola, with an area of 487,788 square miles, a considerable portion of which is above the 4000 feet level, a native population of some 3,000,000 and a European of 40,000, and Mozambique, whose area is 299,973 square miles, native population 4,000,000, European 35,000. In the latter colony two chartered companies, the Mozambique and Niassa Companies, exercise over the areas covered by their charters administrative powers, including the right to tax the native population and to impose labour obligations upon it; but the Colonial Charter which is part of the new Portuguese Constitution of 1933 provides for the transfer of these powers to the State as soon as this can be effected by agreement with the Companies. Each of these Colonies has a Legislative Council with five elected unofficial members.[1]

Portugal also controls the cocoa islands of San Thome and Principe, and Portuguese Guinea, with an area of 13,944 square miles and a population of 365,000.

The Dignity of Labour.—The general aim of Portuguese native policy appears to be a Europeanization even more thorough-going, if possible, than that attempted by the French

---

[1] Colonial Charter, 1933, Section 53.

in their colonies. The Colonial Charter lays down specifically that it is the duty of all Europeans in touch with the native population to foster their attachment to "the Portuguese motherland" and the spread of the Portuguese language. The inculcation of the dignity of labour is regarded, here as elsewhere, as one of the most important elements in the civilizing process. Portuguese views on this subject were defined by General Freire d'Andrade in a controversy with Lord Lugard as to the attitude with regard to native labour which should be taken up by the Permanent Mandates Commission:

"If [the native] attempts to go on living under his present conditions, if he prefers his former habits of ease and idleness, then the Mandatory must intervene and give him to understand that work is a law of nature and that, in communities which hope to prosper, idleness is a punishable offence." [1]

In accordance with these principles, the principle of the "obligation to labour" was given legal force by a decree of 1911 and re-affirmed in the General Native Labour Regulations of 1914.[2] The obligation was deemed to have been met by natives possessing property "the income from which secures them sufficient means of subsistence", or habitually engaged in agriculture, commerce or any profession, and by those who had worked for wages for three months in the year. Those who failed to comply with it were offered work by the local authorities, and, if they refused it, could be allotted to private employers, who must be of good character, for periods varying from three months to one year. A decree of 1921, providing that no native shall be compelled to work without payment even for the State, applies to work of this kind. Anyone who still refused was held guilty of vagrancy, and on conviction was sentenced to "correctional" labour, on public works, rewarded only by food and clothing, for a period of from eight to 300 days. This penalty was also imposed for breach of contract.

[1] Permanent Mandates Commission, Session 7, p. 200.
[2] See International Labour Office Report, *Forced Labour*, 1929, pp. 199 ff.

Natives who declare themselves unable to pay their taxes are offered work as an alternative. Those who merely default are required to work for a period equivalent to double the tax, while those who refuse to do so may be sentenced to six months' correctional labour.[1]

Forced labour imposed merely on the ground of vagrancy has since 1926 been authorized only for urgent public works, but penal labour was employed on private enterprises till 1928. The General Decree on Native Labour of that year abolishes the "obligation to labour", substituting for it the affirmation of a moral principle, so that correctional labour cannot now be employed for mere idleness. It continues to be imposed for breach of contract or non-payment of tax, but may now be employed only on public works. The usual obligation of labour on work of local interest exists, but in the case of all except "the smallest village works" the labour is paid and the obligation can be commuted.

In Mozambique the Niassa Company enacted in 1922 that its officials might forcibly recruit natives who "refuse to carry out the work provided in their contracts". The provision that natives who voluntarily undertake labour for a period of at least three months shall receive five per cent. above the current rate of wages indicates that they are in the minority.[2]

The Prazo System.—In the Zambezi region of Mozambique the *prazo* system obtains. This is a relic of the early days of Portuguese occupation, when individual colonists, practically independent of any central government, exercised over the native population what they took to be the rights of their former chiefs. The land in question is now held to be State property for which the occupiers pay rent. They are responsible for the collection of tax, of which they receive 30 per cent,[3] and till at any rate fairly recently the native inhabitants were required to render tribute and services to their masters. In 1919 the minimum period of labour was fixed by decree at 180 days in the year, but it was stated in 1925 that few natives

[1] Angola Law on Native Taxes, June 4, 1931.
[2] I.L.O. Report, cited.
[3] Portuguese East Africa, *Admiralty Handbook*, p. 145.

work more than three months in the year, as a rule in separate periods of a month at a time. There is no legal restriction on the movement of natives from one *prazo* to another or from *prazo* to State lands.[1] Both these systems appear to have been legally abolished by the Native Labour Code of 1928.

The Colonial Charter of 1933.—The new Colonial Charter of 1933 abrogates all agreements whereby the State is obliged to furnish labour for private employers, or the inhabitants of any area are compelled to give their services (Article 243). The sole function of the administration in connection with labour contracts is a supervisory one (Art. 244); they are to see that they are freely entered into and duly carried out (General Decree on Labour, 1928, Art. 95). The contract is limited to two years of employment within the colony where the labourer resides and three years outside (General Decree on Labour, Art. 123). In case of urgent necessity an employer may conclude contracts without administrative supervision; this is also allowed in the case of workers living near the place of employment who "spontaneously present themselves" (*ibid.*, Arts. 128–9). The duration of such contracts is limited to one year (Art. 131). On re-engagement a native must receive a wage increase of ten per cent. (Art. 159). The period of the contract can be prolonged at the request of the employee, or in exceptional cases where its termination would involve serious dislocation in the enterprise on which they are engaged; subordinate officials may authorize a prolongation for one month, senior officials for two months if the natives were recruited in the same colony, three if they come from abroad (Art. 160).

Breaches of contract liable to penal sanction are, on the employee's part: selling the products of the farm, disturbing order and discipline, absence without leave, habitual drunkenness, immoral acts, refusal to work, disobedience to instructions, theft and wilful damage to property (Art. 352). On that of the employer, making fictitious contracts in order to exempt natives from obligations or prevent them from undertaking other employment; advancing sums to be repaid in labour; giving credit in return for labour; lending money at interest;

[1] I.L.O. Report, cited, pp. 215–6.

concluding contracts which do not contain the obligations upon the employer stipulated by Government; engaging men already bound by another contract; engaging natives on their way to or from work; preventing natives from laying their grievances before the authorities; imposing excessive tasks; exceeding the regulation hours of work (nine per day); or employing natives on other work than that for which they were engaged (Arts. 339, 347).

Conscription.—The natives of the Portuguese colonies are liable to conscription, the period of service being two years for "volunteers and recruits", five years for "contraints et réfractaires", seven for deserters (Decree of January 9, 1931, Art. 33). "Réfractaires" include both persons who have tried to evade their military obligations and those who "will not procure their subsistence by their own efforts" (Art. 55). The term of service may be reduced as a reward for proficiency in learning Portuguese (Art. 64). In calculating the quota of conscripts assigned to each district the authorities are to take into account the density and average physical fitness of the local population, the degree of economic development, and "any abnormal events which might suggest the desirability of heavy demands or the reverse" (Art. 45). In Angola not more than about 2000 men are called up each year.[1]

Plans for Colonization.—Economic development in Mozambique is based on plantation labour. In Angola native production is regarded as important, but colonization is also encouraged. The proposal that the colony should be transferred to Germany, first mooted in 1913 and now sometimes referred to in connection with Germany's demand for a mandate, has produced a determination to intensify its Portuguese character by the encouragement of colonization on a large scale. A decree of March 9, 1928, provides for a survey of the territory with a view to the execution of a comprehensive plan of large-scale settlement. The plan provides not only for grants of land and subsidies to individual settlers but for a system of "collective colonization" in which groups of peasants will be transported from Portugal and settled in villages prepared

[1] I.L.O. Report, cited, footnote, p. 121.

to receive them. "The new Portuguese society of Angola will be solidly organized on a basis of labouring masses with a bourgeoisie represented by ' single or individual ' colonists."

To this end the areas selected for colonization are to be divided into zones, in each of which will be laid out ten hamlets of from 1000 to 5000 hectares in extent, with irrigation works, houses of a type to which the colonists are accustomed, shops, accommodation for carpenters, smiths, bricklayers, etc. (Art. 11).

Each hamlet is to be inhabited by a group of families from the same region in Portugal, their destination being determined on the "solid and indisputable biophysical basis" of the different aptitudes of the various sections of the population. The families are to be selected after a careful scrutiny of their "morphological, psychological, physiological and moral qualities". At least one member of each must be literate. Preference will be given to large families with experience of farming (Art. 5). On arrival they will find awaiting them a house with a surveyed allotment of 100 hectares, one-quarter of which will have been cleared and planted, such implements as are necessary for the cultivation of this area, stock sufficient for ploughing and for breeding on the scale considered necessary by the authorities, and a small fund of money to carry them through the first year (Art. 17). Of these benefits the house, the water supply and the clearing of the ground are free gifts from the State; the rest are to be repaid (Art. 19). A *mission rurale* is to be attached to each district, which will be responsible for the building of schools and dispensaries, experimental farms, transforming factories, etc., and for giving advice to the colonists on the special problems of tropical agriculture and in their relations with the natives (Art. 63). Private companies may also organize collective colonization, though they may not sell land to individuals (Art. 105). They may be subsidized by the State and given exemption for the first ten years from customs duties on seed, stock and machinery (Art. 106).

Individual colonists must possess capital, be married and have children, and will be assisted by subsidies (Arts. 34-6).

Officials with 15 years' service may retire on half-pay and become colonists (Arts. 47–50). The delimitation of zones does not seem as yet to have been carried very far.

Outside the "zones of colonization" concessions are granted on terms regulated by a decree of April 22, 1932. On the plateaux of Malange, Benguella and Huila the maximum area which can be granted is 15,000 hectares, elsewhere 30,000 (Arts. 4–5). Concessions of over 15,000 hectares are granted for seventy years (Art. 12).

In each case they are divided into lots of one-tenth of the possible maximum. The minimum initial rent is three escudos, the maximum thirty, to be increased by 25 per cent. every ten years (Art. 11).

Native Land Tenure.—Native rights are to be respected (Art. 8), a principle which is reaffirmed in the Colonial Charter. Decrees of 1918 for Mozambique and 1919 for Angola establish two categories of native lands; reserves, or land delimited by the Governor for the exclusive use of natives and "other land occupied by natives". In the reserves no individual tenure is recognized; outside a native may at his own request be given a title to land which he actually occupies and cultivates. He can transmit this land to his heirs but cannot otherwise dispose of it, and his title expires if he leaves it uncultivated for more than a year. He cannot be expropriated without compensation. The Inspector General of Colonial Administration criticizes these provisions on the ground that they give the native no greater protection than is implicit in the general principle of respect for native rights. As a means of developing initiative in the native cultivator and checking shifting cultivation he recommends the grant of freehold rights on terms similar to those offered by the Mozambique Company in the *prazos*, where title may be acquired after twenty years' uninterrupted cultivation. In 1932 the Company established a system whereby holdings are offered to natives desirous of growing export crops approved by the authorities. The area offered is one hectare plus an additional half hectare for each wife or adult son. Seed is to be given to natives who cannot otherwise obtain it, in return for the same quantity of seed, plus 5 per cent., after the harvest. Twenty-four months' continuous failure to cultivate renders the owner liable to a penalty.

General Rights of Natives.—The general rights of the native population are laid down in a decree of October 23, 1926, promulgated, apparently with immaterial amendments, on February 6, 1929, on the Status of Natives, applicable to Portuguese Guinea, Angola, and Mozambique. The main principles which it lays down are the freedom of labour and of contract, the restrictions already mentioned on the use of penal and compulsory labour, the right of natives to free education and to the expenditure in their interests of a fixed proportion of revenue. Native political institutions are to be preserved and developed (Art. 6). Native law is to be codified along broad lines, as many different codes being drawn up as divergences in custom make necessary; until these codes are complete, native civil cases are to be decided by precedent (Art. 8). At each administrative headquarters is to be established a Commission for the Protection of Natives, consisting of two members, preferably missionaries, nominated for a period of two years, under the chairmanship of an official of the Native Affairs Department. This Commission may receive complaints against officials, hear native chiefs on the needs of their subjects, hold inquiries, propose measures for the benefit of natives, give advice on matters referred to them by the Governor, and their approval is required for the conclusion of all contracts other than labour contracts (Arts. 22-3).

The Administration of Native Law.—Special courts for natives were established in Mozambique in 1927 (Decree of November 11), and in 1929 their constitution was amended and they were extended to Angola (Amended Decree on Status of Natives). The President is an administrative official: he is assisted by two members selected afresh for each case "on the indication of the parties" from among the chiefs, and two assessors chosen by the President from among natives with local knowledge (Art. 15).

There is an appeal to a superior tribunal in the capital of each colony, which at first was presided over by the Governor-General; since 1929 these have been judicial courts (Art. 21).

It was also laid down in 1929 that cases between natives and non-natives, excluding those arising out of labour contracts and questions of personal status, should be decided by the Portuguese courts *ex aequo et bono* (Decree of February 6, Arts. 30–4). The *dossier* in such cases is to be made up by the local administrative official and to contain a statement of the native law on the point at issue. If a non-native pleads guilty, the witnesses for the prosecution need not be questioned; if a native does, they must still be examined (Art. 7). Natives are subject to European law if they speak Portuguese, do not practise characteristic native customs, and exercise a profession, commerce or industry, or have private means. The native wives and children of non-natives, and the illegitimate children of a native woman and a non-native man, if recognized by the father, are also exempt from native law (Decree of November 12, 1927). The franchise was extended to such natives in 1915.[1]

Native Political Institutions.—Such legal recognition as is given to native political institutions is contained in the decree of November 1933 on the administrative organization of the colonies. This provides that the native population is to be divided into communes and these into villages (Art. 9). The commune boundaries are to coincide with existing administrative divisions, but local tradition is to be respected as far as possible (Art. 92). The mayor of each commune is to be a native chief, but paid by the Government and holding office at their pleasure. Subject to this pleasure succession to the office is to be by native custom (Arts. 94–6). The mayors retain traditional chiefly privileges unless these are specifically abolished (Art. 18). Their duties are to obey orders, to transmit Government decisions to their subjects and their subjects' complaints to the Government, to keep order, furnish men for the defence force, report crimes, register births, deaths and marriages, prevent illicit brewing or trading in liquor, put down sorcery and divining, supervise the movements of natives from outside their territory, present to the local authority persons wishing to settle within it (no change of residence being allowed without their approval), report suspicious movements of non-

---

[1] *Admiralty Handbook*, cited, p. 137.

natives, impound stray cattle, assist the police, encourage the spread of the Portuguese language, report the number of fire-arms in the possession of their subjects, furnish census figures and isolate persons suffering from infectious diseases (Art. 99). They may arrest undesirable characters and hold inquiries, but have no judicial powers (Arts. 100–1). Those "minor village services" which are still an obligation upon all natives, clearing roads and waterways, digging wells and rebuilding villages, are organized by them (Art. 102). They must respect native custom as far as possible (Art. 103). They may appoint councils, but each member must have Government approval (Art. 104). They are forbidden, among other things, to receive bonuses from recruiting agents and to be absent from their area without leave (Art. 108).

The mayors nominate chiefs over groups of villages, who are subject to their orders in accordance with native custom (Arts. 109–10). The work of tax collection is assigned to these chiefs, and the mayors are forbidden to take part in it (Art. 116). No village site may be changed without per-mission, nor may a village chief receive a new subject without permission (Arts. 118–19). These provisions appear to be intended to make it impossible for natives to evade their obligations by changing their residence. Neither chiefs nor mayors have any authority over the expenditure of revenue.

Provision for Native Development.—The proportion of total revenue which must be devoted to native interests is 10 per cent. in Angola and 30 per cent. in Mozambique (Decree of December 30, 1933). In Angola the distribution of this sum is laid down in some detail—50 per cent. to the maintenance of roads, bridges, buildings, and the provision of tools to natives, 30 per cent. to "assistance agricole", 10 per cent. to village hygiene, 5 per cent. to rewards to meritorious chiefs, 5 per cent. to furnishing administrative posts and providing native passes, while any surplus is to be devoted to "other works of advantage to natives" (Decree of June 4, 1931, Arts. 100–3).

In Mozambique primary education is free and compulsory for all native children living within three kilometres of a school between the ages of seven and fourteen years (Decree of May 17, 1930, Art. 9). There is to be one professional school for boys and one for girls in each district: these take children over ten, and teach them crafts appropriate to the locality (Arts. 20, 21). Normal schools give a two years' course, but in the absence of certificated teachers any man with knowledge of Portuguese and arithmetic may be appointed to teach in a primary school (Arts. 27, 47).

Decrees of February and March 1933, in Angola provide for the creation "as soon as resources permit" of an elaborate series of technical services to be at the exclusive disposal of the native population. Every administrative station is to provide for irrigation, village planning, the building of granaries where crops may be stored so as not to have to be sold immediately after the harvest, nurseries for fruit trees, plantations of coffee, palm trees, and apiculture (Art. 11). As preliminary steps, officials are to build dams, construct depots for seeds and machinery, gradually stock them, supply plants and cuttings for plantations, distribute beehives of native type with suitable instructions and "intensify" the technical assistance given to the native cultivator (Art. 3). As a means of encouraging improved methods of cultivation it is laid down that natives using animal traction and manure may receive allotments of ten hectares in freehold, and be exempted from taxation and recruiting for labour (Arts. 6–7). The second decree lays down that each administrative division should possess its own experimental farm with sections devoted to agriculture, stock raising, apiculture and sericulture. Since, however, this is impossible for financial reasons such farms are to be opened one at a time as the Governor decides. "Native princes" are to be lent seed, tools, and stock for communal farms, whose product will be theirs, and is to be distributed in the proportions of 20 per cent. to the prince, 30 per cent. to his notables, and 50 per cent. to the natives who did the work (Art. 53).

CHAPTER VII

SCIENCE AND THE FUTURE OF AFRICA

What does Colonial Development Achieve?—Statements of the aims of various types of colonial policy are no novelty; all the Powers are equally anxious to explain themselves to one another, to public opinion in the home country, perhaps even to their African subjects, and lose no occasion of describing the work which they conceive themselves to be accomplishing. But less attention has usually been paid to the actual results which the pursuit of these aims has achieved. It has been the object of this study to indicate at what points and in what directions African society has in fact been modified, whether as the deliberate or the incidental result of European political programmes.

In a brief general survey such indications can be given only in the barest outline; and, as was pointed out earlier, the regions where the interactions of African and European culture have been analysed in any detail are still very few. It is possible, nevertheless, to form a general picture of the type of development that has been produced by each of the main lines of colonial policy, which is probably on the whole accurate, though doubtless fuller inquiry would reveal many points of difference between different areas.

All such policies do in fact represent attempts at blending two civilizations, though perhaps they have not often been consciously so envisaged. Some recognize more clearly than others the type of blend which it is desired to be produced; and some territories are trying to combine policies whose implications are in fact opposed.

Three Types of Cultural Blend: (1) *A Stratified Society.*— There is a very obvious distinction between those policies which are dominated by the permanent establishment in a colony of a European population with its own political institutions, transmitting its culture to generations which have no other home, or the desire to establish such a population, and those which have not to take this factor into account. The latter again can be roughly divided into the "new and rectilinear"[1] construction of the French and Belgian types, with a comprehensive general plan of development as its ideal, and the slower, more flexible process of adaptation that has now come to be the aim of Indirect Rule. It might be said of the first two types of policy that their ends are clearly envisaged; the question which has to be asked is whether they are attainable. It is inherent in the third that its ultimate result should not be foreseen from the outset; it is of its essence to confine itself to the problems of the day. Here one questions whether its logical implications have been fully realized.

In the White Man's Country policy the central aim is the supremacy of the white community. Its practitioners have no doubts as to the place that the native is to take in the dual society; that place is determined by the one predominant necessity. The African population must be available to do that work which Europeans are not prepared to undertake, especially in those forms of production to which cheap labour is essential. The African must therefore adopt the European attitude towards money, the desirability of material possessions, and the dignity of hard, monotonous work regulated, not by the weather or man's inclination, but by the clock; he must acquire new manual skill, and that degree of literacy and knowledge of some language other than his own which will facilitate communication with his employer. But because the standard of living which makes his labour cheap makes him a dangerous competitor in those occupations which the European does not despise, these must be barred to him, whether by direct prohibition or by refusing him the training that would qualify him to compete. In the political sphere the African population is never to attain a degree of influence which would enable it to modify a social order regarded by the European community as vital to its continued existence.

---

[1] See above, p. 189 n.

Many practitioners of the White Man's Country policy would not recognize it under this description. In the territories where it is followed, there are many individuals who are sincerely interested in native welfare and in the promotion of inter-racial goodwill and co-operation. There is a whole group—the missionaries—who make it one of their aims to give the African an education identical with that enjoyed by the European and thus equip him for competition in the professions. In those areas where the white population do not yet control their own destinies, a policy directed from Downing Street interprets the "paramountcy of native interests" in a manner which tends to be characterized by local settler opinion as blind to practical realities. In the self-governing African territories there is a growing body of public opinion opposed to the policy of frank repression. If this has not yet made much impress on the legislation of South Africa, its effect can be seen in Mr. Huggins' statements of policy, and in the claim so frequently put forward by Southern Rhodesians to have evolved a native policy at once more realistic than that of their northern and more liberal than that of their southern neighbours.

Yet the limiting factor remains the necessity of preserving European supremacy—economic, social and political. No liberal proposal which can be interpreted as a threat to that supremacy has a chance of acceptance. Indifference to native development may give way to a willingness that such development should take place—but not to acquiescence in its taking place at the expense of the white man's privileges. Southern Rhodesia is actually trying the experiment in the encouragement of native maize, balanced by a marketing scheme to dispose of it where the European grower will not feel its competition —a ludicrous example of the limits of liberalism in a White Man's Country.

(2) "*New and Rectilinear Architecture*".—The aims of the second school are equally clear. They look forward to an Africa of industrious peasants, producing for export those crops which in any given area have been found to be most suitable, and of well-fed, well-housed, well-disciplined labourers whose

lives centre in the industrial areas and who can hope to rise there to any position to which their skill and intelligence entitle them. Emancipation from the shackles of tribal custom is one of the benefits of such advancement; while native customs may be temporarily tolerated where the population is too backward to reject them, native institutions even utilized so long as nothing better exists, it is on their disappearance, and on the substitution for them of "civilization" as we know it, that interest is concentrated. The severest measures of compulsion and control are justifiable in the pursuit of this end, since it is the belief of this school of thought that the most efficacious way of introducing a new regime is to impose it by constraint for such period as is required until the persons concerned come to take it for granted.

In this type of policy the European contribution consists in organization and guidance, and in carrying out those parts of the plan which the natives themselves cannot manage—the transformation and marketing of their products, the provision of capital for the introduction of agricultural machines, the organization of mining. Such planned colonial development would appear to necessitate much greater financial resources and a much more numerous administrative staff than are available in the territories to which it is believed to be suitable. The ideas of this school with regard to native institutions are in the main shared by the White Man's Countries; there, in so far as a policy of native development is followed in reserves, it is based on the Europeanization of political institutions.

(3) *Evolutionary Development*.—The third school of thought is the Indirect Rule theory—not the crude belief that "natural" chiefs make the best emissaries of Government, but the whole attitude which informed the administration of Lord Lugard and Sir Donald Cameron, and which is perhaps most succinctly expressed in the phrase "Development of the African on his own lines". The peculiar characteristic of this attitude is its belief that African institutions have a definite value for the peoples who have evolved them, and deserve, not mere temporary toleration, but incorporation into the new civilization which European Powers are creating in Africa. The develop-

ment of large industrial centres, whether, as is nearly always the case, they draw their labour from villages to which the men are expected to return, or whether they seek to retain a permanent labour force in their vicinity, is inconsistent with a theory which recognizes the intimate connection of African institutions with the agricultural life in which they were evolved. Hence it was to Lord Lugard, the originator of the policy, an essential element in it that the economic life of territories so governed should be based on native peasant production; and when it was extended by Sir Donald Cameron to a territory where there was already a demand for wage-labour, he made it one of his aims that no native should be dependent on such labour through lack of alternative means of meeting his obligations. Thus in economic matters the relation of the European settler to the native population is clear in this case too; his enterprise must depend on its own efficiency, not on legislation designed to assist it, and should be confined to types of production requiring large capital which the native cannot provide. An area such as Northern Rhodesia, with its Native Authorities Ordinance taken over from Tanganyika, its large European population and its copper belt, is practising a hybrid policy to which the Indirect Rule theory contributes form rather than spirit.[1] Politically, Sir Donald Cameron laid it down as a principle of administration that the European community should not exercise control over policy until the African community was sufficiently developed—to him one of the aims of Indirect Rule—to have a share in such control.

The peculiarity of the Indirect Rule policy, inherent in the theory which underlies it, is that it makes no definite assumptions as to the nature of the cultural blend which it will ultimately produce. To the other two schools of thought the type of society which it is desired to produce is clear; in the White Man's Countries, a stratified community drawing its wealth from industry or large-scale agriculture, with the native population as the labouring class, such opportunity as they may be given for the exercise of local self-government or the

[1] See above, pp. 100 ff.

practice of skilled pursuits learnt from the European being confined within the limits that are held necessary to ensure the maintenance of European supremacy; in the assimilationist areas, a replica of European civilization with natives, as soon as may be, among the captains of industry and Mayors of Communes. Whether the first of these positions, apparently achieved at present, but admittedly held only through a constantly vigilant defence, can be maintained indefinitely; whether the second is attainable at all, are matters for speculation. There is no doubt as to the end desired.

Indirect Rule is essentially a policy of compromise; for the development of African society on its own lines has never been taken to mean that it is to be left entirely free to make its own adaptation to the demands upon it of modern times. British rule has everywhere brought about at least the minimum of changes deemed necessary to civilized government; more than that, experience has shown that the spontaneous reaction of native society to the new influences that Europe has brought to bear upon it does not take the form of a readjustment giving general satisfaction. Indeed, this is only to be expected; for it is individuals who react, not "a society", and their behaviour is determined by no wider considerations than their own apparent advantage. Exactly the same is true of the reactions of modern Europe to the development of mechanical invention; but modern Europe has no benevolent autocrat to attempt to counteract the result.

Indirect Rule: Theory and Practice.—Hence the realization that active intervention by the ruling Power is as necessary under Indirect Rule as under any other system of administration. What is peculiar to the theory of Indirect Rule is the basis on which the intervention is made; if native institutions are modified, this is to be done only with good reason —not in the interests of a European community nor yet because all European institutions are held to be better than any others.

What then constitutes good reason? Confronted with this question, the Indirect Rule policy appears to be less clear as to its own implications than are its rivals. From the first it has been accepted that African institutions are to be "purged of their abuses", and that with reference, not to the requirements of changed circumstances but to an absolute standard. And even the absolute standard is not fixed. If there is universal agreement in condemning cannibalism, trial by ordeal or the blooding of Masai spears, there are other customs which in the last generation have passed from the realm of the repugnant to that of the tolerated or even admired. The express sanction given by the new South African Native Code to the payment of *lobola* is an example; the incorporation of initiation ceremonies into the rite of confirmation by the Bishop of Masai another; while a striking instance of contradictory standards is the complete tolerance of clitoridectomy by the German missions in Tanganyika and the uncompromising condemnation of the same custom by the neighbours of the Church of Scotland Mission in Kenya. A change of attitude that has not needed to be expressed in such a formal manner is the transition from pity—or contempt—for the "communistic" savage, whose self-advancement is constantly hindered by the claims of his poor relations, to admiration for the beautiful generosity of the African through which no unemployed labourer is ever in want.

Again, why do modern circumstances call for adaptation? They have not come into being of themselves, but are part and parcel of the colonial development which claims as its guiding principle that changes are only to be made when circumstances call for them. The increase in material prosperity, which requires the introduction of new techniques, a new division of labour, new standards of value, a new attitude towards social obligations which conflict with the new opportunities of gain, is generally held to be the foremost aim of colonial development. The inability of the African to exploit to the full the natural resources of his own land is regarded as the ultimate justification for colonial expansion; it is being invoked today against the one remaining independent African State. As an expression of the necessity to an industrial civilization of constantly expanding markets, this postulate is readily acceptable. As an essential element in trusteeship for another race its validity is not so self-evident. It is true that a higher material standard *can* produce a higher level of health, and physical health is one of the few goods which can be recognized as objectively desirable in all circumstances. But it is assuredly not with the aim of improving the physique of the African that colonial administrators are primarily concerned in their ceaseless efforts to increase production; nor yet with that of raising the revenue necessary to pay the expenses of government. What then is the imperative? The answer lies in the realm of faith rather than reason.

Here then we have one European standard imposed without question of its universal validity. The other assumption which is at work in the creation of new situations is related to Indirect Rule in a slightly different way. The missionary bodies who seek to introduce to the African the Christian system of ethics, with the social relationships which that system is held to demand, act with the approval or toleration of Governments, but not as part of their organization. In so far as they are utilized in the educational system, it is with the knowledge imparted and not with the rules of behaviour inculcated that the administration is concerned. It is not held to be an essential function of colonial government to promote those aims which missions set before themselves; indeed French policy, which makes education a government service, is largely indifferent to the work of missions in spreading Christianity.

Nevertheless, the influence of Christian teaching represents another arbitrary element in the situation with which the Indirect Rule policy has to reckon. Here again the modifications which the missionary seeks to bring about in African life are assumed to be good in themselves, without reference to the circumstances of the society into which they are being introduced. Some missions, it is true, have experimented with combinations of native and Christian ritual; the majority have abandoned the attempt to detach their converts entirely from all their old allegiances. To build as far as possible on native institutions is now the avowed policy of the principal Protestant missions. Yet an activity whose whole purpose is the inculcation of new moral standards cannot in the nature of things be guided by an objective estimate of the requirements of a given situation.

In fact, then, Indirect Rule is an attempt to preserve what can still be preserved of indigenous institutions in a situation in which the radical modification of many of them is assumed as necessary and desirable. This the advocates of the policy would readily admit; and their opponents seize on the admission as sufficient to discredit their whole theory. That Africa must be modernized, they say, is common ground. Indirect Rule has repudiated the charge that it means no more than non-interference; in intention it is not a policy of stagnation, whatever it may be in fact. But in that case, what is the use of preserving a few odd anachronisms in the new Africa? A twentieth-century society must have the whole outfit of twentieth-century institutions; only thus can it face "the strenuous conditions of the modern world", and only thus can it satisfy the aspirations which western influences have rightly awakened in those of its members whose intelligence is sufficient to appreciate them. Above all the friends of the native in the White Man's Countries assert that Indirect Rule provides a specious argument for the refusal to allow him to participate on equal terms with the white man in the new dual society; and educated Africans in most territories, seeing in membership of a society organized on European lines the life for which they have been fitted and which they have a right to claim, and in political authority the fitting channel for the exercise of superior knowledge, regard with suspicion a regime which in their eyes has been devised in order to keep out of politics the class that is intelligent enough to criticize the European authorities.

The Contribution of the Scientist.—Is there any objective test by which we can weigh the merits of such arguments, estimate the likelihood that the various policies will achieve their avowed aims, assess their value in terms of that native welfare to which all give at least lip service? As has already been suggested, a final answer could only be given after a detailed comparative study of the actual situations that have been produced. If we believe that scientific analysis can lead to a more rational direction of human affairs, to a clearer perception of the relation between means and ends, then we must hope that some such study will in time be made.

Meanwhile, has science anything to say in the nature of a preliminary estimate of the results as they are already known? Which of the social sciences are relevant to the question, and what can they contribute to its elucidation? For an analysis of the phenomena of social change and the contact of cultures we must look to social anthropology; on certain of the special characteristics of the White Man's Countries economics has also something to say.

The Nature of Social Cohesion.—The crucial issue in the controversy between the assimilationist and Indirect Rule theories is the question of the nature of social cohesion; what are the forces that uphold the institutions of a society, that ensure a degree of obedience to recognized authority, of respect for systems of rules, such that the recalcitrant are never more than a minority whose misdemeanours leave the validity of the system unimpaired in the eyes of the rest? If we can answer this question, we shall know whether it is possible to create authorities of a new type and be assured that their orders will be obeyed, as is desired by those who would do away with the African chief; and whether it is reasonable to hope that codes of behaviour enforced by constraint will in due course become habitual, as is believed by the advocates of regimentation.

In the first place we have to realize that the orderly working of any society, however primitive, depends upon the existence of institutions which regulate the conduct of its members. Such institutions are not wholly or even largely comprised by the spectacularly repugnant customs which European rule has been concerned to put down, or the quaintnesses which the anthropologist is believed to be concerned in preserving. They are more humdrum and often more indispensable. Rules of conduct towards his parents, consort and children, towards other relatives, towards religious or political authority, bind the member of an African tribe as they do the subject of a European State. The conduct prescribed may differ, but the end of orderly social co-operation is the same. Respect for property, for human life, for the sexual code enjoined by the society, are principles of African law as of ours. The bases of economic co-operation are not those to which we are accustomed, but they exist and make possible the production of a regular supply of food and material goods. A recognized discipline trains the child for his adult responsibilities. Many of the rules are irksome; they curb spontaneous inclinations or demand uncongenial effort. Opportunities of evading them, such as are presented by the new circumstances that Europe is creating in Africa, are therefore welcomed, and that part of the liberation from tribal custom which consists in destroying the sense of obligation is easily achieved. But the assumption that the African who has been encouraged to shed the sense of duty with which he grew up will in the same moment adopt that of his European master is altogether too optimistic.

From the studies now being made of those situations in which the contact of cultures offers the individual a choice between conflicting standards over a wide range of behaviour, we may hope to learn much as to the relative strength of different motives in determining human conduct. At present it is too early to formulate laws of social change. But we know enough about the building up of social attitudes in the individual to hazard a judgement as to the relative advantages of putting new wine in old bottles or making all things new. Put shortly, a man obeys the rules of the society in which he lives, partly because he has been brought up to take them for granted, partly because, in the main, obedience pays.[1] In the normal situations of life, unless some particularly irksome obligation is in question, the knowledge that a certain line of action is expected is probably a more efficient motive than any conscious calculation of the advantages of conformity. In most indigenous African societies, in the specific case of obedience to political authority, there were on the one hand recognized limitations to the exercise of authority—for the "absolute powers" of an African chief extended only to his personal relationships, not to interference with what was traditionally established as the

---

[1] This is the gist of the argument advanced by Malinowski in his *Crime and Custom in Savage Society*.

normal conduct of life among his subjects—and on the other recognized ways of expressing dissatisfaction. Thus, situations in which authority could become so oppressive that the advantages which it gave in the organization of security, offensive warfare, justice, provision against famine, and the like, did not compensate for the toll demanded of the subject in tribute or services, were rare.[1] But there was also a tradition of loyalty, inculcated in childhood, which was so powerful that it retains much of its force today, even where the functions of chieftainship have all passed into other hands, and the personal rewards that a loyal subject could once hope for have become illusory in comparison with what he can gain in European service.

Such a sentiment cannot be created by creating an institution and ordering obedience to it. Where it exists, it represents an influence over conduct so strong that it is surely the course of wisdom not to neglect or try to break it, but rather to utilize it as a foundation for the new institutions which are to be built up. If in any African society it has actually already vanished under the stress of modern conditions—as might prove to be the case where a great proportion of the native population live in scattered homesteads as squatters, subject to no authority but that of their white master—it would be no more than sentimental antiquarianism to try to revive it. No thorough sociological study has been made of such a population. But we have evidence that among some urban native groups where the rupture of all ties with the traditional organization would seem to have gone farthest, the sentiment of attachment to the chieftainship appears in a new form, as a rallying point for the nascent nationalism of African groups conscious of the opposition between themselves and a European society in which they are allowed no part.

To point to the existence of this sentiment is not to deny that one of the results of European contact has been to weaken it considerably in certain individuals. This has been the case where the chief has been manifestly set at naught by the European Government; at times it has been an aspect of the

---

[1] I have tried to develop this point more fully in an article, " Chieftainship in Modern Africa ", shortly to be published in *Africa*.

economic independence of the younger generation; it is widely regarded as the necessary and laudable result of a European education. Many take this discontent as proof that the institution is obsolete and needs to be replaced by something more consonant with the requirements of the twentieth century, an attitude inherently akin to that of the impatient reformer at home who holds that only when the present order of things has been shattered can the ideal society be achieved.

Is Revolution an Efficient Mechanism for Cultural Change?— In Europe this kind of reform is called revolution, since in Europe it cannot be achieved without recourse to violence. When they are dealing with European problems, the same liberal thinkers who are for transforming African institutions root and branch would be the first to urge the importance of solving them by constitutional means. To them, it is true, revolution in Europe means something different from revolution in Africa; bloodshed, the uncertainty of the outcome, the dictatorship which at the best is inevitable during the period when the new order is being consolidated. In African revolutions, where the dictatorship is already established, there is no bloodshed and no risk of an unsuccessful struggle. Yet the real reason to suspect the efficacy of revolution as a means of social change is far more fundamental than ethical prejudices against the methods by which it is brought about.

The authors of African revolution would probably be amazed at the suggestion that there was anything in common between their activities and the political upheavals which they associate with the word. Yet the type of social change which they are trying to achieve—albeit not by the use of armed force—is fundamentally similar to that which is the aim of revolution. The revolutionary attempts to anticipate a change in social standards by imposing on a society, usually over a wide range of situations, behaviour which implies the acceptance of the standards that he desires to introduce. It is his recognition of the importance and force of traditional standards which leads the sociologist to doubt whether such an attempt can ever be truly successful —a doubt which is independent of ethical preoccupations.

So long as at any given moment the standards applicable

to the majority of situations remain apparently unaltered, a change can be made in a direction where the need for change is really felt, and the institutions affected will gradually, almost imperceptibly, adapt themselves to it. But if changes in every department of life at once are imposed by the superior will of a law-giver—the only way in which such far-reaching changes can be introduced—no such spontaneous adaptation, if one may call it so, is possible. The standards which the individual takes for granted no longer apply anywhere, and the changes, if they are to become permanent, must be enforced by external compulsion. Such schemes as the Belgian compulsory cultivation system accept this position, in the belief that after a sufficient period of constraint the new ways will become so firmly integrated into the complex of institutions that they will persist when the compulsion is removed.

If this hope were justified, then those who believe that the twentieth century has found the key to all social problems might be encouraged to bring Africa right up to date as rapidly as possible and might set themselves to introduce monogamy, democracy and competitive economic individualism by the same methods as were employed by M. Leplae in the introduction of cotton to the Congo.[1] But the Leplae school are content to disregard the existence of any problem of motive. They do not ask whether constraint can engender sentiments that will take its place when, as it ultimately must be, it is removed. They invoke the word "habit" in complete disregard of the complicated psychological mechanisms by which habits are built up. They forget that a system of regulations which requires constraint to maintain it is by definition not consonant with the standards of the society on which it is imposed, and do not ask whether compulsion is a type of process likely to reverse those standards.

Conditions of Cultural Assimilation.—Herein lies the true indictment of revolution as a means of social change. It is arguable—it is the revolutionary's chief argument—that the end justifies the means; but the argument loses its cogency if the means do not attain the end.

[1] See above, pp. 235 ff.

274

SCIENCE AND THE FUTURE OF AFRICA

I have suggested reasons for suspecting the efficacy of direct constraint as a means of making lasting changes in social institutions. The alternative method open to those who wish to recast an entire society is to create a political authority whose personnel are imbued with the standards which it is desired to inculcate, and allow or encourage them to issue orders tending in the directions desired.

Here the situation is more complex. The element of constraint is present, inasmuch as the orders given by such authorities owe their validity in the last resort to the support of the irresistible European Government, and that that support counts for much more in securing obedience than did the physical force which a traditional authority could command.

But such new creations have in common with the cotton patches of the Congo a subtler element: the fact that no spontaneous impulse from within the native society has gone to their making. They too exist as the product of an external will, uninfluenced by the dictates of prevalent sentiments or accustomed standards of behaviour. And while the cotton patch is something which, given suitable incentives, has readily appealed to an accepted native standard of values, the Native Council is something which existing standards, in an unforced adjustment to new situations, could not conceivably have produced. It disregards the very definite attitudes to authority, its duties and responsibilities, its sphere and limitations, the personal loyalties, the religious sentiments, the expectations of reward and the fear of penalties recognized as just, that combine in any society to secure respect for the political institutions that it has itself evolved. Its advocates are content to believe that a process of election can take their place, and have never stopped to consider how much the validity of political authority in Europe really rests upon the ritual of the ballot box, how much upon the sentiments associated with it, and how much upon entirely other attitudes developed in entirely different contexts.

Many anthropologists have stressed the point that a cultural innovation will not be effectively assimilated unless the behaviour involved in its acceptance is, broadly speaking, in harmony with the standards which already prevail. It is perhaps possible to go further and try to formulate certain general prerequisites of effective assimilation—that is, of an assimilation in which the new type of behaviour is not only generally adopted, but is adopted in a manner that does not damage those institutions upon which the regulation of other aspects of social life depends.

In the first place, it must either present some apparent advantage to the majority of those persons who are to be involved by its introduction in a departure from their accustomed routine of life, or else the circumstances must be such as to create some problem to which it is the only solution; in other words, the constraint of circumstances may do what cannot be done by the constraint of orders backed by penalties. In the first category comes the adoption of more efficient or more easily acquired implements—matches, tools, like European hoes, which enable customary activities to be carried on with less effort, kerosene tins in place of laboriously made baskets or pots—clothes and other goods whose possession represents an approximation to the material standards of the ruling race, and the cultivation of crops for sale.

Wage-labour can belong to either category. In those parts of Africa to which wage-labour was first introduced, the imposition of taxation which cannot be met in any other way has done what the Portuguese laws on the Duty of Labour or the recruiting of the Congo could never do—produced native societies in which the migration to and fro of a large percentage of the adult males, their absence from home for long periods, and the dependence on them of the rest of the community for such requirements as have to be paid for in cash, is accepted as a normal feature of life. The change has been made in response neither to the orders of a superior authority nor the stimulus of apparent advantage. Instead, external circumstances have been manipulated so that the logic of economic necessity presents itself in new terms. But although the first demands of Europeans for labour—involving as they did for the individual concerned not only a departure from the accustomed routine but separation from the whole familiar environment, human and natural—met nowhere with a ready response, at the present day European employment has elements in common with the category of welcomed innovations. Many young men leave home, not under the weight of an irksome necessity but eager for new experience, freedom from authority, and the material possessions that they hope to bring home; and there are now parts of Africa, such as the Northern Territories of the Gold Coast, where, although no taxation has been imposed, spontaneous migration to labour takes place.

The second condition of effective integration is one that is not so readily attained. The adoption by a number of individuals in a native society of those European elements which they find attractive is easy. But if the changed behaviour implied in their adoption is not to affect adversely the working of existing institutions, it will probably be necessary for a number of consequential readjustments to be made: and the attraction of the easy or profitable, of the line of least resistance in a difficult situation, does not necessarily lead in the direction of the readjustment required.

One might quote many examples from the facts recorded in this book. New economic standards, now universally accepted, have produced landlordism in Buganda, political instability in the Gold Coast, discontent on the part of subjects and op-pression on that of chiefs in the Protectorates. In the Belgian Congo a religion which preaches the rejection of tribal authority, and is undoubtedly popular partly for that reason, has weakened native political institutions without establishing the higher standard of morality which was its aim.

These are cases of maladjustment which probably could be remedied. But there are others in which it is simply im-possible for a satisfactory adjustment to be made. The most obvious example is that of the labour market.

An economic organization based on wage-labour presupposes that the rewards of that labour contribute to the subsistence—if they do not wholly provide it—of the community from which the wage-earners are drawn; and in Africa this adaptation, requiring as it would immense changes in the whole economic system, has not been made. Subsistence is still drawn directly from the soil; and the young men who abandon their own plots for a mining centre or a European estate bring back nothing that adequately replaces the loss of their contribution to the food supply and to the whole cycle of village activities. Here, then, is a change for which inducements are not lacking, but whose implications are so wide that an African society retaining its traditional structure is unable to accept them.

Modern political institutions, too, are desired by a certain section of the population—those educated young men who see in them an opportunity to exercise talents that must otherwise be wasted; and, of course, to draw the salaries that those talents should command. But, as has been suggested at many points in this book, the efficacy of political institutions depends upon all the complex of relationships through which certain individuals can count on obedience to their commands—a complex involving religious beliefs, training in early childhood, perhaps the kinship system and organization of family life, the play of ambition and economic interests; and not to be re-placed by a warrant recorded in the Official Gazette. Here, too, the innovation calls for readjustments in so many directions that it is hard to see how they can be readily made. Certainly there is at present no reason at all to assume that any native society, taken as a whole, is prepared to give to an elected council under the presidency of the local European official the obedience, the confidence, the loyalty which the bulk of the people of most native tribes do still give to their traditional heads. Indeed this fact is tacitly accepted by those Governments which, in instituting Native Councils, keep all real authority in European hands.

This is doubtless an efficient method of carrying out public works. But if these councils are really intended to develop into organs of independent local government, one can only say that they lack a relationship with the population at large which, it is suggested, is indispensable for the secure establishment of a political authority not resting on force.

A policy of native development which satisfied the two conditions mentioned above would not deliberately introduce changes so great that the necessary adaptations to them could not be made. It would make its criterion of change the necessity of enabling African society to meet new situations, and where external considerations, such as the demands of European ethical standards or European commerce, were held to render the creation of a new situation imperative, would concentrate on making modifications at the most essential points and allowing native society to make its own adjustments to them. It would have further to be vigilant lest such adjustments should lead to situations felt by the people themselves to be unjust.

Indirect Rule approximates more nearly to these principles than any other African policy. The increasing official interest in the working of native institutions, side by side with the development of scientific field research, should make the approximation closer; though the arbitrary element, in the form both of situations already created and of changes called for by a public opinion whose standards are not those of the scientist, will always prevent it from being complete. Even so, this is the one type of colonial administration which shapes its ends with some conception of the properties of the material in which it is working.

This interpretation of the situation rests on an hypothesis which is admittedly tentative, but which can at least claim to be more objectively founded than the ethical or political considerations that usually dominate discussions of native policy. It is an attempt to evaluate such policies in terms of their chances of attaining the ends they seek rather than of that justice whose nature it is so easy to dispute.

The Economist and the White Man's Countries.—On the narrower question of the organization of production the economist has also something to contribute to the discussion. He would point out that that abundance of material goods which is generally accepted as the criterion of prosperity attains its maximum when production is carried out by methods which are able to pay their way without extraneous aids; since all such aid represents a diversion of productive resources from more efficient to less efficient employment. He would explain that the colour-bar policy, whether in the form of direct prohibition of the employment of Africans or of the restriction of certain markets to Europeans, means in effect that the whole European community is paying a larger price than it need in order to increase the incomes of engineers or maize growers, and is poorer by the quantity of other goods which it has in consequence to forego. If white supremacy is held to necessitate or justify such levies—a series likely to increase to the Gilbertian point where everybody is subsidizing everybody else— well and good; let the price be paid. But it is more than doubtful whether those who vote the levies know what they are paying.

This is a point which no economist would dispute. Restrictive economic policies can only be defended on non-economic grounds. The Indirect Rule policy, however, meets with certain criticisms which do claim to be as objectively based as the arguments by which it has been here defended. They attack it on the ground on which it has been here upheld —its chances of attaining its avowed aim. Such criticisms may be generally described as appealing to the lesson of history.

The Appeal to History.—History, we are told, demonstrates the culmination in representative government of all political development. It shows how one nation after another has discarded other forms of government in favour of the one which they have all come to recognize as the best calculated to secure equal consideration for the needs of all sections of the community. It teaches that the spread of education creates an irresistible demand for a democratic system in which authority shall depend on popular consent and not on hereditary privilege.

But what is the history that teaches these lessons? It is a study that is only beginning to have sociological relevance as the facts which every schoolboy knows are fitted into the context of the social structure in which the events so frequently appealed to in isolation did actually take place. So long as it can appeal only to the broad analogies which pass for "historical laws", so long as the type of detailed analysis of processes of change that is being carried out by the anthropologist in his study of living cultures has not been extended to research into the past, the argument from history has only a spurious validity.

Moreover, the facts to which this argument appeals can be interpreted very differently. We know that all the European nations have at one time or another had a system of representative government; we also know—a fact which this argument conveniently ignores—that several of them have discarded it, as their rulers hope, permanently, in favour of dictatorships whose subjects have far less freedom than those of an African chief. If we are to regard representative government as the outcome of an evolutionary process, then it seems impossible to avoid considering modern dictatorships as a further step in the same process; if, again, the process is an inevitable one, we must resign ourselves to seeing Africa follow in the path of Europe, but we shall surely become less eager to accelerate it.

But what real ground is there for assuming this inevitable development? That an event is known to have been repeated several times does not constitute it a law of nature. Until a chain of causation is established, its repetition may be no more than a coincidence, and in the field of phenomena with which history deals, the causes leading up to a single conspicuous event are so numerous and complex that it is all but impossible to take any repetition as evidence of a general law; the search for such laws, inspired by an analogy with biological processes which does not really hold good in the realm of cultural development, has led to a concentration on broad similarities which entirely ignores the local variations that characterize the "democracies" of the various occidental nations.

Again, the argument from history tends to see the evolution from despotism to democracy as a telescoped process in which the beginning and end are clearly marked, but the intervening stages disregarded. We are reminded that once all Europe was ruled by feudal monarchs under a system not unlike that of the most highly centralized African societies; therefore, it is asserted, African society can—and, if it is to hold its own in the twentieth century, must—advance with all speed to the point that

Europe has now reached; though not, as has already been noted, the furthest point.

But the question of the intervening stages is all-important; for it is to those stages that the hypothesis that has been advanced here with regard to the nature of cultural change is relevant. If we look to our own history, we see, not a sudden transition, but a series of gradual modifications, which cannot be dismissed as stages in the process of trial and error, to be left out now that the final solution has been discovered. It is more pertinent to point out that in each the demand for change came from persons who had some specific cause of dissatisfaction with the existing system and sought to remedy that specific grievance. In no case was the change such as to call for any great modification in the normal life of the population at large, as is the case when an African tribe is at one and the same time endowed with a modern form of government and called on to pay rates for the public works decided upon by that government. And at no time—obviously—was there a group of reformers, imbued with the ideas of societies centuries ahead in development and thousands of miles away in space, and demanding, not to find a remedy appropriate to some particular complaint, but to imitate in all respects those distant institutions. One might hazard the suggestion that it is because of its gradual, unforced development that our own political system, open as it is to criticism, still functions with relative stability and efficiency and is not yet threatened with forcible overthrow.

Again, in so far as history does repeat itself, it does so in part because ideology does not change. The nations of Europe adopted parliamentary government during the nineteenth century, not as the result of an irresistible evolutionary force, but because it was widely held that this was the most desirable form of political organization. It is now beginning to be almost as widely held that it is obsolete; and if the controllers of African policy ceased to regard its rapid introduction into Africa as desirable, there is no reason to suppose that a development of African society in which no modification was made except when some specific need called for it would result in a political system closely resembling anything known in Europe.

The Attitude of the Educated African.—There is, as we are constantly reminded, an important factor to be reckoned with in forecasting the future—the demands of the educated African. He firmly believes the truth of what his European teachers have told him—that representative government is one of the sources of European superiority, one of those blessings which Europe has discovered. He sees in it the opportunity for a career such as his training entitles him to claim, whether as a member of an elected council or as its expert servant. He publishes newspapers in which the denial of this blessing becomes a symbol of alien oppression.

Several arguments are advanced for making this class, rather than native society as a whole, the basis of new developments. It is said that all reforms have come from thinking minorities; that this class represents an *élite*, as is proved by their ability to profit by European education; that their ultimate triumph is inevitable.

The first argument has already been implicitly accepted in the statement that demands for change have come from those groups—necessarily minorities—which have specific grounds for discontent; but if the reforms they have introduced have adequately met the unsatisfactory situation, it is because they have done their thinking in terms of the situation and not in an entirely different context.

That the educated class are an *élite* in the sense that they are endowed with abilities superior to their fellows is a proposition open to doubt. For an African to complete the course of education provided in his country, and perhaps proceed to a British university, may require greater perseverance than is called for in societies where a long period spent at school and college is taken for granted; on the other hand, he may well have an easier life during this time than he would have had at home. For some it may represent financial sacrifice; for many the accident of wealthy parentage, rather than individual merit, makes higher education possible. To pass in English the examinations taken by English students is certainly an intellectual achievement showing great ability; but is this necessarily the type of ability called for in the political field?

We have to accept a serious responsibility towards the educated African. European policies have brought him into being, and the figure which they have created is in many ways tragic. He has been taught that the knowledge he possesses makes him superior to his fellows, but he is often unable to turn his knowledge to account in any way that will give him a superior status. He has been encouraged to believe that African society in its present state is no place for him, but we neither admit him into European society nor let him make his own culture into something that he can endure living in. But is his superiority over his fellows so great as to justify their sacrifice to his interests? Those who would remould Africa on a plan whose main object is to find a place for him would not admit that any sacrifice was involved, and are prepared to dismiss the anthropologist's arguments as antiquarian romanticism. The hypothesis which I have here put forward, however, does not rest on any sentimental glorification of the past, but on the inherent necessities of the situation; if it is accepted, then a transformation of native society on lines admittedly felt as desirable by only a small group must mean the sacrifice of the rest.

The argument that the triumph of the educated class is inevitable is of a different order. It is not a matter of scientific generalization; it is an estimate of the outcome of a particular situation, given the probable attitudes of the persons who will in fact control future developments. It is very probably true. It is equally probable that those European countries which are not yet under the rule of dictatorships will eventually be so; but those who regard dictatorship as an undesirable form of government do not feel compelled for that reason to change their views. This last argument does not affect the results of sociological analysis one way or the other. To the politician emotionally in sympathy with the aspirations of the educated African it is a source of assurance in putting his case. To the scientist it merely means that once again the facts which it is his task to discover will be disregarded by those to whom they are disagreeable.

The Place of the Scientist in Politics.—It seems to be widely believed that the function of the scientist is to enable the politician to carry out with greater facility plans of action which have already been decided upon. If his investigations lead him to the conclusion that the means selected are unlikely to achieve the ends desired, he is told that he has no contribution to make to practical affairs, or even, where a policy which ignores his conclusions has been sufficiently long established, that his theories are out of date.

The scientist claims at once more, and less, than popular opinion allows him. He does not judge his hypotheses by their acceptability to those whose interests they affect, holding that his business is to state the facts as he sees them. He does consider that action based on knowledge is more likely to produce satisfactory results than action taken in the dark, and that dispassionate research is the most effective way of increasing knowledge. When questions of actual policy are under discussion, he can supply data which should be relevant to their decision. He does not demand that these should be the deciding factor; it is for the politician to determine, in a conflict of interests, which considerations are of supreme importance. But where a line of action is proposed, which, in the light of his data, seems likely to create further difficulties—as does the establishment of artificial native governments to which their subjects are bound by no ties of tradition, or the periodical absence of large numbers of young men from their homes— he feels justified in asking those responsible at least to count the cost. He knows only too well that their readiness to do so will be inversely proportioned to the interested pressure of an uninstructed electorate. He does not claim infallibility, and where governments have decided to pay the cost, or have acted before it could be calculated and subsequently regretted it, he cannot unmake their mistakes any more than a doctor can cure a case brought to him too late; he can only advise that the next case be treated differently. It is no reproach to a science which studies the functioning of social institutions if it cannot offer a constructive programme for the development of populations whose institutions have been systematically destroyed; if the anthropologist's analysis of the nature of cultural adaptation leads to the conclusion that in such a situation all the conditions requisite for successful adaptation are lacking, he cannot be expected to go further and save the creators of the situation from the consequences of their actions.

The ideal union between science and policy would be one in which action was taken only in the light of all the knowledge available as to its probable consequences; where such knowledge carried greater weight than the clamour of conflicting desires, and was accepted as a reason for abandoning desires that in achievement must be disastrous. But that is a hope that no one who makes human nature his study would be so foolish as to indulge.

APPENDICES

NOTE.—In these Appendices I have put together, for convenience of reference and comparison, various facts and figures whose inclusion in the body of the text would have made it rather cumbrous. It has seemed preferable to indicate here the sources used rather than to dazzle the eye with an array of footnotes on every page. For British Colonies I have referred mainly to the official *Annual Reports* and the *Statesman's Year Book*. The figures of population density for South Africa are taken from those which Professor Macmillan quotes in his *Complex South Africa* from the 1921 Year-Book. I took those for Kenya from the evidence presented to the Carter Commission, and those for Northern Rhodesia from the Reports of the Reserves Commissions. Wage-rates and numbers in employment in South Africa are given by the Native Economic Commission. For South-West Africa I am indebted to Mr. Ifor Evans' *Native Policy in Southern Africa*; for the Protectorates to the Pim Reports, to Messrs. Hodgson and Ballinger's *Basutoland* and *Bechuanaland*, to a private communication from Dr. Hilda Beemer, and to Professor I. Schapera's various articles on the Ba Kxatla of Bechuanaland. The figures for the Belgian Congo come from the Reports of the 1931 Labour Commission. The data on labour obligations and the period of contract are taken from Major G. St. J. Orde-Browne's *The African Labourer*; this contains an admirable comparative analysis of labour legislation in all African territories to which the reader is referred for further

I

AREA AND POPULATION OF THE TERRITORIES DISCUSSED, WITH LAND DISTRIBUTION

(Areas in Square Miles)

Territory.	Population.		Total Area.	Area open to Native Occupation.	Area subject to European Rights or Reserved for European Ownership.
	Native.	European.			
South Africa (excluding mandated area)	6,000,000 (estimated)	1,828,175	472,550	33,984	438,566
South-West Africa .	241,733	31,600	317,725	11,623 in Police Zone (plus non-delimited native territories outside)	—
Swaziland .	110,295 (1921)	2,205 (1921)	6,705	2,661	3,787
Basutoland .	495,937 (1921)	1,603	11,716	11,716	Negligible
Bechuanaland .	150,185	6,743	275,000	102,000	7,500
Southern Rhodesia .	1,154,500	52,950	150,344	64,422	50,000 (includes estimated share of undetermined area)
Northern Rhodesia .	1,382,705	10,533	290,320	76,280 (includes estimated share of undetermined area)	13,672
Nyasaland .	1,608,023	1,817	37,596	not delimited	6,193
Kenya .	3,107,645	17,249	219,370 land area approx.	53,084	16,700
Tanganyika .	5,022,640	8,217	340,000 land area approx.	not delimited	3,125
Uganda .	3,604,135	1,854	80,558 (land)	77,843	300
Nigeria (with mandated area) .	19,928,171 (total) Europeans not given separately		372,674	not delimited	403
Gold Coast (with mandated area)	3,268,411	3,140 (non-Africans)	91,843	not delimited	2,361
Sierra Leone .	1,546,905	5,685	28,070		
Gambia .	199,120 (total)		4,068		
Sudan .	5,728,551	51,471	1,008,100		
Belgian Congo .	9,467,503	17,588	918,000		
French West Africa .	14,376,811	27,331	1,604,159		
French Equatorial Africa .	3,318,968	4,661	912,049		
Mozambique .	4,000,000	35,000	289,973		
Angola .	3,000,000	40,000	487,788		

information. Figures for numbers in employment appear sporadically in various departmental reports; that for Kenya comes from the evidence taken by the Carter Land Commission, that for Northern Rhodesia from the Merle Davis Report, *Modern Industry and the African*, that for Nyasaland from the 1935 Commission on Emigrant Labour.

I am myself responsible in some cases for working out population densities and the conversion of areas to square miles. I do not claim that the figures given are more than approximations.

II

PRINCIPAL EXPORTS

SOUTH AFRICA.—Gold, wool, fruit, diamonds, sugar, iron and steel, hides and skins.

SOUTH-WEST AFRICA.—Diamonds.

NIGERIA.—Palm-oil, palm-kernels, cotton, cacao, ground-nuts, hides and skins.

GAMBIA COLONY.—Ground-nuts.

SIERRA LEONE.—Palm-kernels, palm-oil, kola-nuts, ginger, piassava fibre.

GOLD COAST.—Cacao, gold, diamonds, manganese.

KENYA.—Cotton, maize, coffee, tea, hides and skins, wattle-bark.

TANGANYIKA.—Sisal, cotton, coffee, ground-nuts, hides and skins.

UGANDA.—Cotton, coffee.

NYASALAND.—Tea, tobacco, coffee, cotton.

NORTHERN RHODESIA.—Copper.

SOUTHERN RHODESIA.—Gold, silver, copper.

BASUTOLAND.—Wool, angora hair.

BECHUANALAND.—Gold, cattle, dairy produce.

SWAZILAND.—Tin, tobacco, cotton, wattle-bark, hides, cattle.

III

POPULATION DENSITY IN DELIMITED NATIVE AREAS

	Per square mile.	Percentage permanently resident in European areas, Cape Province.
UNION OF SOUTH AFRICA:		
Transkei . . .	58·59	14
Zululand . . .	24·06	—
Natal . . .	35·76	48

	Per square mile.	Percentage permanently resident in European areas, Cape Province.
UNION OF SOUTH AFRICA:		
Transvaal . . .	70·90	93
Basutoland . .	42·44	—
Swaziland . . .	38	16·6
Bechuanaland . .	1 to 22	—
South-West Africa . .	(Police Zone only)	75

SOUTHERN RHODESIA . Average 20, range 2½ to 60

NORTHERN RHODESIA:	
Eastern Luangwa .	38·7
Tanganyika . .	8·5
Railway Zone . .	6·89
Barotseland . .	12·16

KENYA:	
Kavirondo . .	157–1100
Kikuyu . . .	200–500
Masai . . .	3·5
Akamba . . .	25
Samburu . . .	1
Turkana . . .	2·5
Suk	7·8
Kamasia . . .	2
Elgeyo . . .	40
Marakwet . . .	28
Nandi . . .	66

IV

LABOUR OBLIGATIONS OF NATIVES

(*Periods given are legal maxima*)

BASUTOLAND.—Duty of cultivating chief's field when summoned.

SWAZILAND.—Tribal obligations remain in force.

BECHUANALAND.—Tribal obligations remain in force.

SOUTHERN RHODESIA.—Duty to obey orders from chiefs valid in native custom.

NORTHERN RHODESIA.—Sixty days per annum on road maintenance or emergency work.[1]

[1] In these territories the obligation is one not regularly imposed, but available for use in case of emergency.

NYASALAND.—Sixty days per annum on public works; exemption for two months' previous work on contract.[1]

KENYA.—Sixty days per quarter on public works in native areas; exemption for natives in employment or employed for three months in the preceding twelve.[1]

TANGANYIKA.—Sixty days per annum on essential public services.[1]

UGANDA.—Thirty days on local works; can be commuted for cash payment.

NIGERIA.—Road maintenance for native authorities (unpaid).

GOLD COAST.—Twenty-five days per annum on road maintenance.

BELGIAN CONGO.—Sixty days per annum on emergency work or cultivation of export crops.

FRENCH COLONIES.—Fifteen days per annum "prestations" for local labour.

V

TAXATION OF NATIVES

SOUTH AFRICA.—Poll-tax, 20s., plus 10s. local rate in native areas.

SOUTH-WEST AFRICA.—Dog tax, 10s.

SWAZILAND.—35s. for monogamists; for polygamists, 30s.+30s. for each plural wife up to £4, 10s.

BECHUANALAND.—28s.

BASUTOLAND.—28s.+25s. for each wife beyond one.

SOUTHERN RHODESIA.—20s.+10s. for each wife beyond one.

NORTHERN RHODESIA.—7s. 6d. to 12s. 6d.

NYASALAND.—6s.+6s. for each wife beyond one.

KENYA.—Masai, 20s. Other tribes, 12s.

TANGANYIKA.—4s. to 12s., plus 50 per cent for each wife beyond one.

UGANDA.—5s. to 21s.

NIGERIA.—Southern Provinces: graduated tax on incomes over £30. Northern Provinces: graduated tax on incomes; amount varies from 2s. to 13s.

GOLD COAST.—No direct taxation.

BELGIAN CONGO.—Basic tax, 25 to 75 francs. Tax per wife, 12 to 25 francs. Contribution to native treasuries, 1 to 5 francs (in two cases there is an additional contribution per wife of 50 c. and 2·50 francs respectively).

[1] In these territories the obligation is one not regularly imposed, but available for use in case of emergency.

VI

NUMBERS IN EMPLOYMENT, WITH PERCENTAGE OF ADULT MALES ABSENT FROM NATIVE AREAS

	Numbers in Employment.		Percentage of Adult Males absent from Native Areas.	
	Maximum.	Latest Figures.	Maximum.	Latest Figures.
South Africa		315,000 (1930) (mining only)	—	40–70 (1929)
Swaziland		10,000	—	—
Bechuanaland		8,759 (1929)	—	40 (1933)
Basutoland	95,864 (1926)	51,856 (1933)	—	50 (1933)
S.W. Africa	7,645 (1930) (mining only)	1,230 (1934) (mining only)	—	—
S. Rhodesia	90,000 (1926)	79,000 (1934)	—	—
N. Rhodesia	102,700 (1930)	—	34·45 (1930)	10–20 (1932)
Nyasaland		120,000 (1935)	—	2–65 (1935)
Kenya	152,346 (1926)	145,000 (1934)	—	5–62 (1927)
Tanganyika		139–140,000 (1927)	—	—
Uganda		49,685 (1933)	—	—
Nigeria		45,000 (1928) (tin mines and Cameroons plantations only)	—	—
Gold Coast	16,453 (1933); (mining only)	16,453 (1933) (mining only)	—	—
Belgian Congo, maximum reached in 1929		490,262 (1927)	—	—

VII

MAXIMUM PERIOD OF LABOUR CONTRACT [1]

SOUTH AFRICA—

Cape Province.—Five years (written), one year (oral).

Transvaal.—Five years (written), one year (oral).

Natal.—Three years.

Orange Free State.—Two years (written), one year (oral).

[1] In most areas the average contract is made for a shorter period than the maximum. In the Belgian Congo, however, it is part of the "stabilization" policy to offer special advantages to workers engaging for the full term.

KENYA.—Two years.

TANGANYIKA.—One year.

SWAZILAND.—Three hundred and sixty working days. *

NYASALAND.—No legal limit.

NORTHERN RHODESIA.—Two years.

SOUTHERN RHODESIA.—Three years.

UGANDA.—Two years.

GOLD COAST.—Three years (Home contract); thirteen months (Foreign contract).

NIGERIA and CAMEROONS under British Mandate.—Two years.

BELGIAN and PORTUGUESE TERRITORIES.—Three years.

FRENCH TERRITORIES.—Two years.

VIII

WAGES EARNED BY NATIVES

(Figures for 1933, unless otherwise stated. Rates per month, unless otherwise stated)

SOUTH AFRICA.—Agriculture, £15, 4s. to £30 per annum (includes estimated value of squatter privileges and payment in kind (1928 and 1929)). Mining, £1, 3s. 7d. to £2, 4s. Urban areas, £3, 5s. per month.

SWAZILAND.—Mines, 2s. 1d. per shift. Roads, 1s. 6d. a day.

BECHUANALAND.—Mines, 2s. 1d. per shift.

NORTHERN RHODESIA.—Clerks, £2 to £7. Artisans, £1, 10s. to £4. Mining, 17s. 6d. to 37s. 6d. Agriculture, 6s. to 10s.

NYASALAND.—Unskilled labour, 6s. to 10s. Skilled labour, 15s. to 120s.

KENYA.—Unskilled labour, 6s. to 14s.

TANGANYIKA.—Agriculture: unskilled labour, 6s. to 14s.; semi-skilled labour, 12s. to 15s.; skilled labour, 20s. to 180s. No figures for mining.

BELGIAN CONGO.—Unskilled, 22·50 to 40 francs. In urban areas in Equator Province, 45 to 75 francs. Skilled labour (Equator Province), 300 to 1000 francs.

UGANDA.—Unskilled, 5s. to 16s. Skilled, 16s. to 150s.

GOLD COAST.—Agriculture, £3 to £10 a year, plus rations. Mining: unskilled, 1s. to 1s. 9d. a day; skilled, 1s. 9d. to 10s. a day.

NIGERIA.—Porterage, 4d. to 6d. a day. Other labour, 4d. to 9d. a day.

IX

LEGISLATIVE COUNCILS IN NON-SELF-GOVERNING AREAS

SOUTH-WEST AFRICA.—12 elected, 6 nominated members.

NORTHERN RHODESIA.—5 *ex-officio*, 4 nominated official, 7 elected unofficial members.

NYASALAND.—4 official, 4 nominated unofficial members.

KENYA.—11 *ex-officio*, 9 nominated official members; 11 elected Europeans, 5 elected Indians, 1 elected Arab; 2 nominated unofficial to represent native interests.

TANGANYIKA.—13 official, 10 nominated unofficial members.

UGANDA.—7 official, 6 nominated unofficial members.

NIGERIA.—30 official, 4 elected unofficial, 15 nominated unofficial members (for the Colony and Southern Provinces only). The unofficial members are mainly native.

GOLD COAST.—15 official, 14 unofficial members, who include 6 elected chiefs and 3 elected native municipal members.

BIBLIOGRAPHY

CHAPTER II

SOUTH AFRICA

BALLINGER, W. G., *Race and Economics in South Africa*, 1934.
BROOKES, E., *The Colour Problems of South Africa*, 1934.
MACMILLAN, W. M., *Complex South Africa*, 1929.
ROGERS, H., *Native Administration in the Union of South Africa*, 1933.
SCHAPERA, I., *Western Civilisation and the Bantu*, 1934.
WALKER, E., *History of South Africa*, 1928.

Official Publications:
> Native Affairs Commission, 1903–5, Report and Evidence.
> Zululand Lands Delimitation Commission, 1904, Report.
> Native Economic Commission, 1930–32, Report.
> S. H. Fazan, Memorandum on the Transkei, in Kenya Land. Commission Evidence, 1930.
> Report on the Financial and Economic Condition of Swaziland, Cmd. 4114, 1932.
> Report on the Financial and Economic Condition of the Bechuanaland Protectorate, Cmd. 4368, 1933.
> Report on the Financial and Economic Position of Basutoland, Cmd. 4907, 1935.

SOUTHERN RHODESIA

HOLE, H. M., *The Making of Rhodesia*, 1926.

Official Publications:
> Native Affairs Commission, 1910, Report.
> Native Education Commission, 1924, Report.
> Native Land Commission, 1927, Report.
> Annual Reports of Chief Native Commissioner, Director of Native Development, Native Land Board.

Periodicals:
> East Africa.
> The Round Table.

NATIVE POLICIES IN AFRICA

KENYA

HUXLEY, E., *White Man's Country* (2 vols.), 1935.

ROSS, W. MACGREGOR, *Kenya from Within*, 1927.

Official Publications:
    East Africa Commission, Report, Cmd. 2387, 1925.
    Labour Commission, 1927, Report.
    Commission on Closer Union, Report, Cmd. 3234, 1929.
    Select Committee on Closer Union, Evidence, Cmd. 4093, 1932.
    Kenya Land Commission Report, Cmd. 4556, 1934.
    Kenya Land Commission, Evidence, Colonial No. 91, 1934.
    Legislative Council Proceedings.
    Annual Reports of Native Affairs and Education Departments.

NORTHERN RHODESIA

MERLE DAVIS, ed., *Modern Industry and the African*, 1933.

Official Publications:
    Native Reserves Commission Reports, 1925 and 1928.
    Legislative Council Proceedings.
    Annual Native Affairs Reports.

NYASALAND

Official Publications:
    Commission on the Occupation of Land, 1921.
    North Nyasa Reserves Commission, 1929.
    Legislative Council Proceedings.
    Annual Reports—General; Native Affairs; Agriculture.

CHAPTER III

NIGERIA

GEARY, W. N., *Nigeria under British Rule*, 1927.

LUGARD, F. D., *The Dual Mandate*, 3rd ed., 1935.

TEMPLE, C. L., *Native Races and their Rulers*.

Official Publications:
    LUGARD, *Political Memoranda*.

WARD PRICE, H. L., *Land Tenure in the Yoruba Province*, 1933.

CAMERON, D., *Note on Land Tenure in the Yoruba Province*, 1933.
    Principles of Native Administration and their Application, 1934.
    Permanent Mandates Commission Proceedings.
    Nigeria Gazette.

BIBLIOGRAPHY

Annual Reports, Northern and Southern Provinces, and Education Department.
Northern Nigeria Lands Committee, Cmd. 5102, 1910.
Recent Disturbances in Owerre and Calabar Provinces, Commission of Enquiry, 1930.

TANGANYIKA

Official Publications:
CAMERON, D., *Native Administration Memoranda*, 1933.
Government Circulars:
Special Labour Report, 1927.
Land Development Survey Reports, 1928–32.
Annual Reports to League of Nations.
Proceedings of Permanent Mandates Commission.
Legislative Council Proceedings.
Annual Reports—Provincial Commissioners; Labour Department; Land Department.

GOLD COAST

Official Publications:
West African Lands Committee, Draft Report, Colonial Office Library, No. 13080 folio.
Legislative Council Proceedings.
Annual Reports.

UGANDA

MAIR, L. P., *An African People in the Twentieth Century*, 1934.
Official Publications:
Report on Land Tenure and the Kibanja System in Bunyoro, 1931.
Annual Reports, General and Education Department.

THE SUDAN

MACMICHAEL, H., *The Anglo-Egyptian Sudan*, 1934.
Annual Reports.

CHAPTER IV

ABADIE, M., *Nos Richesses Soudanaises*, 1928.
BUELL, R. L., *The Native Problem in Africa* (2 vols.), 1928.
GIDE, A., *Voyage au Congo*, 1927;
   Le Retour du Chad, 1928.
GIRAULT, *Colonization et Legislation Coloniale*, 5th ed., 1929.
GUERBIER, M. L., *L'Afrique Champ d'Expansion de l'Europe*.

GUY, C., *L'Afrique Occidentale Française*, 1929.

HARDY, G., *Une Conquête Morale*, 1917.

HOMBERG, O., *La France des Cinq Parties du Monde*, 1927.

LYAUTEY, J. P., *Empire Coloniale Française*, 1931.

MERCIER, R., *Le Travail Obligatoire dans les Colonies Africaines*, 1933.

OLIVIER, M., *Six Ans de Travail Social au Madagascar*, 1931.

SARRAUT, A., *La Mise en Valeur de nos Colonies*, 1923.

Official Publications:
> Débats Parlementaires.
> Journal Officiel de la République Française.
> Journal Officiel de l'A. E. F.
> Journal Officiel de l'A. O. F.
> Reports to the Permanent Mandates Commission and Minutes of the Permanent Mandates Commission.
> Circulaires sur la Politique et l'Administration Indigène. Gorée, 1932.

Periodicals:
> L'Afrique Française, with supplement, Renseignements Coloniaux.
> Industrial and Labour Information (International Labour Office).

CHAPTER V

CATTIER, F., *Etat Independant du Congo*, 1906.

FRANCK, L., *Etudes de Colonisation Comparée*, 1924.

VERLAINE, L., *Notre Colonie*, 1929.

WALTZ, *Konzessionswesen in Belgischen Kongo*, 1917.

Official Publications:
> Débats Parlementaires.
> Minutes of Permanent Mandates Commission.

Periodicals:
> Congo: in which all important official publications and many articles in other journals are summarized.
> Société Belge d'Expansion et d'Etudes.
> Industrial and Labour Information.

CHAPTER VI

International Colonial Institute Yearbook of Compared Colonial Documentation.

International Labour Office, Report on Forced Labour, 1929; Report on Recruiting of Labour, 1935.

INDEX

INDEX

INDEX

AFRICA SOUTH

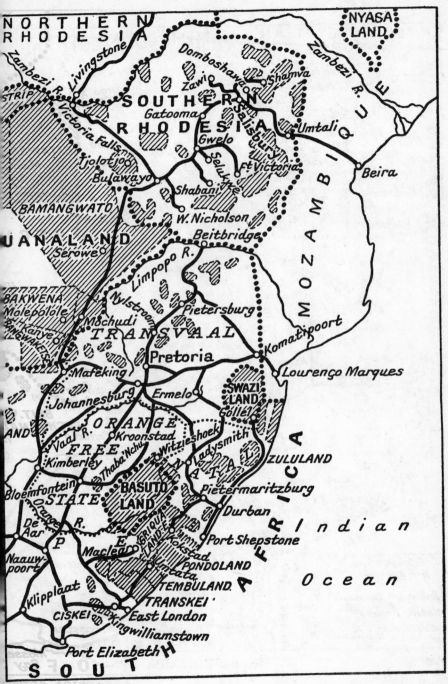

OF THE ZAMBEZI

ANGLO-EGYPTIAN SUDAN

ABYSSINIA

L. Stefanie

Kitgum

NORTHERN

Arua

Gulu

Lodwar

Moroto

Moyale

Nile

Lira

Masindi

EASTERN

Soroti

Kacheliba

NORTHERN

Wajir

L. Albert

Hoima

Namasagali

Mbale

Kyoga

Elgon

Kitale

RIFT

FRONTIER

Ft. Portal

Mubende

Tororo

Butere

Kakamega

Solai

Thomson's Falls

Ruwenzori

Kampala

Nanyuki

WESTERN

Entebbe

Kisumu

Kenya

Mbarara

Masaka

Kericho

Nyeri

Ft. Hall

L. Edward

Bukoba

Lake

Sotik

Naivasha

CENTRAL

Kitui

Victoria

Musoma

Maga

Nairobi

Machakos

Masongaleni

Biharamulo

Mwanza

L. Natron

Kilimanjaro

Lamu

Shinyanga

L. Manyara

Kinyangiri

Arusha

Moshi

Voi

Malindi

Samburu

Kibondo

L. Eyasi

NORTHERN

Taveta

Kasulu

Nzega

Singida

Kondoa

Buiko

Mombasa

Kigoma

Usinge

Tabora

Mlagara

Ugalla R.

CENTRAL

Manyoni

Mpwapwa

Handeni

Pemba I.

Kibwesa

Dodoma

Bagamoyo

Pangani

Zanzibar

Karema

TANGANYIKA

EASTERN

Dar es Salaam

Kipili

Kilosa

Morogoro

Sumbawanga

L. Rukwa

IRINGA

Iringa

Ruaha R.

Rufiji R.

Mafia I.

Kasanga

Mahenge

Utete

Mbeya

Tukuyu

Kilwa

NORTHERN RHODESIA

Njombe

Liwale

Lindi

Mikindani

LINDI

Songea

Masasi

MOZAMBIQUE

Ruvuma R.

English Miles

0   50   100 150

Railways ——

Native Areas

Boundaries of Provinces ••••••

MAP 2   BRITISH EAST AFRICA

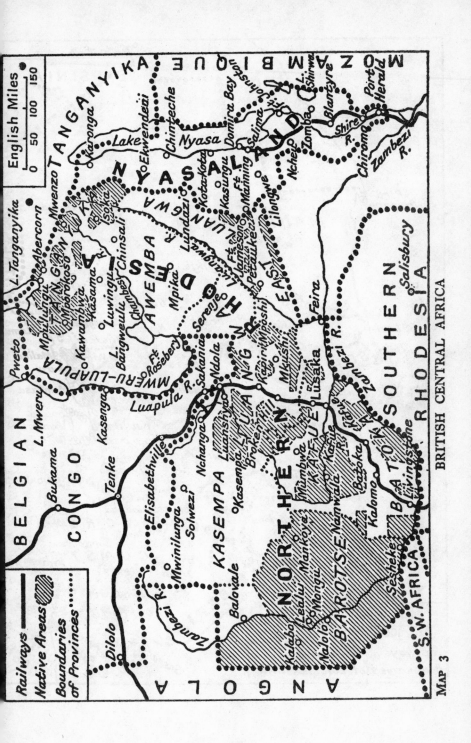

BRITISH CENTRAL AFRICA

MAP 3

MAP 4

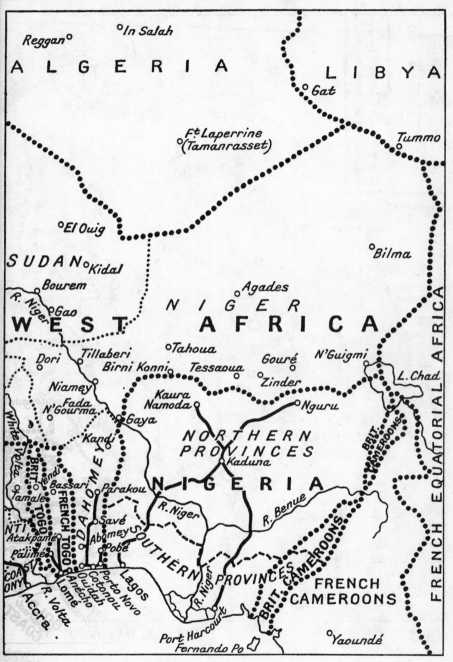

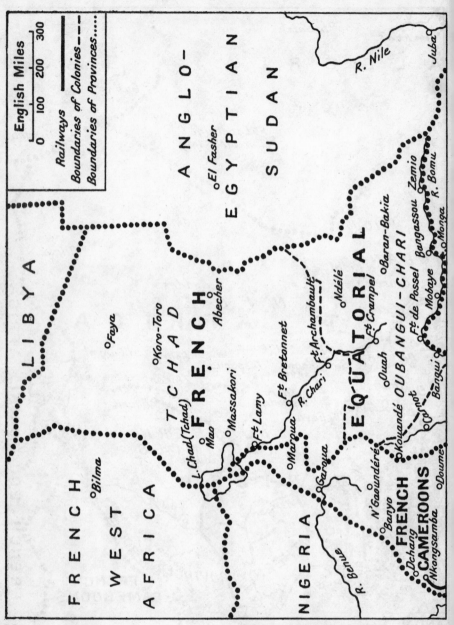

MAP 5   FRENCH EQUATORIAL AFRICA